QMW LIBRARY

D1351644

DATE DUE FOR RETURN

23. FEB 93		16 MAY 2006
19. APR 93		
06. MAY 93		
21 MAR 1995		
03 MAY 1996		WITHDRAWN FROM STOCK QMUL LIBRARY
21 MAY 1996		

Brief Chronicles

Also by Martin Esslin

BRECHT: A CHOICE OF EVILS

THE THEATRE OF THE ABSURD

BERTOLT BRECHT [COLUMBIA ESSAYS ON MODERN WRITERS]

Edited by Martin Esslin

SAMUEL BECKETT [CRITICAL ESSAYS]

THE GENIUS OF THE GERMAN THEATRE

014 3410
16.3.83

Brief Chronicles

ESSAYS ON MODERN THEATRE

Martin Esslin

*... the players ... are the abstract
and brief chronicles of the time*
HAMLET

Temple Smith · London

WESTFIELD
UNIV.
LONDON
COLLEGE

Copyright (©) 1961, 1962, 1963, 1966, 1967, 1968, 1969, 1970
by Martin Esslin

This book was first published in Great Britain
in 1970 by Maurice Temple Smith Ltd
37 Great Russell Street, London WC1

ISBN 08511 7000 5

Printed by Western Printing Services Ltd, Bristol

Contents

Foreword

To be faced with a collection of one's more or less fugitive pieces is, of necessity, a daunting experience. Articles written to meet a casual request, lectures transcribed from tapes, essays written as contributions to a controversy, introductions to volumes of plays, records of interviews with playwrights—how can they add up to a meaningful whole?

And yet there is a case for collecting at least a proportion of this work: there are, for one, the repeated requests for reprints in other people's anthologies, so there must be a case for keeping the material in a readily available, accessible form. Moreover, the very spontaneity and casualness of these writings might, at times, be an advantage. They reflect one's thought and, in the case of a critic, one's immediate reactions in the very process of formation and, as such, may acquire some value simply as a record of that process. Much of the material in this volume, for example, consists of footnotes, or second thoughts, or changes of mind, about subjects dealt with in my more deliberately composed books. To make these available is only fair to those readers who have treated the books themselves with sufficient respect to take what they said seriously.

Inevitably the confrontation with so much of one's work that came into being without deliberation as the by-product of one's natural working process also raises the fundamental question: Why should one be so concerned with the theatre, with drama at all? Is it worth while in an age of great and tragic happenings to take so seriously what might well be regarded as a mere pastime, and a pastime of a dwindling minority at that!

To reply merely that, after all, this happens to be one's chosen field and one might as well go on working in it as long as there is a demand for one's contributions, would surely be totally unsatisfactory. Yet the question is a real one, and it must be answered.

One approach to an answer, I think, is this: *any* examination in depth of *any* manifestation of the human spirit, of *any* form of the life of any society, should ultimately be worth while, simply because each part contains and sheds light on the whole. A study of, say, Victorian advertisements, table manners, horse racing or, for that matter, Victorian theatre or music hall, might throw as much light and point up as significant an aspect of that society as a study of industrial production or the movement of trade. Indeed, as a reflection of the true state of society, its problems and neuralgic points, the theatre, in spite of its minority status, is probably as valuable a source of insights as any other social activity. Ibsen is as valid a critic of nineteenth-century society as Marx; his direct influence on life may not have been as great, but that it was of considerable impact is beyond doubt.

If this is true in studying and evaluating the past, it must surely be equally true in one's attempts to understand the present. The arts express the collective consciousness—and conceal the collective subconscious—of our society. A constant awareness of its state must therefore clearly be a matter of considerable importance. In the personal sphere, rational control of our own actions depends on our degree of self-knowledge; the same is true in the social sphere. The process of critical evaluation of current output in the arts and literature is therefore merely society's struggle for self-awareness of its own mental and emotional state at any given moment. The innumerable errors made by the critics, who represent an extremely wide cross-section of different levels of discernment, knowledge, and even intelligence, are no different from the innumerable errors each individual makes in his constant endeavour to reach an awareness of his own position. What matters is that these errors are part of a process of trial and error. As time passes valid judgments do emerge. That is why time is the only true test of greatness in literature. To play one's part in this process in all humility and in the full awareness of one's inevitable fallibility seems to me a justifiable social role for the critic of drama and the theatre. Particularly as drama, being a social form of art, has special significance as a social symptom. Although the audiences for drama are a minority, they are an influential minority of trendsetters for society as a whole.

But I should go even further: each individual's—and society's—self-awareness is becoming increasingly important in the present state of our culture's technological and social development. We live in an age of leisure, ever increasing leisure, and in an age of the manipulation of minds, ever increasing degrees of manipulation by the mass media. Herbert Marcuse rightly points to the fact that the manipulation of man's consciousness by those who control society does, even in a formally free society, amount to complete totalitarian subjection of his mind. This is merely another way of saying that the mass of human beings is so naïve, so uninformed about the true workings of society and about the technique of mind manipulation, that they are unable to resist.

Where I disagree with Marcuse is in the remedies he proposes: he wants to *ban* the expression of certain views, to suppress certain techniques of mass communication. In other words, to the covert totalitarianism of one form of society, he opposes simply overt totalitarianism. The remedy here seems to be worse than the disease. Surely the way to defeat the hidden manipulators is to make their audience aware of what is going on and to give them the tools to detect their intentions. That is to say, they must learn to understand society and its workings and train themselves to be critical of the techniques of communication. The criticism of drama and of performance in the theatre, however, should be able to provide something like a training ground for these skills. In many ways the mass media are *extensions*—and perversions

—of theatrical techniques; and the theatre has remained a potent training ground for the practitioners of the mass media.

Hence the steadily increasing importance, in my opinion, of criticism, the critical attitude, the techniques of evaluation in this and kindred fields. Already in Britain the critical discussion of television programmes—and television commercials—has became part of the curriculum of some schools. Far from posing as arbiters of taste who dictate the success or failure of productions in the theatre, the critics should therefore become no more, and no less, than working models of the critical attitude in action. It is not their opinions but their methods and attitudes that the public should learn to adopt and copy. The manipulators of the subconscious can be defeated only by the creation of a truly critical, self-aware, fully conscious public. Only those who are completely in control of their own responses can claim to be more than mere automata.

These are extravagant claims for the social function of the critic—in the theatre as in other fields. They are certainly not made for this critic in particular, but merely to explain why it is that he feels justified in having produced the articles and essays in this volume. They will have to speak for themselves; I am content if they provoke discussion and contradiction.

This book would not have come into being without the help of Anne Freedgood. I am deeply grateful to her.

MARTIN ESSLIN

The Making of the Contemporary Theatre

New Form in the Theatre

Form-smashers ought certainly to be encouraged. But at the same time we should know what is being smashed; and what is taking its place.

What is form? A set of rules or prescriptions handed down through habits of craftsmanship, academic teaching, or critical practice. Some of these may be wholly arbitrary, based on considerations that have been long forgotten; others are the congealed expression of philosophical assumptions, some of which may still be valid, while others are equally forgotten and have long since become obsolete or need to be re-examined. Others again are derived from fundamental realities, such as the laws of the psychology of perception; these will resist the smashers—but even they may be swept away, for even the conditions of perception change with time. Men's wits become sharper, their eyes and ears quicker in their response, chords that grated on the ears of one generation may be tolerable or even beautiful to those of a later age.

So most forms may be, and should be, smashed. What we must remember, however, is that the new forms that take their place will also, inevitably, present new and different *contents*. It is a fallacy to think that there is a division between *what* is said and *how* it is said; ultimately form is content and content form—it would be quite impossible to have the statement made by Picasso in *Guernica* repainted in the style of Rubens or Velazquez; and when Picasso did repaint *Las Meninas* of Velazquez in his own style in a long series of new paintings, these turned out to have an entirely different content. Equally, you could not express the subject matter of *Hamlet* in the form of Racine or Eugene O'Neill, let alone in the form of a musical. *West Side Story* may be a retelling of *Romeo and Juliet*—it certainly does not say the same thing that Shakespeare said.

To make a musical out of *Romeo and Juliet*, however, is not an act of form-smashing; it is a perfectly traditional method of taking inspiration from the theme of an older work. The form-smashers aim at breaking up the basic rules of the art form itself.

Let us take a simple example of an established aesthetic dogma smashed—and not by revolutionaries either. For decades the aesthetics of the cinema were based on the traditional proportions of the screen; the origins of these were wholly arbitrary, probably due to such accidents as the format of the first cameras, or the standard size of film made available by industry to the early film makers. Once cinema houses around the world were equipped with screens of a certain size and shape, it became extremely difficult to change the proportions of the picture projected, and the original coincidence was elevated into a formal principle that seemed destined to assume eventually the sacred stature of an eternal aesthetic law; film theoreticians accepted it and derived their philosophies from it. If a few directors, like Abel Gance, rebelled against it in one or two films, they could not move the established principle. Yet the day came when technical developments and economic forces coincided; when the competition of television created a demand for more spectacle and larger vistas, and technical developments in the form of various wide-screen and panoramic processes were at hand. So Cinemascope and Cinerama smashed what, a bare half century after the birth of the cinema, had come to be regarded as its basic form. It now became possible to create a much wider picture within a frame of different shape—or even a picture so large that its edges lay outside the field of vision of a pair of eyes focused on the centre, so that it became possible to suggest an unframed picture, like that perceived when we are looking at reality itself.

It was soon apparent that these new forms must present a

different type of content. On the Cinemascope screen, montage and quick cutting, which make up the basic grammar of the language of the normal cinema, become much more difficult, simply because it takes much longer to absorb a wider picture and therefore quicker cutting would be bewildering. In Cinerama, which attempts an illusion of reality itself, quick cutting is found to give the audience a violent physical jolt and be positively uncomfortable. So, on that very large screen, the picture has to be almost as stable as in the old live theatre; the real value of the process lies in the purveying of landscape: only one type of content, the travelogue, ideally fits that particular new form.

In other words, the old form has not been smashed; it has not been superseded. The language of the cinema has been extended in one particular direction. If the new very large screen process became the only standard of cinematic art, we should have lost a valuable form of expression.

This certainly is a very humble and a very limited example. But it makes its point; the origins of an aesthetic may be arbitrary, but once the arbitrary step has been taken, it sets up its own framework of by no means arbitrary rules which are dependent on the psychological and perceptual basis of the experience involved. Thus the origins of Greek tragedy are still obscure: we do not know *why* it was originally confined to one actor and chorus, to which another actor and later— by a daring and revolutionary innovation—a third were added. It was certainly a highly arbitrary form. Yet it is from these limitations that the character—and range of expressiveness—of Greek tragedy stemmed. And it was a form perfectly adapted to the content it was designed to express. But to that content only.

It was from that very limited, and arbitrarily limited, art form that Aristotle deduced what were for centuries regarded as the immovable laws of the aesthetics of drama. At that point a tyranny of form was established. For it is a fatal fallacy when principles deduced from existing works of art *a posteriori* are elevated into *a priori* rules. For many centuries, while certain aspects changed, it was considered an eternal principle that the drama must imitate nature, that it was based on a plot with a beginning, a middle, and a solution, and on the delineation of characters that must be consistent throughout the action.

It was against this form that Beckett, Ionesco, Genet, Harold Pinter, and a host of other dramatists rebelled. Some of them have written plays that lack plot, others have created characters that lack consistency and change their personalities completely in the course of an evening—not by logical development, but arbitrarily. They have written plays that start without a formal exposition and end without a solution. In other words they have produced a theatre that, by that *a priori* definition of the theatre, is neither possible nor permissible and could certainly not be successful. Yet, undoubtedly, these authors have written for the stage and they have been successful.

This is a case where not only have some of the rules of form been revealed as arbitrary, but where, moreover, the philosophical assumptions on which the convention rested have changed. Plays with a rationally constructed plot that start from the exposition of a problem, moral, social, or philosophical, and then proceed towards a solution presuppose a world order that is rational and known to man. Characters who remain consistent throughout the development of an action presuppose that each individual has something like an immutable and eternal essence of which all his various manifestations from the cradle to the grave are temporal and more or less fortuitous modifications: in other words, that each individual has his immortal essence, his immortal soul.

For the avant garde in the theatre of today neither of these basic assumptions holds good: they see the world as essentially mysterious and unintelligible, certainly devoid of rational purpose and hence of clearly deducible rules of conduct. And these authors have also digested the findings of modern

psychology, which sees human character not as an eternal
essence but as the sum of physiological and psychological
factors that are in constant flux. In Beckett's *Waiting for
Godot*, Pozzo appears as a self-confident and overbearing
man at one moment, as a blind and defeated man at another.
No explanation is given for the change; there is even room
to doubt that the two manifestations of personality are the
same man. In Ionesco's *Rhinoceros*, men change into beasts
without warning or explanation, the victims of a psychological and physiological change that is regarded as a disease.
With the loss of intelligible purpose in the universe and with
the disappearance of consistent character, the drama can no
longer be an equation starting from a number of known
constants and working towards a solution of the unknown
factors according to a well-established and sure formula. We
now work with a much higher number of unknown factors
and the certainty that there is no easy solution.

Here, then, in contrast to the merely technical change in
the example from the cinema, we are faced not so much with
an *attack* on an arbitrary form as with its internal collapse.
To these avant-garde authors the traditional form of the
theatre no longer makes sense because it is based on implied
philosophical assumptions in which they no longer believe.
This is why, say, the usual Soviet play or the Victorian melodrama strikes us as unconvincing: they express systems of
values that have, to us, lost their relevance. But so, to the
avant garde in the contemporary theatre, have the basic, unspoken, and implied assumptions of the usual drawing-room
comedy or socially relevant play, with its careful delineation
of character and neat solution. To writers like Beckett, Ionesco, or Pinter, the fact that boy gets girl in the last act, or
that the desirability of racial tolerance is convincingly
demonstrated, is irrelevant. The boy and the girl still face an
absurd universe; no social reform will alter its mysterious-
ness. By tackling a small, and to these writers irrelevant,
segment of the reality of the human situation, the conventional theatre presents a distorted and unreal picture.

The attack on the *form* of the traditional theatre is thus revealed as an attack on its *content*. And if a play attempts to deal with the new content in the conventional form of logical construction, consistent characterization, and coherent language, the implied assumptions behind its form will belie its apparent content. In that sense even the blackest existentialist plays of Sartre and Camus, which present a philosophy closely akin to that of the plays of Beckett and Ionesco, contradict their explicit content by the implied content that shines through their logical and traditional construction.

The identity of form and content is even clearer in the most obvious aspect of the attack the avant-garde dramatists have launched against the traditional theatre: their resolute destruction of language and discursive thought on the stage. One of the main contents of this new theatre is the demonstration of the difficulties of communication between human beings—the inadequacy of language in establishing contact. Here, too, the smashing of form expresses a changed philosophical basis: the time has passed when an identity was believed to exist between the structure of language, the structure of logic, and the structure of reality. That is the content expressed by the formal means of the dissolution of logical discourse in the avant-garde theatre.

The destruction of old rules, old forms that fitted old contents does not, however, lead to the destruction of *all* rules, *all* form. On the contrary, plays that can do without exposition, development, solution, closely observed characters, or even logical discourse, require an even stronger discipline, an even more acute and original formal sense from their authors. For, having dispensed with the traditional means of capturing their audience's attention, having jettisoned the clichés that helped them to follow what was going on, they *must* create their own *new* convention: no communication can exist without some common ground between the transmitter of a message and its recipient. That is why the loosest of all forms of communication, lyrical poetry, has the most rigid formal patterns: regular rhythms, rhyme, highly formalized groupings of lines into stanzas. That is also the reason why abstract painting is more formally patterned than illustrative pictures. In a non-discursive, lyrical theatre of concretized images, therefore, the need for form, *new* form, but form nevertheless, is *greater* than in the naturalistic theatre. All successful examples of this kind of theatre are in fact built according to the strictest formal patterns: the correspondence between Acts I and II in *Waiting for Godot* is as close as the rhyme scheme of a sonnet; the silences of Pinter's *The Homecoming* give that play the rhythmic formality of a string quartet.

The form-smashers of the contemporary theatre, therefore, are anything but frivolous iconoclasts. They are expressing fundamental changes in contemporary thought—and they are expressing them in the only way that will give them adequate expression in terms of the stage. In doing this they may not be destroying the traditional basis of the theatre, but they are certainly adding a new dimension to it, widening, in fact, the range of its content and subject matter.

The Theatre of the Absurd has opened up a new possibility for poetry on the stage. Having renounced the function of telling a story, of exploring character, of discussing ideas, of solving problems, it has been able to concentrate on the presentation of what is essentially a *sense of being*, an intuition of the tragicomic absurdity and mystery of human existence. As such the Theatre of the Absurd is an existentialist theatre which puts a direct perception of a mode of being above all abstract considerations; it is also essentially a poetic, a lyrical theatre, for the expression of intuitions of being is the field of lyrical poetry. So, paradoxically, the theatre that attacks language, and above all language that is beautiful and poetical for its own sake, is a deeply poetical theatre, only its poetry is a poetry of situation, movement, and concrete imagery, not one of language. Plays like *Waiting for Godot* or Ionesco's *The Chairs* eminently prove this point.

So, in this field at least, the form-smashers are not form-smashers at all; rather are they explorers who penetrate into new fields and open up new vistas. Instead of destroyers of old forms they are the bringers of new contents.

This is not to say that everything that seems avant-gardist must be good. Once the basis of a new approach has been understood, the grammar of a new kind of language learned, standards of judgment will immediately become apparent. If it is recognized that the avant-garde theatre is concerned with the presentation of complex imagery, with the exploration of the human condition in terms of an intuition of the mystery, the tragedy and comic absurdity of existence, then obviously its plays will have to be judged, not by any truth of character drawing or any ingenuity of plot, which they renounce, but by the quality of their imagery, the depth of their intuition, the validity of their poetic imagination.

Just as we have learned to discriminate between good and bad abstract painting and no longer attack Picasso because he paints women with two noses when we all know that in nature they have only one, so it should be the function of drama critics to make a minimum effort to find out the terms of reference of avant-garde writing in the theatre and judge its works within those terms and standards. There may be some form-smashers in the avant-garde theatre who have nothing to say and are therefore purely negative. Any critic worth his salt should easily be able to distinguish these from the writers who smash old forms because they feel that they have become inadequate to express new contents.

And these form-smashers, certainly, ought to be encouraged.

Naturalism in Perspective

Nothing tastes staler than the revolutions of the day before yesterday; the bitter flavour of great expectations disappointed clings to them; they make us feel superior for having seen through their ridiculous pretensions and sorry for our fathers and grandfathers for having been taken in by them. That naturalism in the novel and in the theatre still leaves such an aftertaste on our palates is, in a way, a tribute to the intensity of emotion it aroused in its day and the length of time during which it acquired and held a dominant position. After all, it was in the 1870s that Zola shocked the world with his new concept of naturalism; Ibsen's *Ghosts* was first published in 1881; Strindberg's *The Father* in 1887, his *Miss Julie* in 1888; Hauptmann's *Vor Sonnenaufgang* had its first performance in 1889; Chekhov's *The Seagull* in 1896. Yet the expressionism of the 1920s, Brecht's epic theatre of the thirties and forties, the Theatre of the Absurd of the fifties and sixties were still, essentially, reactions *against* naturalism, or at least against its latter-day exponents who still dominated —almost to this day—the more conservative sector of our theatre: Broadway, the London West End, and the Paris boulevard, not to speak of Moscow. What started out as a furious attack on the conventions of what was then regarded as the well-made play, as an iconoclastic, revolutionary onslaught against the establishment, has now turned into the embodiment of 'squareness', conservatism, and the contemporary concept of the well-made play. In the West End of London early Shaw and Ibsen have become safe after-dinner entertainment for the suburban business community, the equivalents of Scribe, Sardou, and Dumas fils in their own day—the very authors whom they wanted to replace because they were safe and establishment-minded.

Such, however, is the dialectical law of historical development: each hour has its own necessity, its own imperative; and what is essential is precisely the insight and the courage needed to obey it. Once the hour is passed, the new moulds have been created, lesser spirits will inevitably continue to use them; and that is how the revolutionary contents and forms of yesteryear turn into the safe, conservative clichés of today.

What matters, therefore, for any objective assessment of a movement like naturalism is to see it in its historical context; to understand the moral and artistic impulse behind it; and to pursue its manifestations into our own time. We shall then find that the impulse behind the naturalist movement is still very much alive, very relevant for our own time, and well worth our study and understanding.

The mid-nineteenth century was one of dismal stagnation in the European theatre; the achievements of the classical and romantic movement in Germany, of the romantic revolution in France had frozen into an empty routine; the theatre was discredited as a serious art form. Looking back on those days, Strindberg reported that

> if one wanted to submit a play to the Royal Dramatic Theatre in the sixties and seventies the following conditions had to be met to get it performed: the play had to have five acts, each act had to run to about six sheets of writing paper, thus the whole play to 5 times 24 = 120 foolscap pages. Changes of scene within the acts were not liked and were considered a weakness. Each act had to have a beginning, a middle, and an end. The curtain lines had to give rise to applause, through oratorical figures; if the play was in unrhymed verse, the last two lines had to rhyme. In the play there had to be 'turns' for the actors which were called 'scenes'; the monologue was permissible and often constituted a highlight; a longish emotional outburst or invective, a revelation, were almost compulsory; there also

had to be narrative passages—a dream, an anecdote, an event. . . . This dramaturgy had a certain justification and even a certain beauty; it stemmed in the last resort from Victor Hugo and had been a reaction against the obsolete abstractions of Racine and Corneille in the thirties. But this art form degenerated like all others when it had had its day, and the five-act form was used for all kinds of subjects, even for insignificant minor history or anecdote.

Strindberg here confirms the diagnosis Zola made in his preface to *Thérèse Raquin* (dated 25 July 1873):

> Drama is dying of its extravagances, its lies, and its platitudes. If comedy still keeps on its feet in the collapse of our stage, that is because it contains more of real life, because it is often true. I defy the last of the romantics to put onto the stage a heroic drama; the old iron of the Middle Ages, the secret doors, the poisoned wines and all the rest would only make one shrug one's shoulders. Melodrama, the bourgeois offspring of romantic drama, is even more dead in the affection of the people; its false sentiment, its complications of stolen children and recovered documents, its impudent grandiloquence have brought it, at long last, into such disrepute that one holds one's ribs at any attempt to resuscitate it. The great works of the 1830s will remain as milestones of a struggle, as literary red-letter days, as superb efforts that brought down the classical trappings. But now that all this is overturned, the cloaks and the daggers have become unnecessary. The time has come to create works of truth. To replace the classical tradition by a romantic tradition would amount to a failure to make use of the freedom which our elders won for us. There must be no more schools, no more formulae, no more literary panjandrums of any kind. There is just life itself, an immense field where everybody can explore and create to his heart's content.

No more schools, no more formulae, no more literary panjandrums of any kind! Here lies the impetus behind the naturalist movement which is still alive, still active, still immensely relevant today. No wonder that Zola's impassioned manifesto reads so well, that is seems fresh and topical to us, almost a hundred years after it was written. The romantic movement had overthrown the dominance of the rigid formula of French classical drama; but it had imposed its own narrow conception of subject matter, technique, and objective on all serious drama. Comedy, stemming from Molière and his realism of observation and language, had remained much freer from the blight of the schoolmen. Now the naturalists called for a fresh start in *complete* freedom; art, like philosophy, was making the transition from a *closed* to a totally *open* system. The naturalists were the first to formulate such a new, open view of aesthetics.

It had taken half a century for Auguste Comte's positivist philosophy to be taken up by the creative artists—Comte's *Système de philosophie positive* had appeared in 1824. It reached Zola via the works of a physiologist, Claude Bernard, notably his *Introduction à l'étude de la médecine expérimentale* (1865), and a literary and social historian, Hippolyte Taine, whose epoch-making *Histoire de la littérature anglaise* had appeared in 1864. What Zola took from Claude Bernard is no more and no less than the basic concept of the *scientific method* of painstaking inquiry through observation, hypothesis, and the testing of hypotheses through experiment. Zola's essay *Le Roman expérimental*, the basic formulation of the naturalists' creed, is little more than an anthology of quotations from Claude Bernard's book on experimental medicine. 'All experimental reasoning must be founded on doubt, for the experimenter must have no preconceived ideas when confronting nature: he must always preserve his freedom of mind.'

Bernard had stressed that the scientific, experimental method implied a *determinist* view of nature; experimentation uncovers the chain of cause and effect behind seemingly arbitrary phenomena. But is was from Taine that Zola took his own specific determinism. In his history of English literature Taine sought to explain each writer through three main factors that determined his nature and his style: *race, milieu, moment*—race, environment, and the particular historical circumstances of his time. This concept allowed the naturalists to reintroduce the classical source of tragedy, pre-ordained, inescapable *fate*, into the drama in a new and highly respectable 'scientific' guise. Men were predetermined, their individual fate was preordained through a combination of heredity, environment, and history. (Taine's ideas of race and heredity came to hideous fruition in Hitler's racialism and the extermination camps of the Second World War.) It was this idea of heredity that stalked through Ibsen's *Ghosts* and Gerhart Hauptmann's *Vor Sonnenaufgang* or Strindberg's *Miss Julie*.

Taine's determinism was an oversimplification and in itself scientifically untenable. (Modern genetics soon showed that the real workings of heredity were far more complex than Taine, or even Darwin, had imagined, that neither Oswald's syphilis nor the alcoholism Hauptmann's Helene in *Vor Sonnenuntergang* seemed destined to inherit would in fact have been transmitted from father to son, from father to daughter.) But—and this must be stressed again and again in the face of a present-day tendency to scoff at the naturalists precisely for being scientifically out of date—these mistakes of scientific detail are not of the essence of their attitude. Their fundamental and essential belief has not become obsolete:

> Naturalism, in literature . . . is the return to nature and to man, direct observation, correct anatomy, the acceptance and the depiction of that which *is*. The task is the same for the scientist as for the writer. Both have to abandon abstractions for realities, ready-made formulas for rigorous analysis. Hence no more abstract characters in our works, no more mendacious inventions, no more absolutes, but real people, the true history of everyone, the web and woof of daily life. It was a matter of a totally new start, of getting to know man from the very well-springs of his being, before reaching conclusions in the manner of the idealists who invent their types. Writers from now on are constrained to build from the foundation upward, by bringing us the largest possible number of human documents, presented in their logical order. (Zola, *Le Naturalisme au théâtre*)

This spirit of free inquiry, totally unprejudiced, unburdened by preconceived ideas, liberated immense energies. That it consciously aimed beyond the immediate techniques and subject matters of the moment is clearly shown by, for example, the manifesto with which Otto Brahm, the great critic and director of German naturalist drama, opened the Berlin *Freie Bühne* (Free Stage) on 29 January 1890:

> Once upon a time there was an art which avoided the present and sought poetry only in the darkness of the past, striving in a bashful flight from reality to reach ideal distant shores where in eternal youth there blooms what has never happened anywhere. The art of our time embraces with its clasping organs everything that lives, nature and society; that is why the closest and subtlest relations bind modern art and modern life together; and anyone who wants to grasp modern art must endeavour to penetrate modern life as well in its thousand merging contours, in its intertwined and antagonistic instincts. The motto of this new art, written down in golden characters by our leading spirits, is one word: truth; and truth, truth on every path of life, is what we are striving for. Not the objective truth, which escapes the struggling individual, but individual truth, freely arrived at from the deepest convictions, freely uttered: the truth of the independent spirit who has nothing to explain away or hide; and who therefore knows only one adversary, his arch-enemy and mortal foe: the lie in all its forms.
>
> No other programme is to be recorded in these pages. We swear by no formula and would not dare to chain into the rigid compulsion of rules that which is in eternal flux—life and art. Our striving is for that which is in the act of becoming and our eyes are directed far more attentively onto the things which are about to arise than onto those elements of an eternal yesterday which have the presumption to tie down in conventions and rules once and for all time mankind's infinite potential. We bow in reverence before all the greatness that past epochs have preserved for us, but it is not from them that we draw the lodestone and the norms of life; for it is not he who ties himself to the views of a dead world, but only he who freely feels the demand of the present hour, who will penetrate the spiritual powers activating our age as a truly modern man. . . .

No barrier of theory, no sanctified model of the past must inhibit the infinity of development, which constitutes the essence of our species. . . . Friends of naturalism, we want to stride along with it for a fair stretch of the way, but we shall not to be astonished if in the course of this journey, at a point we cannot as yet foresee, the road might suddenly turn, opening up surprising new vistas in art or life. For the infinite development of human culture is bound to no formula, not even the newest; and in this confidence, in this faith in infinite potentiality, we have erected a free stage for modern life.

These are noble words; they show the genuine freedom of the spirit, transcending all the narrow dogmatism of literary movements or coteries, that inspired the best minds among the champions of naturalism. Seldom in the history of literature has the call for *absolute truth* been voiced with such uncompromising conviction, such absolute courage.

Artistic literature is called so [wrote Chekhov in 1887] because it depicts life as it really is. Its aim is truth—unconditional and honest. . . . I agree with you that the 'cream' is a fine thing, but a littérateur is not a confectioner, not a dealer in cosmetics, not an entertainer; he is a man bound, under compulsion, by the realization of his duty, and by his conscience; having put his hand to the plough, he must not plead weakness; and no matter how painful it is to him, he is constrained to overcome his aversion and soil his imagination with the sordidness of life. He is just like an ordinary reporter. What would you say if a newspaper reporter, because of his fastidiousness or from a wish to give pleasure to his readers, were to describe only honest mayors, high-minded ladies, and virtuous railroad contractors? To a chemist nothing on earth is unclean. A writer must be as objective as a chemist; he must abandon the subjective line; he must know that dung heaps play a very respectable part in a landscape and that evil passions are as inherent in life as good ones. (Letter to M. V. Kiselev, 14 January 1887)

The decisive and truly revolutionary element in this attitude —this I believe must be stressed above all—was its passionate proclamation of the *primacy of content over form*, the conviction that any subject matter could be treated, and that each subject matter would call for the form most adequate and suitable to express it. Artistic form thus came to be seen as the *organic expression* of its content.

We are through with intrigue, with artificial plot, through with the play as a kind of chess game; the ability to perceive and to express, which is the secret of each true artist, is his natural style, his inner form, his inner turn of phrase. In these the great rhythm and the great dynamism of life are reduced to an individual rhythm, an individual dynamism. There may be a tradition in this, but it has become flesh and blood, a tradition that, like those of eating and drinking, is carried by ever new hunger and thirst. Traditional, external dogmas cannot have a bearing on this process. Such useless and pointless external dogmas are: the dogma of plot, the dogma of the unities of space and time, the dogma of exposition in twenty to thirty lines at the opening of the first act, and others. (Gerhart Hauptmann, c. 1910)

Yet in their demand for truth, for the primacy of subject matter over form, the naturalists were never—as is nowadays often thoughtlessly assumed—naïve enough to believe in the possibility of a truly objective representation of nature. In the above quotation Hauptmann insists on the artist's individual ability to perceive and to express as the starting point. And Zola himself coined the famous slogan: '*Il est certain qu'un oeuvre ne sera jamais qu'un coin de la nature vu à travers un tempérament.*' (It is certain that a work of art will never be anything but a corner of nature seen through a temperament.) This recognition of the subjective nature of all perception marks the really decisive breach with any theory of art that believed in the possibility of embodying absolutes, eternal verities, in great enduring works. As such the naturalists were the first conscious existentialists in the realm of aesthetics. (The link from Kierkegaard to his fellow Scandinavian Ibsen is only too clear, although Ibsen was at pains to stress that he had 'read little and understood less' of Kierkegaard. Mere awareness of the debate around Kierkegaard must have been enough to acquaint him with the essence of his ideas. While denying that Kierkegaard had been the model for Brand, Ibsen added: 'But, of course, the depiction of a man whose sole aim in life is to realize his ideals will always bear a certain resemblance to Kierkegaard's life.')

There is no contradiction between the ruthless pursuit of truth, observed, scientifically tested, experimental truth on the one hand, and the continual awareness of a subjective point of view on the part of the observer. Indeed, the notion that the observer's subjectivity will always have to be reckoned with is the hallmark of a truly scientific attitude. Zola used the term *document humain* to show that any truthful description of human experience, however subjective, also has an objective value as a contribution to man's knowledge of himself. Hence Strindberg's violent denunciation of the tyranny of women over men could be seen as equally valid as Ibsen's and Shaw's passionate advocacy of the rights of women. Each one of these dramatists was ruthlessly truthful, precisely *because* he gave the fullest possible expression to nature seen through *his* temperament.

From this acceptance of the individual's point of view there also follow the rejection of any ethical absolutes, the denial of the previously held notion that it was art's purpose to propagate the accepted moral code. 'The idealists,' says Zola, 'pretend that it is necessary to lie in order to be moral, the naturalists assert that one cannot be moral outside the truth. . . .' Truthfulness, accuracy of observation, and the courage to confront the results of this observation thus become the only moral absolutes of the artist. And this is the impulse that inspires the literature of today—as indeed it does all the other arts.

Once one realizes that the view of naturalism as a mere attempt to create photographic reproductions of external reality is a very superficial one; that, indeed, the essence of the naturalists' endeavour was an existential, value-free, scientific, and experimental exploration of reality in its widest possible sense (including the subjective reality of the artist's temperament through which he perceives external reality), and that this approach logically led to the rejection of all ready-made formal conventions and implied the acceptance of organic form dictated by the nature of the subject matter—all else follows.

The earliest naturalists did not, to be sure, all have the ability or the desire to follow the theoretical implications of their views to their logical consequence. Zola's own *Thérèse Raquin* had more in common with a well-made play à la Dumas fils than with later naturalist drama (while its basic highly effective melodramatic image, the paralyzed observer unable to communicate his knowledge of a crime to his visitors, comes directly from that arch-romantic novel by Dumas père, *The Count of Monte Cristo*). Ibsen's great social dramas used the stage technique of Sardou, while Shaw openly proclaimed his determination to use the convention of popular drama to put over modern ideas in a play like *You Never Can Tell*. But who, on the other hand, would doubt that Ibsen's later symbolic myths were the direct and logical development of his determination to explore his inner as well as his external reality; that Strindberg's dream plays continued the impulse behind his naturalistic explorations?

As early as 1887 Georg Brandes pointed out that Zola constantly invested the nature he was describing and exploring with symbolical, mythical significance; that in fact his naturalism took far more from Zola's own poetic temperament, his way of looking at the world, than from the mere transcription of external phenomena. Art, unlike experimental science, deals with a reality that includes the *emotional* reaction of the observer; even the most prosaic object, seen in a human context, becomes a symbol: Hedda Gabler's pistols, Solness' church tower, Hedwig Ekdahl's wild duck, transform themselves into images of inner, psychological realities, become the embodiments of dreams and dark desires.

It is often said that naturalism soon lost its impact because its main practitioners turned to symbolism and neo-romanticism. This is true only in so far as the dramatists concerned—Ibsen, Strindberg, Hauptmann—followed their initial impulse to its logical conclusion. In Hauptmann's *Hannele* the sick child's dream vision leads us straight from the ultra naturalist environment of a workhouse into the poetic world of neo-romantic visions of the Saviour surrounded by angels. Likewise Strindberg in plays like *The Ghost Sonata* or *To Damascus* merely translated the psychological situation of the brief character of a play like *The Father* into a direct concrete image of his nightmares and obsessions. Oscar Wilde's *Salomé* (1892) and Hugo von Hofmannsthal's *Elektra* (1903) are both clearly derived from naturalism in their ruthless determination to delve into the depths of human nature, yet at the same time they also bear the mark of aestheticism and neo-romanticism. Max Reinhardt, the greatest of the neo-romantic directors, took over from Otto Brahm, the founder of the *Freie Bühne*, and also excelled as the interpreter of the naturalists. He can, indeed, be regarded as the founder of the truly naturalist style of acting by his creation of the *Kammerspiele*, a chamber theatre specially designed for intimate dialogue and subtle psychological effects (1907). Quite analogously, Stanislavsky, the other great originator of naturalistic acting and production, developed his style toward neo-romanticism and invited Gordon Craig to direct a highly stylized neo-romantic *Hamlet* (1912). 'The theory of environment ends where the subconscious starts,' Stanislavsky declared—in other words, the naturalism of external reality merges into the dreamlike reality of man's inner life.

This, of course, is not to say that symbolism, neo-romanticism, and expressionism are *identical* with naturalism in its accepted sense, but merely to draw attention to the fact that once the basic position of the naturalists had been reached a *new phase* of art history had begun, a phase in which the same basic impulse carried all before it so that—as indeed Otto Brahm had predicted—new vistas quite naturally opened up at bends in the road and the wayfarers travelling on it naturally entered a succession of new landscapes: Ibsen, who had consciously chosen the path of realism with *Pillars of Society* ('I believe I may say with certainty that we shall both be satisfied with this play of mine. It is modern in all respects and completely in tune with the times . . .' Letter to F. Hegel, 29 July 1877—six years after Zola's *Thérèse Raquin*), almost imperceptibly turned into a symbolist; Hauptmann into a neo-romantic; while Strindberg gradually evolved from a ruthless naturalist (*Miss Julie* was subtitled 'A Naturalistic Tragedy') into the first expressionist; and at the end of *The Cherry Orchard* even Chekhov, the most rigorous naturalist, could not resist introducing that famous, mysterious symbolic sound, like the breaking of a string.

This line of evolution was dictated not only by the logic behind the basic philosophical concept that had inspired the naturalist movement but also by the parallel logic of the development of the *organic form* which, of necessity, had to follow the subject matter. Zola, Becque, Ibsen followed the formal pattern of the well-made social melodrama of the Parisian boulevard. Yet with the gradual implementation of the underlying theory, with its rejection of intrigue and artificial shape, dramatists tried to implement Jean Jullien's slogan that drama should become a *tranche de vie*—a slice of life.

It was Hauptmann who perfected this new technique in plays like *Die Weber* (*The Weavers*) or *Florian Geyer*. Each act of these massive dramas became a series of loosely connected snapshots, with characters emerging from the crowd and then sinking back into it, half-finished episodes out of which the total picture gradually coalesced, like a mosaic, which is composed of thousands of tiny coloured pieces. These plays could dispense with the old division of the cast into heroes and supporting actors. *The Weavers* has no hero; its principal character is the mass of the Silesian weavers, just as the subject of the play is not the fate of one man but that of a whole social class. This is the multifocal technique of playwriting that was used with such immense effect by Gorky in *The Lower Depths* (triumphantly produced by both Stanislavsky and Reinhardt) and by Chekhov. (Elmer Rice's *Street Scene*, Saroyan's *The Time of Your Life* and O'Neill's *The Iceman Cometh* belong in the same category. O'Neill is, of course, also a notable example of the closeness of the naturalistic and the expressionist impulse; his development closely parallels Strindberg's.)

The multifocal snapshot technique makes the playwright concentrate on a single, static segment of *time*. Hauptmann tended to build his plays in this style from a sequence of such static pictures. But he was at the same time aware that there might be subjects requiring a completely different approach. In a note dated 9 August 1912 he remarked: 'The modern dramatist, being a biologist, may sometimes strive for a drama which like a house, a work of architecture, stands still in one spot without moving from its position. Or he may have cause to comprehend life in a horizontal direction, having already grasped it in the vertical. He might prefer the *epic flow* of life to its *dramatic stasis*. The true biologist will not want to do without either of these two possibilities of form. . . .' Here Hauptmann clearly anticipates Brecht's idea of an epic theatre in which the loving depiction of multifarious minute detail gives way to the swift flow of action in a horizontal direction through time. That Brecht's concept of the theatre as a sociological laboratory also stems from the original impulse of the naturalist's experimental concept hardly needs to be stressed. His demand for a theatre that would be able to deal with reality in an age of science very closely resembles Zola's original manifesto. Equally his view that drama should be used to stimulate thinking in the audience has much in common with Hauptmann's view— which he expressed in 1912—that 'drama as literature is not so much the ready-made result of thought as the *thinking process* itself. It is the living presentation of the socially manifested content of consciousness. From this it follows that none of the truths it presents can lay claim to final, absolute, self-contained validity. Each is valid only in so far as it is conditioned by the inner drama,' i.e., the particular conception of a particular poet's consciousness of a particular event.

Hauptmann saw the dramatist as a biologist, Zola took his basic concepts from the physiologist Claude Bernard. It is surely no coincidence that Georg Büchner (1813–37), the greatest forerunner of naturalistic drama, who inspired both Hauptmann and Brecht, was a physiologist, that Brecht was once a medical student, and that both Chekhov and Schnitzler were practising physicians. Arthur Schnitzler (1862–1931), another great dramatist who is far too little known in the English-speaking world, wrote in both a strictly naturalistic and a neo-romantic style and also used drama as a means of exploration—of depth psychology. His series of dialogues, *Reigen* (1900), was the first attempt to put the sexual act on the stage and to illustrate, with bitter irony and sparkling wit, the extent to which the purely physiological side of sex is over-shadowed by social ambition, snobbery, and the struggle for domination. Sigmund Freud regarded Schnitzler as a kind of double of himself, a co-discoverer of the world of the subconscious. On the occasion of Schnitzler's sixtieth birthday he wrote to him:

> Again and again, in looking into your creations, I have thought to find, behind the make-believe of poetry, the same endeavours, interests, and results that I knew to have been my own. Your determination as well as your scepticism—what people call pessimism—your being captivated by the truths of the unconscious, of the instinctive nature of man, your disruption of the securities of cultural convention, your preoccupation with the polarity of love and death, all this has always struck me with an uncanny familiarity. . . . Thus I gained the impression that by intuition—but in fact by subtle self-observation—you know all that I have uncovered in painstaking work on other people. Yes, I believe that fundamentally you are a psychological depth explorer, as honestly unprejudiced as any. (Letter to Schnitzler, 14 May 1922)

Among the explorations Schnitzler undertook was one of the earliest examples of a work of literature that consisted entirely of the thoughts and feelings of an individual—*monologue intérieur*. This was naturalism driven to its utmost consequence—nature as perceived through a single temperament, an attempt to encompass the totality of the existential process of a human being. Schnitzler's novella *Leutnant Gustl* (1901) —the thoughts of a young officer compelled to commit suicide by a ridiculous 'affair of honour'—marks, among other things, a point of contact between the novel and the drama. (In his essay *Le naturalisme au théâtre*, Zola had deplored the fact that 'an increasingly deep gulf' had opened up between the two.) The very fact of being couched in the form of a monologue—a soliloquy—turned the short story into a dramatic representation of reality: the reader was made to *witness* a sequence of events *as it happened* rather than being told about it as an event that had taken place in the past. Here again the naturalists' rejection of rigid categories and preordained forms had led to a creative merging of ancient categories. The internal monologue was to become one of the main forms of the vast literature of introspection that arose in the twentieth century.

Leutnant Gustl was one of the earliest examples of internal monologue. The very first came from France: Edouard Dujardin's short novel, *Les lauriers sont coupés* (1887), which James Joyce regarded as the model for his own use of internal monologue in *Ulysses* and *Finnegans Wake*. Here then is the direct link between the naturalists and the avant-garde literature of introspection, dream, and fantasy, which culminated in surrealism and the Theatre of the Absurd. Again, as in the case of the link between the naturalists and neo-romantics, the connection is narrow, organic, and initially so gradual as to amount to an imperceptible merging. Joyce started as an admirer of Ibsen; he learned Norwegian to read Ibsen in the original, and his first works of fiction were meticulously observed slices of life. The step from the careful description of external reality to the plan to encompass not only the outside but the inside of the hero's life was logical and inevitable. In the French novel, and in the wake of Dujardin, certainly by the same inner logic, Proust's monumental attempt to capture the process of time through his hero's consciousness also led to an *internalization* of the concept of reality: the same scenes, the same people, appear differently to an eager young and a disillusioned middle-aged Marcel. And this, again, is a process entirely analogous to the subjective vision behind Strindberg's *The Ghost Sonata, A Dream Play*, and *To Damascus*.

Antonin Artaud directed Strindberg's *Dream Play* in 1928. Arthur Adamov derived his inspiration for his first absurdist plays from Strindberg as well as from Artaud himself; and Samuel Beckett's dramatic *oeuvre* forms part of a wider exploration of the inner world of the internal monologue closely related to the ideas and example of James Joyce. Thus we can observe the initial impulse behind the naturalist revolution spreading, and still active, in the manifold manifestations of contemporary theatre.

However revolutionary the ideas of the early naturalists may have been, they themselves saw themselves as part of a tradition. Zola proclaimed that 'Naturalism is Diderot, Rousseau, Balzac, and twenty others.' He even regarded Homer as a naturalist—in his own fashion—and consciously emulated passages from Homer. Taine, who admired English literature so much, derived many of the ideas that later inspired Zola from the English realistic social novel of the eighteenth and early nineteenth centuries. In Germany the dramatists of the *Sturm und Drang* period (Lenz, Zacharias Werner, Klinger) as well as the early Goethe and Schiller must clearly be regarded as forerunners of naturalism; and so must Kleist and Büchner, Grabbe and Hebbel. In Russia Gogol, Tolstoy, Dostoyevsky, and Ostrovsky exercised a powerful and decisive influence on Chekhov and Stanislavsky, Gorky and Leonid Andreyev. In the English-speaking theatre T. W. Robertson's *Caste* (1867) must be regarded as a trail-blazing forerunner of the realism of Shaw and Granville-Barker.

The coming of the naturalist revolution was inevitable. It was an expression of the *Zeitgeist*—the rapid industrialization of Europe and North America, the growth of science, the impact of Darwinism, positivism, and the consequent collapse of old certainties and established faiths. What the early pioneers and theoreticians of naturalism achieved was no more than the systematization and clear, programmatic expression of the spirit of their age. Nevertheless, the effect was overwhelming—a feeling of excitement, of liberation. And it was this excitement that released the most valuable element in the naturalist revolution: by opening up a vast new field of subject matter, by removing age-old inhibitions and taboos, by destroying time-honoured rules and recipes for writing dialogue and structuring plot, naturalism opened the floodgates for a vast stream of new poetic possibilities in the theatre.

Whatever their ideas, their social purpose, their political commitment may have been, the great naturalists Ibsen, Strindberg, Shaw, Hauptmann, Chekhov, Gorky, Schnitzler must ultimately be judged as great poets, poets of a new kind; they discovered the magic that lies behind the seemingly commonplace surface of ordinary life, the tragic greatness of simple people, the poetry of silences and reticences, the bitter ironies of unspoken thoughts: Mrs Alving hearing the ghosts of the past in the next room, the old drunken doctor, Chebutikhin, washing his hands on the night of the fire in *The Three Sisters*, the 'Baron's' barely articulate account of his life in *The Lower Depths*—these are examples of a poetry *of* the stage with an intensity and poignancy that could not have been achieved with the rules and methods of an earlier theatre, a poetry arising out of, and entirely in tune with, an industrialized, urbanized society and the image of man that, for better or for worse, it had created. To have bridged the gulf between literature and the theatre, which had opened up so disastrously in the middle of the nineteenth century, to have restored the dignity of the stage not only as an art but also as an instrument of serious thought and inquiry, and to have created a new kind of poetry—these are the true achievements of the early naturalists. The contemporary theatre to a very large extent draws it impetus and energy from their ideas, their courage, their liberating influence.

Ibsen

AN ENEMY OF THE PEOPLE
HEDDA GABLER · THE MASTER BUILDER

It was from Rome on 23 November 1881 that Ibsen wrote to his publisher, F. Hegel: 'I am busy with plans for a new comedy in four acts, a work which I had in mind before, but which I laid aside because *Ghosts* forced itself on me and demanded all my attention.' That play, which eventually grew to five acts, was *An Enemy of the People*. On 21 June 1882 Ibsen announced to Hegel that the play was finished: 'Yesterday I completed my new play. It is titled *An Enemy of the People* and is in five acts. I am still uncertain as to whether I should call it a comedy or a straight drama. It has many of the characteristics of comedy but it also has a serious theme. . . .' On 9 September 1882, Ibsen sent Hegel the last section of the final manuscript. 'I have enjoyed writing this play,' he wrote from Gossensass, his Tyrolean mountain retreat, 'and I feel quite lost and lonely now that it is out of my hands. Dr Stockmann and I got on so very well together; we agree on so many subjects. But the doctor is more muddle-headed than I am; and moreover he has other peculiarities that permit him to say things which would not be taken so well if I myself said them. . . .'

Ibsen did not in fact call *An Enemy of the People* a comedy, but subtitled it simply 'A play'. Too much serious matter, too much bitterness had crept into it while he was writing it, under the influence of the storm and scandal that had followed the publication of *Ghosts*. And so Dr Stockmann did indeed become a mouthpiece of his author and the play a very personal declaration—Ibsen's defiant answer to the critics who accused him of being a corrupter of youth, a

fanatic who threatened the peace of society by exposing its
hidden shames and sources of infection.

An Enemy of the People is Ibsen's most directly *political*
play. In most of the other realistic plays of his middle period
Ibsen deals with social rather than political problems. But
here he boldly tackles the municipal politics of a Norwegian
town and exposes the hypocrisy and cowardice of the very
circles who had seemed his natural allies, the liberals, the
progressives, the democrats. It is they, here represented by
the town's newspaper the *Herald* and its editor Hovstad, who
'go on proclaiming day after day the false doctrine that it's
the masses, the multitude, the "solid majority" who are the
keepers of liberal doctrine and morality!—and that vice,
corruption, and depravity flow from culture. . . . Fortunately,
the idea that culture is demoralizing is just another fabrica-
tion that's been handed down to us! No, it's ignorance,
poverty, and dirt that do the devil's work . . . !' More than
eighty years after Ibsen wrote *An Enemy of the People* these
are still highly topical sentiments.

In Ibsen's hand the most prosaic subject turned into a
structure of powerful symbolic images. The infectious waste
products that flow from the tannery into the water of the
public baths in Stockmann's home town become a telling
metaphor of the lies, the hypocrisies, and the puritanism that
Ibsen so hated. 'A community that lives on deceit,' cries
Stockmann at the climax of the play, the public meeting in
the fourth act, '. . . ought to be razed to the ground. All men
who live by lies should be exterminated—like vermin!'

Dr Stockmann utters these radical opinions in the white
heat of passion, when he has been intolerably provoked. And
Ibsen was right when he said that his hero was somewhat
more muddleheaded than he himself. No wonder a good
American democrat like Arthur Miller, who made a well-
known adaptation of *An Enemy of the People*, felt compelled
to tone down some of the seemingly anti-democratic opinions
voiced by Dr Stockmann and to argue that its message lies in
a plea for the protection of unpopular minorities. Ibsen cer-

tainly makes that last point, but his view is less optimistic, far more bitter and resigned than Miller's. He was fully aware of the tragic position of the man of vision, insight, and genius in a society where the majority must, of necessity, be less intelligent, less perceptive, and more cowardly than the lonely vanguard who can see farther and deeper than the masses and is capable of facing unpleasant facts more boldly. 'You are, of course, right,' Ibsen wrote to Georg Brandes in June 1883, 'when you say that we must all work for the spread of our ideas. But I maintain that a fighter in the intellectual vanguard cannot possibly gather a majority around him. In ten years the majority will possibly occupy the standpoint which Dr Stockmann held at the public meeting. But during those ten years the doctor will not have been standing still; he will still be at least ten years ahead of the majority. The majority, the mass, the mob will never catch up with him. And he can never have the majority with him. As regards myself at least, I am quite aware of such unceasing progress. At the point where I stood when I wrote each of my books there now stands a tolerably compact crowd; but I myself am no longer there. I am elsewhere; farther ahead, I hope.'

So it is not only that Dr Stockmann happens to be unpopular as the herald of one particular and peculiarly unpleasant truth in one particular case. The holder of the truth, the man who can see the essence of the situation, is *bound* to be unpopular, and bound to remain so, even if the masses catch up with his ideas in due course. That is the meaning of Stockmann's final summing up, the oft-quoted line: 'The strongest man in the world is he who stands alone!'

There is a certain arrogance, a certain aristocratic intolerance, in this attitude. *An Enemy of the People* is not a difficult play, it is built on the model of the most successful kind of nineteenth-century French drama; but its subject matter is closely akin to Ibsen's most ambitious and most difficult work, the great poem *Brand*, the hero of which also is a man who feels strongest because he stands alone and whose stubborn determination not to yield an inch brings ruin to all around him. In a certain sense Dr Stockmann is a popularized version of Brand, reduced in size and without Brand's fanatical destructiveness. At the end of *An Enemy of the People* we are left without any indication whether Dr Stockmann's courageous stand, his decision to face his adversaries on his own home ground rather than to move elsewhere and start afresh, will in fact bring ruin to his family. There are grounds to assume that Ibsen wanted the audience to be reassured on this point. Writing to Edvard Fallesen, the director of the Royal Theatre at Copenhagen who was about to stage the play, Ibsen expressly asked that Captain Horster, one of the few who remain staunch supporters of Dr Stockmann, should be played as a *young* man, so that in the fifth act it should be possible to infer that an 'intimate and warm friendship' might be about to grow up between him and Stockmann's daughter Petra, thus compensating her for the painful disappointment she suffered in the editor, Hovstad, in whose progressive ideas she had previously shown a more than merely theoretical interest. That is why *An Enemy of the People*, though not a comedy, still keeps clear of being a tragedy. Dr Stockmann, unlike Brand, will survive; he will, indeed, eventually win his point, even though, by that time, he will have incurred unpopularity for some other reason.

It is highly characteristic of Ibsen that he could also see the other point of view. His very next play, *The Wild Duck*, demonstrates the destructiveness, the humourlessness of a fanatic of the truth, Gregers Werle, who in destroying the lie by which the Ekdahls live also destroys their happiness. This is the other side of Brand and to some extent also of Dr Stockmann. But there is also an essential difference between Gregers Werle and Dr Stockmann: while the former's concern is with the destruction of a *private* lie which does not harm society, the latter causes trouble and unhappiness by insisting on exposing a social evil based on the *collective* lie of a whole community.

Many of Ibsen's attacks on the social evils of his time have inevitably dated—the social conditions he criticized, notably the status of women and the squeamishness of the nineteenth century about the open discussion of sexual and moral problems, have undergone a radical change for the better since Ibsen's day. Being a political rather than a social play, *An Enemy of the People* has curiously, at first glance almost paradoxically, escaped this process of dating. On closer reflection this will appear natural enough. While social conditions change from century to century, politics remain essentially the same. The struggle for power, for the support of the majority in one form or another, was the essence of politics then as it is now and as it has been in any other historical epoch. Always politicians have been involved in the dilemma, that, to retain their power and influence, they must serve the sectional interests of their supporters, even if they can clearly discern the long-term advantage of short-term sacrifices on their part. Today as in Ibsen's time the politician who tries to win his election by concentrating on the cost of living in his own constituency, while neglecting some major world problems of mass starvation or war in other continents, re-enacts the dilemma of Dr Stockmann's brother the mayor and of Hovstad, the editor. And Aslaksen, the leader of the taxpayers' association, is the eternal symbol of the electorate themselves for whom all long-term social, cultural, and ideological issues ultimately reduce themselves to pounds, shillings, and pence. The clarity of the vision, the economy of the technique with which Ibsen has succeeded in compressing these eternal elements of all politics in to the compass of a small, compact community, of a single dramatic conflict, is a truly astonishing proof of his genius.

This is also clearly the reason why this particular play of Ibsen's has so frequently been revived, so frequently been adapted to fit into different national idioms and milieux. Whether in American, German, or Norwegian, *An Enemy of the People* will always prove itself one of the archetypal images of political conflict, even if it is not Ibsen's most poetic or most profound play.

It is also a play that presents the producer with a healthy challenge in one of Ibsen's relatively rare crowd scenes, the public meeting in the fourth act. Ibsen was very anxious that the numerous small parts in that scene should be cast with highly accomplished actors, so that the crowd itself, the stage image of the mob Dr Stockmann—and Ibsen—confront, should be seen to be composed of individuals, not generalized types.

Apart from this one scene, *An Enemy of the People* has the simplicity of all technically perfect structures. That the two main antagonists, the medical officer of health and the mayor, should be brothers is a fine poetic stroke: it deepens the purely political conflict into a battle within one family, with an echo of the struggle of Cain and Abel.

The two journalists from the *Herald*, Hovstad and Billing, both young men, both progressives, play a particularly vital part in the mechanics of the play. For while the mayor is clearly shown as a reactionary, and Aslaksen as a 'moderate' (i.e., a cautious and somewhat cowardly supporter of liberal ideas from the start) these two young men are Dr Stockmann's intimates and admirers; their defection comes as a surprise, the mercenary nature of their attitude (also shown in the episode of the English novel Petra has been asked to translate) is a painful revelation. As always in Ibsen's plays, the characters balance each other in such a way that the features of each act as a foil to those of his opposite number. Each character has his definite function in the plot. It is the elegance of the structure that it rests on the utmost economy of means. The Ibsen of *Peer Gynt* may have been an exuberant romantic. The Ibsen of *An Enemy of the People* is a master of the 'well-made play'.

Hedda Gabler, which Ibsen completed in 1890, is the last of his strictly realist plays. It lacks, at first sight at least, the intense preoccupation with social problems that dominated Ibsen's work in the middle period of his career as a dramatist, the period between his youthful romantic and poetic phase (from *Catiline*, 1849, to *Emperor and Galilean*, 1873) and his last plays (from *The Master Builder*, 1892, to *When We Dead Awaken*, 1899) in which the allegorical and symbolic elements predominate.

Hedda Gabler is a realistic play without an obvious social objective. It is first and foremost about a human being, not about an idea: a human being composed of mystery, malevolence, evil, and at the same time overwhelming charm and fascination. Certainly, as a dramatic portrait of a complex and ambivalent character *Hedda Gabler* has few rivals. And yet the social preoccupation, the critique of society, is nevertheless present in the play, provided one probes beneath the surface. For *Hedda Gabler* is also a penetrating exploration of what was in Ibsen's time, and still is in a different form, one of the basic social problems—the position and role of women in the modern world. *Hedda Gabler* is, then, a violent attack on social convention and conformist respectability.

But—and this is the artistic triumph in *Hedda Gabler*—the fusion of the two elements of character portrayal and social comment is so completely successful in the play that the central character *is* the social comment; and the social comment consists in the character of Hedda Gabler. Such an integration of abstract content and concrete human reality must be regarded as the highest aspiration of any dramatist, its achievement his ultimate goal. Hence it could well be argued that *Hedda Gabler* is one of the high points of Ibsen's *oeuvre* and most likely to remain fresh and vital in the future. Precisely because the social comment is so completely integrated in the character of the heroine—or anti-heroine—the play strikes our generation as vividly as it did audiences in its own time.

Among Ibsen's working notes on *Hedda Gabler* there is one headed 'Main Points' which reads:

1 They are not all made to be mothers.

2 They are passionate, but they are afraid of scandal.

3 They perceive that the times are full of missions worth devoting one's life to, but they cannot discover them.

It is obvious enough that 'they' in this context stands for 'women.' How then do these considerations find expression in the character of Hedda Gabler?

Most critics see her essentially as a wicked woman:

> . . . one more variation of the Femme Fatale of the Romantics —la Belle Dame sans Merci; that strange type of woman who through the ages has curiously fascinated many men—partly as a challenge to their aggressiveness, as the Matterhorn tempts the climber; partly as an allurement to their masochism.[1]

> Hedda Gabler has no ethical ideas at all, only romantic ones. She is a typical nineteenth-century figure, falling into the abyss between the ideals which do not impose on her and the realities she has not yet discovered. The result is that though she has imagination, and an intense appetite for beauty, she has no conscience, no conviction: with plenty of cleverness, energy, and personal fascination she remains mean, envious, insolent, cruel in protest against others' happiness, fiendish in her dislike of inartistic people and things, a bully in reaction from her own cowardice.[2]

> Hedda Gabler is strong in her intellectual dishonesty. She will not face her life, her limitations or her creditors. Hedda has neither self-awareness nor responsibility. . . . There is neither progression nor conflict in her character. From the beginning she is shown as eaten up by envy and pride, in all the malignancy of impotence.[3]

These harsh assessments are undoubtedly true, applying as they do to a woman who marries a man whom she does not love but despises and treats with open contempt; who deliberately ruins and drives to his death another man whom she has loved, but whose achievement as a creative thinker, whose happiness in love she envies; a woman who so loathes life, herself, and her obligations that she kills not only herself but the unborn child she carries.

[1] F. L. Lucas, *Ibsen and Strindberg* (London, 1962) p. 222.
[2] Bernard Shaw, *The Quintessence of Ibsenism* (London, 1913) p. 110.
[3] M. C. Bradbrook, *Ibsen the Norwegian* (London, 1946) p. 116.

And yet, could such a loathsome creature become the heroine of a tragedy, an object of deep pity and compassion—as Hedda Gabler undoubtedly does—if she were really so utterly without redeeming features? Surely her beauty alone would not be enough to win the readers' and audiences' sympathies; nor her preoccupation with beautiful things, her 'aestheticism' as F. L. Lucas calls it. Even the desire to 'die beautifully' would, in such a character, be no more than foolish and grotesque romantic sentimentality. Why is it that we cannot but feel for Hedda Gabler, that we are on *her* side while observing her wicked and destructive actions?

I think the reason lies in the fact that Ibsen clearly conveys to us his deep conviction that Hedda Gabler is not so much a wilful destroyer as a victim: a victim of society, its conventions, and its heartless denial of human dignity to a woman of spirit and talent. It is not envy and impotence that are Hedda's outstanding features so much as *frustration*. That Hedda has imagination and intelligence, that she has a deep craving for everything that is beautiful, is evident enough. So, in fact, she is potentially an artist, a creative human being. But this potential is unrealized; she herself is only dimly aware of it. Or, as Ibsen put it in his note, she perceives 'that the times are full of missions, worth devoting one's life to, but [she] cannot discover them'. Why? Because social conventions about the upbringing of girls, social conventions about the life women are to lead, have denied her the possibility of learning enough about the world and herself to realize that she might make use of her imagination, her craving for beauty, her intelligence. A stunted artist, a maker nipped in the bud, unaware of her potential, Hedda Gabler must be a profoundly frustrated personality. Hence her restlessness, her envy, her destructiveness, her death wish. With the hand of the true master Ibsen clearly shows *us*, the audience, the sources of Hedda's frustration, of which she herself is totally unconscious.

If Hedda were a man she could be master of her own fate,

free to choose and to pursue a course of action. It is no coincidence that General Gabler's pistols are one of the central symbols of the play. These pistols are tokens of masculinity in more senses than one: sex symbols as well as symbols of sport and male pursuits, the freedom of the hunter and the adventurer. If Hedda clings to these pistols, she does so because she longs for the creative freedom of the world of men. On the other hand she is shown loathing the conventional female role: she refuses to be a housewife, she hates the idea of motherhood. ('They are not all made to be mothers.') She longs to participate in Eilert Lovborg's creative work and is fiercely, destructively envious of the woman who has succeeded in becoming Eilert's helpmate, the mother of his spiritual child, his book.

Of all this she is but dimly aware. But why does she not take the step towards emancipation, which was quite possible by 1890, why did she not become Eilert Lovborg's lover and companion? Why did she marry Tesman, the dull, pedantic, uncreative scholar? Because—and here her case becomes truly tragic—her upbringing as a member of the respectable upper class, as the General's daughter, has conditioned her, more mercilessly than any of Pavlov's dogs, to react as a member of her class, and of her stunted and degraded sex. When Lovborg offered her emancipation and free love, she could not but reject him with indignation. And when the time had come by which girls of her class must get married if they did not want to decline into despised maiden aunts, life's ultimate failures, condemned to become mere hangers-on, vicarious participators in the life of luckier members of their family, like Aunt Julia, she simply had to take the best offer there was, George Tesman's hand. She envies Mrs Elvsted's courage that enabled her, the less brilliant, the less wellborn woman, to break the shackles of convention and to face the disapproval of the world in leaving her husband to live with Eilert Lovborg. But then Thea Elvsted does not carry the burden of convention, of pride, of social conditioning, that has formed a general's daughter. Precisely because Hedda has more breeding, is stronger-willed, nobler—which means haughtier, more aware of her social position and obligations —she is denied the capacity to break her chains.

That is why Hedda despised Thea at school and why she pulled her hair: it is the superior family's pride that makes even its children cruel toward inferiors in wealth, or status, or manners. It is that pride, that sense of superiority, however, that keeps the products of such conditioning chained to the conventions of their class. They simply could not give up the standards that procure them that most pleasurable of all satisfactions—the sense of being better than others. What makes the case even worse for the women produced by this social conditioning is that, having been impregnated by this sense of superiority, this pride, they are still condemned to the traditional role of their sex, which is submissiveness and the acceptance of their husbands as their lords and masters. Being above Tesman socially, and also intellectually, Hedda cannot but resent her position, cannot but loathe poor kindly George and his angelic but fussy aunt.

Social superiority may be no more than empty pride which makes those infected by it into heartless and cruel people; but its worst side in Hedda's case is that this sense of social superiority prevents her from realizing her genuine superiority as a potentially creative personality. If the standards prescribed by the laws of noblesse oblige had not prevented her from breaking out into the freedom of moral and social emancipation, she might have been able to turn her passionate desire for beauty (which is the hallmark of real, spiritual, as distinct from social, aristocracy) to the creation of beauty, living beauty rather than merely a beautiful death. It is the creative energy, frustrated and dammed up, that is finally converted into the malice and envy, the destructive rage, the intellectual dishonesty that lead to Hedda Gabler's downfall. Because all this wickedness springs from a perverted creativeness, and because we sense that the depths of this evil are the reverse side of high potential achievement chained and turned upside down, we feel for Hedda Gabler and see her as a truly tragic figure. One is tempted to think that Ibsen, who like all great playwrights must have been able to identify himself completely with his characters, and who must, to some extent, *be* Hedda Gabler too, began by imagining what he himself with all his rebellious thirst for freedom and all his creative power, would have felt like if he had been born a woman, a member of a superior family. It is as though the horror at the thought of all the creativeness that would then have been bottled up inside him, the rage at the waste of so much creative energy, pervaded the suffering, the restlessness, the cruelty and wilful wickedness of Hedda Gabler. Beauty, intellect, and creative power turned into evil from sheer frustration is a truly heartbreaking spectacle. And that is why *Hedda Gabler* is a truly heartbreaking, tragic play; why Hedda herself, in all her heartlessness, is a truly heroic character.

As a dramatic structure *Hedda Gabler* is a masterpiece of economy: six main characters, three men and three women, balance each other and, by subtle contrast, focus and vary the play's argument. If Tesman is the pedantic, uncreative man, Lovborg is the unruly, creative one. If Hedda stands for the superior, aristocratic woman who is the slave to the pride of her caste, Thea Elvsted represents her exact counterpart, socially, intellectually, and physically inferior, but because of those very drawbacks more successful, more adaptable, better able to survive. And Aunt Julia, condemned to a life of selfless abnegation in which she loses her own individual existence, subtly sets off both Hedda and Thea, exactly as Brack, the cynical epicurean, emphasizes Tesman's homespun goodness and Lovborg's lack of cynicism in his dissipation. Each of the male characters also has his female counterpart: Hedda and Lovborg are both creative and morally weak; Thea and Tesman, both kindhearted and uncreative; Aunt Julia and Brack present the two poles of male and female unmarried middle and old age, the maiden aunt and the elderly Don Juan. It is a microcosm that Ibsen puts before us but so subtly shaded and so delicately balanced that it becomes an image of the world itself.

Hedda Gabler is a profound character study and a profound social analysis, hardly less relevant today than it was in the 1890s, for even if women have gained social equality of sorts, many creative outlets are still denied to them, and the ill consequences of social snobbery and heartless pride are no less evident in our own time than in Ibsen's Norway. The play is also a poem. An entrance or an exit, a figure standing by an open door, a shot ringing out in what seems an idyllic scene, all these may contain more poetic feeling than a dozen finely written speeches. It is as a sequence of stage images of this kind that a play like *Hedda Gabler* must also, and perhaps essentially be judged. And here again it is the image of Hedda herself that is the centre and the triumph of the play: Hedda radiant, Hedda bored and restless, Hedda burning the manuscript, Hedda dying beautifully—an unforgettable figure that imposes itself on any actress who undertakes the part, one of the truly immortal characters of world drama, an image of infinite complexity and depth.

It is the peculiarity of masterpieces that they reveal a new facet of their significance to each generation, that they change and grow with the times, expand and contract and even oscillate between the tragic and the comic. There is something mysterious about this Protean quality of great works of the imagination: 'How is it possible,' we ask, 'that contemporary audiences can find meanings in *Hamlet* or *Don Quixote*, *Faust* or *The Brothers Karamazov* of which Shakespeare and Cervantes, Goethe and Dostoyevsky themselves must have been completely unaware? How can a play or a novel say more than its author wanted to say?'

Part of the answer surely lies in the fact that no work of the human imagination or intellect can ever exist *in vacuo* and completely independent of its audience. A work of literature is an act of communication; and communication takes place between the mind that utters and the mind that perceives. A piece of Greek sculpture may have been charged with deep religious significance to its maker and his contemporary audience; this religious significance has evaporated

for us who admire the same piece of sculpture two or three
thousand years later; *our* attention is held by the harmony of
the proportions, the quality of craftsmanship. These qualities
are nothing new, they were equally present two or three
thousand years ago; but at that time the religious significance
was so powerful that it may have *drowned*, as it were, the
purely aesthetic excellence we now regard as the work's chief
claim to our attention. And our preoccupation with proportions, harmony, and craftsmanship may, in its turn, make
way for a rising interest in some other aspect, equally present
from the very beginning, of which neither the original Greek
audience was nor we, in the mid-twentieth century, may as
yet be aware.

No writer of the comparatively recent past demonstrates
these truths and mysteries more conclusively than Henrik
Ibsen. To his contemporaries the plays of his maturity and
old age appeared above all as acts of defiance of social and
political taboos. His introduction of a subject like syphilis
into drama in *Ghosts* (1881), his plea for social and sexual
equality for women in *A Doll's House* (1879), or his defence
of an adulterous relationship in *Rosmersholm* (1886) made
him a subject of scandal and concern, the storm centre of
impassioned controversy. So strong were the emotions Ibsen
aroused that these controversial aspects overshadowed all
others. Today, when these issues have long been overtaken by
events and the process of social change, it is difficult for us
to imagine the bitterness and intensity of the passions aroused
by Ibsen's plays. And indeed, in the case of a play like *The
Master Builder* it is well-nigh impossible to visualize any
reason whatever why, at its first English production in 1893,
it should not only have been condemned by the press as being
obscure to the point of total unintelligibility ('Dense mist en-
shrouds characters, words, actions, and motives'—*Daily Tele-
graph*; 'Rigmarole of an Oracle Delphic in obscurity . . .
Three acts of gibberish'—*Stage*) but also denounced as un-
wholesome, blasphemous, and unchaste.

Today *The Master Builder* seems to invite the very opposite criticism, namely that it shrouds its sexual subject matter in a veil of conventional symbolism which is both obvious and trite; several decades of schooling in Freudian psychoanalysis have made the meaning of church towers to be scaled and secret kingdoms to be conquered so commonplace as to empty them of any poetic validity, let alone any power to shock. And Hilda Wangel, that embodiment of the new woman, who reduced her contemporaries to apoplexies of righteous indignation by defying convention to the point of setting out into the great wide world on her own before she reached the age of twenty and boldly challenging a middle-aged man of distinction to leave his wife and home for her sake, that same Hilda Wangel today strikes us as a charming period character, a Victorian suffragette, sensibly dressed, decorous, romantic, and utterly respectable in spite of her wild talk.

These aspects of *The Master Builder* were apparent fairly soon after the play had been written—Ibsen completed it in 1892, when he was sixty-four—and already between the two world wars the critics and the audiences that were still thrilled by it looked for and found other points of significance and relevance in it. In a period in which the younger generation was deeply shaken by the disaster in which the blunders and follies of their elders had involved them, *The Master Builder* was seen as primarily a dramatization of the conflict between the older and the younger generation. Halvard Solness became the personification of the hollowness of success, a symbol of the evil hold those who have reached the top establish on its fruits. Poor Hilda, who had believed in the great man's ability to scale the heights, must learn that he suffers from vertigo; and that the incident when she saw him climb to the top of a tower was an exceptional occurrence by no means typical of his personality. For us, this reading of the play has also become something of a cliché; there have been too many plays on similar themes since the twenties.

And yet *The Master Builder* continues to hold our attention, to move, to shatter us. Why?

Perhaps because it is only after the layers of social defiance and iconoclasm, of the more obvious psychological implications, have been stripped away that we finally penetrate to the simpler human content and to the poetry. For—and this becomes clearer with every decade that passes—Ibsen was, in the last analysis, a great poet—a great poet of the stage—with the supreme ability to make an entrance or an exit, the juxtaposition of two scenes, into shattering emotional experiences. This is—at least in the plays that are written in prose—not so much a matter of language as of dramatic structure: the conciseness of the action, the precision of its construction, the perfection of the timing with which events unfold. And this poetic quality lies in the core of genuine human experience, deep human suffering that the playwright has embodied in his text.

That *The Master Builder* is the outcome of a deep emotional crisis in Ibsen's life is by now well known: his meeting, at the age of sixty-one, with a young Austrian girl, Emilie Bardach, at Gossensass in the summer of 1889. One must beware of going too far in trying to establish too close a parallel between the events of that holiday in a South Tyrolean resort and the content of the play. It is, however, clear enough that the experience of meeting a young woman of the then rising and highly unconventional generation, the discovery on Ibsen's part that he was still able to make a powerful emotional impression on such a young woman, and his eventual decision to resist any temptation to take advantage of the hold he had established over her, confronted the aging playwright with aspects of his own situation and personality which form the basis of the creative process behind *The Master Builder*.

It is this level of the play that holds the greatest interest for our own time: the poetic projection onto the stage of the existential experience of a man of genius at the point of his existence when he comes face to face with the process of aging and death. Halvard Solness, who never qualified as an architect, is only a master builder, but the English term is far too heavily charged with the social implications of lower-class and artisan status. In Norwegian *Bygmester* may have the same associations, yet it is also a far more poetic, a far larger term than architect, with implications of creativeness, of mastery in the artistic sense that go beyond anything the dryer, more precise qualification could contain. There can be little doubt that Solness is—up to a point—a self-portrait of his creator (as is the sculptor Rubek in *When We Dead Awaken*). And Solness, who wanted to build churches when he was young and became rich by turning to the building of small houses for the people, Solness who laid the foundations for his financial success at the cost of his wife's happiness, carries his 'good luck' about with him 'like a great raw wound in [his] breast'. And it was precisely this strange, magic power of making things happen as he wished them to (which is the same as the creative power of an artist of genius) that led Solness into his tragic situation. He is afraid of this magic power. For it is this magic power that made Hilda Wangel resolve to come and seek him out when she grew up; it is this power to make people believe in him that makes them ask the impossible, the scaling of the heights by an aging man who has always felt dizzy even when standing on his first-floor balcony. It is the fundamental contradiction in the life of most men of genius that they create an image, a persona, of superhuman dimensions for their public. This image is based merely on the creative aspects of their personality. Rousseau, who revolutionized mankind's ideas about enlightened education, put his own children into an orphanage; the film star who appears as a symbol of sex to millions may be a lonely and frigid woman. What kills Solness is the image of himself he has instilled in Hilda Wangel, his public persona as the great artist who soars to the heights to the music of the harps of heaven, the hero who is bound to conquer all before him.

Here Ibsen touches the problem around which so much of modern literature revolves, the problem of human identity. Which is the true Solness: the mean and cowardly man who exploits his talented subordinates by preventing them from striking out on their own, who has ruined the man who gave him his first chance in life, who feels, and perhaps is, responsible for his wife's distress? Or that other Solness, whose buildings testify to his genius, his soaring spirit, the man whom Hilda Wangel saw climbing up onto the heights, the man who made homes for multitudes of human beings? It is by no means a foregone conclusion that it is the private Solness who is the true one. For that private Solness may lie with a crushed skull down there in the quarry, but the tower he has built still stands, and so do the many other buildings he created. That is why, in the last line of the play, Hilda Wangel continues to look up at the tower, where she can still see her master builder. A creative genius' private personality is short-lived and—in the eyes of future generations—irrelevant. His creative part endures and will increasingly be seen as his true self.

But this is scant consolation to the human being behind the creative persona—and that is why I think *The Master Builder* remains a true tragedy even for our own epoch. The human being would much rather stay reduced to the dimensions of his private self and feels the demands made upon him by those who see him as a superhuman figure as cruel intrusions, however flattering, however hard to resist they may be. That is why Hilda Wangel, who comes to be carried off by a wild Viking raider, whose admiration drives Solness to climb to a height from which he is bound to topple, is seen as both desirable and cruel, a bird of prey swooping down on its victim. There is a special irony in the fact that it was Ibsen as much as any other man of his time who had helped to mould the 'new woman' Hilda represents: independent, always ready to take the initiative, conscious of her right to happiness and her right to choose her own sexual partner. In *The Master Builder* this new woman has become a threat to her own aging creator. After all it was Solness himself who moulded Hilda's entire emotional life by inspiring her with the ideal he himself is unable to live up to. The man of genius can be a sorcerer's apprentice who will be destroyed by the creatures he himself has brought to life.

Hilda Wangel has much in common with Gregers Werle in *The Wild Duck*, who also destroys a family by his excessive belief in the talent of one of its members; only Hjalmar Ekdahl is really a pathetic fraud, while Solness is a man of genuine creative powers. This makes the destruction of Solness more tragic than that of the Ekdahls, and Hilda Wangel a far more dangerous character than poor Gregers Werle.

It is undeniable that the character of Hilda has become dated, if only in some of its more superficial aspects—the knapsack and the walking stick, the sensible clothes, etc. That of Mrs Solness, on the other hand, the third main character in the play, has, if anything, become more contemporary. As a study of neurosis Aline Solness is a masterly creation, and the unfolding of her character a supreme example of a great playwright's craft; while at first we are led to believe that her plight is the fairly conventional one of a woman who mourns her dead children, she herself, by a stroke of supreme irony, reveals to us in the end that in fact it is not her children she mourns but her dolls—i.e. the lost innocence of her childhood—and that, in fact, she was responsible, if only subconsciously, for the death of her children, whom she rejected as one of the responsibilities of the maturity she did not, or could not, attain. So Aline is in fact the woman that Nora in *A Doll's House* refused to become, the child wife Helmer wanted, but aged and broken by an event that propelled her too far into the reality of suffering. She is thus, very profoundly, the antithesis of Hilda Wangel—the passive, infantile, and probably also frigid woman as against the active, autonomous, and passionate new feminine personality. That is the reason Aline has not dated for us. She is an eternal type, while Hilda is essentially of the late nineteenth century. The infantile, passive, unawakened female is still with us; it is the mature, autonomous woman who has developed and progressed into a completely different type.

If Ibsen portrayed himself in the character of the Master

Builder, the play triumphantly justifies the title. As a dramatic structure it is a supreme example of architecture: concise, economical, beautifully balanced, *The Master Builder* must be regarded as one of the finest achievements of dramatic technique. Every word, every sentence, every pause appears in its inevitable place, the only one that could possibly be right. The dovetailing of exposition and action, that most difficult aspect of the playwright's craft, is here seamless and perfect; and so is the integration of the subsidiary plot, the emancipation of Ragnar Brovik and the death of his father, with the main action. As always in Ibsen's realistic plays, a great deal of the action has happened in the past and is recounted by the characters. But, unlike most of the other plays of this type, here the feeling that we are treated to complicated narrations is completely absent. Hilda's account of her first meeting with Solness and Solness' revelation about his past are dramatic events in their own right, which create their own peculiar tension and movement. The perfection of its form and the richness and depth of the human experience it expresses ensure the enduring success and validity of *The Master Builder* through the constant flux of taste and changes in the audience's interests, which make some of the surface features of the play more or less topical in succeeding periods. Ibsen, the master craftsman, has built an edifice of perfect proportions and a solid basic structure that is bound to outlast some of its decorative detail.

Pirandello:
Master of the Naked Masks

Among the creators of the contemporary theatre Luigi Pirandello stands in the very first rank, next to Ibsen, Strindberg,
and Shaw. And even though his plays may be less frequently
performed in the English-speaking world than those of either
Shaw or Ibsen today (Strindberg is equally unjustly neglected), his living influence in the work of the dramatists of our
own age is far stronger, far more active than that of those
two giants. For Pirandello more than any other playwright
has been responsible for a revolution in man's attitude to the
world that is comparable to the revolution caused by Ein-
stein's discovery of the concept of relativity in physics: Pirandello has transformed our attitude to human personality and
the whole concept of *reality* in human relations by showing
that the personality—character in stage terms—is not a fixed
and static entity but an infinitely fluid, blurred, and *relative*
concept. People appear different to different fellow human
beings, they act differently in different contexts, they react
differently to differing situations. And where is the Archi-
medean point outside that fluid reality from which we might
judge which of these different manifestations of a human
personality is the true, the *real* one? There is no such point,
just as there is no fixed point in the physical universe from
which all velocities could be measured.

A man keeps his wife confined to his house, and that makes
the neighbours talk. He does not even allow his mother-in-
law to come and see her. All she may do is to look at her
from the street as she appears at the window. The man has
his explanation: he has lost his first wife in an earthquake in
another town and has now remarried. The dead woman's

mother will not believe that she is dead and he cannot bring himself to hurt her, so he pretends that the old lady still *is* his mother-in-law but keeps her from his wife in order to spare her the shock of finding someone else in her daughter's place. But the mother-in-law also gets a chance to tell *her* story. She knows that her son-in-law thinks he has remarried, but in fact the earthquake so unhinged his mind that he thought his wife was killed and in order to make him go on living with her the family had to pretend that he has remarried. Each of the two explanations is put forward with perfect logic and apparent sanity, each would perfectly fit the situation. But only one of them can be true. Finally the young woman at the centre of the dispute appears, heavily veiled. She is asked: Which of the two are you? And replies: 'I am the old lady's daughter and I am this man's second wife. And for myself, I am nobody! Nobody at all!' But the by-standers object, she must be either one or the other. 'No! As far as I am concerned, I am just whoever you think I am. . . .'

And indeed the alternative between only *two* possible solutions is far too simple. There is an infinity of other solutions. The young woman may be neither the daughter of the lady nor the second wife of the husband. She may be trying to keep two equally disturbed minds from cracking up. Or she herself may suffer from a form of insanity which makes it necessary for her to think that both characters she embodies must co-exist. In other words we are faced with a multiple system of delusions which is kept in a precarious balance, and each of these delusions undermines the foundations of the other two. It is a closed system without an exit: each person's illusions are *his* reality.

Again and again this basic problem of illusion and reality, so neatly and logically worked out in the plot of the play *Right You Are If You Think You Are*, occurs in different variations in Pirandello's vast *oeuvre* of more than forty plays, seven novels, and some two hundred stories.

He himself lived his life caught up in such an inextricable net. He was the son of wealthy owners of sulphur mines near his native Sicilian city of Girgenti (today renamed Agrigento). At the age of twenty-six he married the daughter of one of his father's partners. Nine years later a mining disaster caused the ruin of the family fortunes of Pirandello's own and his wife's parents. Signora Pirandello was paralyzed as a result of the shock; she could not move her legs for six months and after that developed the symptoms of extreme paranoia. She was so jealous of her husband that no woman was allowed to enter their home, maidservants had to be more than fifty years of age and were not permitted to live in the house. Pirandello had to hide his manuscripts as his wife suspected secret love letters in any piece of paper with writing on it. He never went out without taking one of his children with him, so as to have a witness for every minute of the day. Yet Pirandello loyally suffered all these tribulations rather than have his wife removed to an asylum. It was only after sixteen years, in 1919, that her condition made it necessary for her to go to a sanatorium, where she survived for another forty years.

So he himself was confronted with the problem: in his wife's disturbed mind he appeared as a totally different character from the image he had of himself. And yet, who was to decide which image was the true one, which was illusion, which reality? Who is sane? Who is mad? The mad are convinced *they* are sane. So every one of us who swears that he is sane may in fact be mad without knowing it.

The hero of Pirandello's greatest play, *Henry IV*, is a case in point. As a young man, while impersonating the German Emperor Henry IV in a historical pageant, he fell from his horse as a result of a practical joke engineered by his rival in love. For many years, in consequence of the blow he suffered, he has been mad, thinking that he actually *is* the medieval Emperor. So as not to expose him to an unbearable nervous shock he has been surrounded by costumed servants in a reconstructed medieval court. Then one day the patient realizes the masquerade, he becomes sane, but because he rather likes the comfort of living outside his time, he keeps up the deception, he continues to pretend that he believes himself a medieval Emperor. His friends, unaware of his state of mind, prepare an elaborate shock therapy to cure him: they will confront him with the daughter of his former love, who resembles her exactly, so as to take him back to the exact point where his madness started. As he has long seen through his masquerade the shock treatment does not have the desired effect. He merely gets so furious with his erstwhile rival that he kills him, knowing he will have to go on pretending to be insane to escape the consequences of the murder. This is a complex enough pattern, but as Eric Bentley has pointed out in a brilliant essay on *Henry IV*, it is in fact still more complex: is the hero's withdrawal from reality, after he has realized that he is living in the twentieth century and not in the eleventh, the act of a sane man? Hardly. It might be seen as a different type of insanity. And is the murder of his old rival in a fit of rage the action of a sane man? Surely not. So in fact our hero may believe himself to have returned to normality, but this itself is merely a further illusion. . . .

The man who thinks he is the Emperor Henry IV wears elaborate medieval costume, he is *masked* in the sense in which the costumed participants of a masked ball are referred to as *masks*. Pirandello gave the edition of his collected plays the over-all title *Maschere nude* (*Naked Masks*). We all in our daily lives, he suggests, are like the masks in a masked ball, the masks of the old Italian Commedia dell'Arte, stereotyped characters with roles prescribed by long tradition. He, the dramatist, sets out to strip these masks off his characters, to tear off their disguise, their conventional costume, to get at the naked truth. But he finds that it is impossible ever to establish the absolute truth about any living human being, simply because, life being change, change in the observer as well as in the observed, there can never be an absolute—that is, *fixed*—truth about anyone.

If we are all costumed masks enacting stereotyped roles, then the dividing line between the actor on the stage and the spectator in the stalls becomes blurred. Many of Pirandello's plays deal with the problem of stage illusion versus illusion in life, stage truth versus truth in life. His most famous play, *Six Characters in Search of an Author* (first performed in 1921), poses the problem in the most ingenious manner. A theatre is invaded during a rehearsal by a group of six characters who have been conceived in the mind of an author but discarded by him as being too melodramatic. Once brought to life, however, they demand their existence on the stage. They enact their predicament. The actors become interested and try to make them the basis of a play. So now the roles are taken by the actors. But, the characters protest, the actors only translate the truth of the imagination of an author back into stage stereotypes. The fiction is more real than its enactment by flesh-and-blood professionals.

This is the core of Pirandello's concern, the nature of human consciousness of itself, of reality as reflected in our minds. If it is impossible to find an objective yardstick of reality we are thrown back into a universe of interlocking subjective viewpoints between which it is impossible to determine a greater or lesser degree of objective truth. As Pirandello told Domenico Vittorini in 1935 (a year before his death): 'The last generation looked upon nature and man as something existing in unchanging, clear-cut and solid form outside of us. To me reality is something that we mould through the power of our imagination. . . . We say "I am one" and we look upon ourselves as well as upon fellow men as solid and clear-cut personalities, while in reality we are the juxtaposition of infinite, blurred selves. . . .'

Pirandello, who had spent some time as a student at Bonn University in Germany and had been greatly influenced by German philosophy, embodied some of the principal trends in modern thinking—Bergson's dynamic vitalism with its insistence on the fluidity of human personality, phenomenology, existentialism—in a vigorous and original type of philosophical drama. He was aware of this. In the preface to *Six Characters in Search of an Author* he distinguished between two types of writers: those who merely want to tell a story 'are . . . historical writers. But there are others who, beyond such pleasure, feel a more profound spiritual need on whose account they admit only figures, affairs, landscapes which have been soaked, so to speak, in a particular sense of life and acquire from it a universal value. These are, more precisely, philosophical writers. I have the misfortune to belong to these last.'

Yet, while he used the stage as a laboratory for the demonstration of a philosophical view of the world, Pirandello was anything but a cerebral dramatist. He was, above all, a man haunted by images. The subject matter of *Six Characters in Search of an Author* is, after all, basically a dramatization of the playwright's mind haunted, invaded, by characters who simply will not let him alone. The scene at the core of the play, that of the father, who furtively frequents houses of assignation, being confronted by his own stepdaughter, who is forced to eke out her existence by selling herself, is one the author does not want to deal with, that he discards, and yet one to which the figments of his subconscious mind force him to return. In that sense the stage itself that the characters invade is simply the author's own subconscious. He wants to repress the Oedipal, incestuous situation that haunts him, but he cannot do it, the play insists on being written: 'Creatures of my spirit, these six were already living a life which was their own and not mine any more, a life which it was not in my power any more to deny them.'

Pirandello was fully aware of the uncontrollable forces at the basis of human personality. As he told Vittorini: 'There are emotions and acts that are uncontrollable because of the blurred character of our personality.' One might put it the other way round: Because our personality is composed of forces that are beyond our conscious control, it is bound to be fluid and blurred; because we are not wholly conscious of our own motivations we cannot distinguish between illusion and reality. Pirandello's plays can therefore be studied, not merely as the product of a brilliant philosophical mind, but also as the expression of a personality haunted by images welling up from the depths of a deeply troubled soul.

Pirandello's influence pervades all contemporary drama. His contribution is so rich that the most diverse tendencies have been able to find nourishment in aspects of Pirandello's thought or practice. His insistence, for example, that the stage is an illusion shot through by the reality of the actors themselves, who become real precisely when they fall out of their roles and address the audience as themselves, undoubtedly had its influence on the anti-illusionist theatre of Brecht. Brecht's alienation effect, after all, is based on the recognition that the audience should be made aware of the illusionistic character of the stage, so that the actors could be in a position to comment themselves, as themselves, on the action they are demonstrating to the audience.

The same Pirandellian idea, in a completely different guise, appears in Genet's mirror technique in plays like *The Maids*, *The Balcony*, and *The Blacks*. The opening scene of *The Balcony* where we are shown a bishop confessing a sinner, only to discover that the bishop isn't a bishop at all but a little man who comes to a brothel where he indulges himself in dressing up as a bishop, derives directly from Pirandello's *Henry IV*. Similarly in *The Blacks* we are gradually made to realize that the action we have been watching was merely put on for our benefit in order to distract attention from a real murder which has been happening off stage; in other words, Genet is using the Pirandellian concept of various levels of illusion between stage and reality.

Anouilh uses a similar device in a number of his plays. In *Le Rendezvous de Senlis*, for example, the hero engages two actors to impersonate his parents so as to give his beloved the illusion that he has a solid family background. And in one of his latest plays, *La Grotte*, Anouilh confronts us with an author who is trying to write a play by producing the characters for us on the stage and trying them out in various situations, with the characters finally becoming autonomous

enough to refuse to go along with their author. Thornton
Wilder has used many Pirandellian ideas and techniques in
plays like *Our Town* and *The Skin of Our Teeth*.

The dramatists of the Theatre of the Absurd who put the
images of their dreams and obsessions on the stage without
even the pretence of a realistic framework continue Pirandello's subjectivist approach to reality. In *Six Characters* we
still have a background of a real theatre with real actors
against which the creatures of the author's imagination are
contrasted. In the plays of Ionesco or Beckett the characters
are clearly enough merely the emanations of the playwright's
subconscious. Yet at the same time both Ionesco and Beckett
retain the Pirandellian effect of letting the audience become
aware of the fact that these fantasies are being embodied by
actors who are real people and do not always pretend to be
the characters they portray. The two tramps in *Waiting for
Godot*, the master and the servant in *Endgame* frequently
refer to their position as actors on a stage.

In a play like Peter Weiss's *Marat/Sade*, Brechtian alienation effects and absurdist projections of the consciousness of
madmen onto a stage are cunningly mingled, but ultimately
the whole elaborate structure of interlocking levels of subjectivity, of madness encompassed in madness, derives from
Pirandello: these are Sade's characters who are trying to
liberate themselves from their author, while we the audience
of today are confronted by an audience of 1809 watching a
play portraying events of 1792, illusions within illusions on
the pattern of Pirandello's *Henry IV*.

Moreover, by confronting stage reality and the reality of
life and showing both up as illusions, Pirandello can also be
said to be a forerunner of the Happening. A play like *Each
in His Own Way*, which Pirandello visualized as being staged
in the foyer of the theatre as well as in the auditorium and
on the stage, is a case in point. The play opens with the
direction: 'The performance of this play should start on the
street outside the theatre. . . .' Newsboys are to distribute a
newspaper containing an item referring to an event that is

said to have been made the subject of the play. As the audience enters the foyer it is to witness the attempts of three elegant gentlemen to dissuade a lady, the supposed subject of the play, from going to see the performance. And the performance itself is to be constantly interrupted by the supposedly real characters, who are the models of the fictitious characters on the stage, protesting against the way they are being dealt with, the whole thing finally ending in such an uproar that the manager has to announce the abandonment of the performance.

This surely must be one of the first scenarios for a Happening. Much of it is embodied in a detailed script, but a good many incidents are left to be improvised by the actors, and of course, once the scandal has broken out, it might well acquire a degree of spontaneity that even Pirandello did not bargain for.

Indeed, the objectives of the Happening are largely identical with Pirandello's. The participants in the Happening are to be made aware of the shifting ground on which they stand—that reality may be illusion, illusion reality, and that the world itself is a vast stage on which illusion merges into reality, which in turn may reveal itself as just another layer of illusion.

Pirandello received the Nobel Prize for Literature in 1934. He died in 1936. Today, more than a hundred years after he was born, the time seems ripe for an intensive revival of interest in Pirandello's work for the theatre. There are still many of his plays that have not yet been performed in English, that have not even been translated. For sheer inventiveness there are few dramatists' *oeuvres* that can rival the as yet untapped wealth of Pirandello's massive achievement.

Some Contemporary Dramatists

Brecht in 1969

I require no tombstone, but
If you require one for me
I wish it to be inscribed,
He made suggestions. We
Accepted them.
By such an inscription we should
All be honoured.

BRECHT from Volume VII
of his *Collected Poems*)

On 10 February 1968 Brecht would have celebrated his
seventieth birthday. It makes one realize how young he died
on 14 August 1956, and how rapidly, since he died, he has
acquired the status of an established international classic.
Ten years earlier, in 1946, he was little more than an unknown, neglected German exile tramping the streets of Los
Angeles and New York in search of recognition. So rapidly
does obscurity turn into fame in an age of instant mass com-
munications, an age of an educational explosion without
parallel in history with an unprecedented consumption of
authors who must be turned into material for theses, disserta-
tions, and essays as soon as they have established some claim
to significance.

Is it the significance of Brecht that has engendered the
Brecht industry, or is it the Brecht industry that makes Brecht
seem so significant? The question can certainly be asked,
although in the case of Brecht the man's significance is far
less subject to doubt than in that of many another object of a
literary industry. Brecht's character as a man, his persona as
an author, and his methods of work make him a peculiarly
fertile ground for academic research and scholarly exploration: his life covered a multitude of countries and left a

bewildering array of documentation behind; his habit of theorizing about his artistic practice, and of practising his aesthetic theories, provides rich material for critical analysis; and his readiness to rewrite his own texts again and again furnishes a plentiful harvest for generations of textual editors to come. And, to cap it all, Brecht's complex political involvement makes him an ideal centre for controversies of all kinds. Eric Bentley has very shrewdly drawn our attention to the fact that Brecht not only displayed a remarkable degree of aggression in many of his political pronouncements, but that he also seems to bring out the maximum of aggressiveness in those who concern themselves with him as writers, critics, or researchers (not to speak of translators).

If I may be allowed a personal remark in this context, I slithered into all this unawares. Ever since, at the age of fifteen, I came across Pabst's *Threepenny Opera* film, I had been enthusiastic about Brecht, had casually acquired any of his writings that came my way (many of them are now precious first editions), and had collected any records of Brecht's songs I could find. And so when Brecht, thanks to Kenneth Tynan's impassioned though at that time not particularly well-informed advocacy, had become a snob talking point in England shortly before he died, I decided that it might be useful if a modicum of hard fact could be inserted into all the woolly and wild debate for and against an artist about whom practically nothing was actually *known* in England at that time.

Originally I planned little more than a brochure; I thought that there was not enough material at hand for a full biography so soon after Brecht's death (he died as I started my preparatory work). Yet, as I assembled the material, it became clear that in fact there was a great deal of it there to be found and used if only one went to the right sources. The *external* sequence of the events of Brecht's life could be traced through an abundance of documentation in newspapers, periodicals, the memoirs of contemporaries already in print at the time, and of course in the living recollections of the many people who had met, worked with, and quarrelled with Brecht. Indeed, there seemed to be a certain urgency to get this material recorded before the generation that had been closest to him disappeared.

Besides, a thorough reading of Brecht's own work—and most of it was after all available and published even at that time, even though one had to go to first printings not readily available (luckily I had my own collection of early editions at hand)—showed very clearly how the established and verifiable external facts of his life mirrored themselves in his writings—dramatic, lyrical, narrative, or theoretical.

So gradually I became convinced that it was possible to attempt a preliminary over-all assessment of the man and of his work. Moreover, it soon became clear to me that such a first survey, which would fix the major outline of Brecht's development, was not only possible but very necessary for the simple reason that the fury of the controversy about Brecht between Communists and anti-Communists, the unscrupulousness of those who wanted to turn the eternal non-conformist into the Communist equivalent of a virtuous Boy Scout hero on the one hand, into the depraved villain of some anti-Communist cartoon strip on the other, was rapidly encrusting the framework of verifiable facts with a rank jungle growth of naïve legend. The sooner the verifiable facts and their sources could be assembled and organized into a sober record, the better.

Already Ruth Fischer was painting a picture of Brecht as a GPU agent, while the East Germans were selling little tracts proclaiming that Brecht had hurried back to the Communist part of Berlin as soon as the war had ended and the wicked Americans had granted him an exit visa (at a time when the chief punishment for a foreign Communist in the United States was deportation!). These are only two examples among many of the myths that swept through the world's press in the East as well as the West. And all the time the evidence, factual, sober, and incontrovertible, was available to anyone who cared to look it up in a multitude of more or less readily accessible sources. So the book grew rapidly enough and was first published in the autumn of 1959, just over three years after Brecht died.

I certainly had not reckoned with the violence of the reactions it provoked. The Communist party line, in reply to the recital of some of the more uncomfortable facts, was simply that the time was not yet ripe for a biography of Brecht; such a biography would have to wait till all the voluminous material in the Brecht Archive was published. The start of a great historical and critical edition of Brecht was said to be imminent, and this would, it was claimed, be concluded with an edition of his diaries and letters. Which meant that it would take about twenty years to reach that section if publication started immediately. It was quite clear that in fact the content of many of Brecht's personal writings would be highly embarrassing for the East German regime, and that therefore the chances of this material ever being included in a complete edition were slight. Since then ten years have passed and not even the first volume of a critical and historical edition has appeared. The whole project now seems to be dormant. In other words, the argument that it was necessary to wait for complete publication of the letters and diaries amounted, even then, to an attempt to delay any biography of Brecht indefinitely. That would have meant a clear run for all the hagiography and pious legends of the East, all the malice and calumny of the anti-Communist West.

The main contention of my exposition of Brecht's life and political career was that, while he was a fervent believer in the Marxist creed, he had been highly critical of the party's theory and practice and bitterly opposed to the official doctrine of socialist realism; that he had hesitated a good deal before finally deciding to settle in East Berlin and in accepting the East German invitation had been largely motivated by his desire to get his own theatre; that, once settled in East Berlin, he had been subjected to a good deal of harassment in the final phase of Stalinism and had consistently, albeit

very prudently and diplomatically, opposed the more op-
pressive manifestations of totalitarianism and state inter-
ference in the arts; that the workers' revolt of 17 June 1953
had deeply shaken him; and that his disillusionment with
the realities of life in a Communist-ruled country might have
been a contributory factor in his early death.

I had arrived at these conclusions largely by a careful scru-
tiny of generally available factual evidence. But I had also
drawn to a certain extent on information privately received
from individuals who had been involved in the events concerned; and in these cases I was not always in a position to
disclose my sources.

In the ten years that have elapsed since the publication of
my book a great deal of new material has come to light. A
great many of Brecht's hitherto unpublished writings have
been published and a good many important documents have
also become accessible, not to speak of numerous works of
reminiscences by personalities who, in one way or another,
had been close to Brecht. All this has tended to confirm the
picture I had drawn in my account of Brecht's life and
personality.

For example: the long delay before Brecht returned to East
Berlin had been flatly denied by the followers of the Communist party line, which has always been that he was burning to return to the Communist part of Germany. It has now
been more than fully explained by the publication of a
number of Brecht's own letters. While the official account
of Brecht's life published in East Berlin maintains 'that
Brecht indefatigably worked for his return to Germany from
Switzerland',[1] Brecht himself wrote to his old friend and
mentor in Marxism, Karl Korsch, from Switzerland in April
1948: 'We have not yet got to Berlin, in spite of some efforts;
now we have to try and get Swiss travel papers, as the others
won't take us any further and I do not want at this moment
especially to settle permanently in Germany.' From this it is

[1] *Bertolt Brecht: Leben und Werk*, Volk und Wissen (East Berlin,
1963) p. 151.

quite clear that Brecht, who could have gone back to Germany whenever he wanted, did in fact want non-German travel documents precisely because he wanted to keep his line of retreat open; what was difficult at that time was for a German to *leave* Germany, not to get in.

Brecht's position was further clarified by the German critic Siegfried Melchinger, who was able to publish the correspondence between Brecht and the Austrian composer Gottfried von Einem concerning Brecht's efforts to acquire Austrian citizenship.[1] In the official East German version Brecht's return to East Berlin is usually dated October 1948. At that time Brecht did indeed visit East Berlin, but he returned to Zurich (having managed to get permission to return to Switzerland before venturing on that visit). And it was at this time that he took very energetic steps to further the realization of a project that had started in the spring of 1948 and that consisted of no less than the creation of a base for himself at Salzburg, as artistic director of the Salzburg Festival. Gottfried von Einem, at that time very influential in circles trying to revive the artistic pre-eminence of Salzburg, had discussed the matter with Brecht in Zurich. Brecht was to write a morality play to take the place of Hofmannsthal's *Everyman* on the Salzburg Cathedral Square; it was to be called *The Salzburg Dance of Death*. One scene from this play has now been published together with Brecht's letters. The plot concerns an Emperor who makes a pact with Death to spare him and his friends in a future war. They agree on a secret sign that will exempt those who make it. But when war comes Death in his excitement forgets the sign and the Emperor also dies.

There was also a plan that Brecht should do an adaptation of Goethe's *Faust* for the Goethe bicentenary year, 1949. In April 1949 Brecht wrote to von Einem:

Dear von Einem, I am sitting here [in Zurich] with Cas [Brecht's friend, the designer Caspar Neher] and we have been

[1] *Stuttgarter Zeitung*, 5 January 1963.

talking about the festival play [*The Salzburg Dance of Death*] and it looks feasible. And I also know now of a quid pro quo which would be more valuable to me than any monetary advance; that would be a place of sanctuary, i.e., a passport. If that were at all possible it should of course be done without any publicity. And perhaps something on these lines might be best: Helle [Helene Weigel, Brecht's wife] is after all a born Austrian—Viennese—and, like myself, stateless since 1933. And now there is no German government. Could she get an Austrian passport back? And could I then, as her husband, also get one? You understand, I don't know the legal way. However, a passport would indeed be of enormous importance to me. I cannot, after all, settle down in one part of Germany and thereby be dead for the other. Perhaps you could really help me? Cordially yours, Brecht.

Von Einem sent Brecht the forms to be filled in for an application for Austrian citizenship. In his application addressed to the Austrian Minister of Education and the governor of the province of Salzburg, Brecht wrote on 20 April, 1949:

My longing for Austria is by no means due to external circumstances, but to be explained by the fact that at the age of fifty I should like to work in a country which offers a congenial atmosphere. And that is Austria. . . . I should like to stress that I feel myself solely a writer and that I do not want to serve any specific political ideology, let alone want to be proclaimed an exponent of such an ideology. For certain reasons I decline to be repatriated to Germany.

The Salzburg project progressed slowly, and Brecht agreed to go to East Berlin where, after the great success of the production of *Mother Courage* he had supervised at the end of 1948, he had been offered the opportunity to start his own company, the Berliner Ensemble. Yet from East Berlin he continued to urge von Einem to continue his efforts to get him an Austrian passport, writing on 12 October 1949: 'I have no official function or obligation of any kind in East Berlin and receive

no salary.' On 2 March, 1950, he was still urging von Einem
to press the matter of Austrian naturalization:

> Dear von Einem, Cas tells me there is only one more paper
> missing and that you have written to me about it. But I have not
> received any letter from you on the subject and therefore do not
> know which paper it might be. Believe me, I am as interested
> in this as ever, indeed more so. You *must* help me. So much
> depends on it for my work (and collaboration) as an artist, as
> many countries, among them West Germany for one, might
> become inaccessible without a travel paper.

Brecht's naturalization as an Austrian citizen finally came
through in April 1950.

This episode is of crucial importance to an understanding
of Brecht's attitude. While he was a convinced supporter of
the Marxist ideology, he did not want to expose himself to
the risk of becoming completely identified with the East
German Communist regime.

The publication of Walter Benjamin's conversations with
Brecht in the years 1934 and 1938 fully confirms the description of his ambivalent attitude to the Soviet Union in Stalin's
time that I gave in my book. Walter Benjamin (born 1892,
died as a suicide while fleeing from the Nazis in 1940) was
one of the great German critics of his time, the first major
literary critic to recognize Brecht's greatness. Here are a few
extracts from his conversations with Brecht in his Danish
exile at Svendborg:

> 6 July 1934: Brecht during yesterday's conversation: 'I often
> think of a tribunal before which I might be interrogated. "How
> is it with you? Are you really serious?" I should then have to
> admit: I am not entirely serious. I think too much of artistic
> matters, of what might be good for the theatre, ever to be
> completely serious. But, having given a negative answer to this
> important question, I would add another, even more important
> assertion: namely that my attitude is *permissible*.'
> 28 June 1938: Brecht speaks of his deeply rooted hatred
> against priests, which he has inherited from his grandmother.
> He hints that those who have made the theoretical teachings of

Marx their own and devote themselves to them will always form a priestly camarilla.

Talking about the problems of writers in the Soviet Union, Brecht is quoted by Benjamin as saying that 'authors over there are having a hard time. It is regarded as an intentional act when the name of Stalin is not mentioned in a poem.'

21 July 1938: The publications by Lukács, Kurella and others [in the debate about socialist realism vs. formalism] cause Brecht much uneasiness. I transpose the problem into the political sphere. But there too he does not restrain himself in his expressions: 'The socialist economy does not need war, that is why it cannot stand war. The Russian people's "love of peace" is an expression of this fact, and this fact alone. There cannot be a socialist economy in a single country. Through armaments the Russian proletariat has been thrown back very seriously, and partially into phases of historical development that ought to have been long passed. Among others the monarchical phase. In Russia there is personal rule. Only blockheads could deny that.'

29 July 1938: Brecht reads several polemical replies to Lukács, drafts of an essay he is to publish in *Das Wort* [the German literary review published in Moscow of which Brecht was co-editor]. These are camouflaged but violent attacks. Brecht asks me for advice about publishing them. As he tells me at the same time that Lukacs is at this moment occupying a very important position 'over there' I tell him I could not give him any advice. 'This is a question of power politics. Someone over there would have to give you his advice. After all you have friends over there.' Brecht: 'As a matter of fact I have no friends there. And the people in Moscow themselves have no friends—like the dead.'

The recently published collection of Brecht's *Writings on Literature and Art*[1] fully confirms Walter Benjamin's account of these conversations. Volume II contains a number of essays by Brecht directed against the official line represented

[1] *Schriften zur Literatur und Kunst*, 3 vols. (Frankfurt, Suhrkamp, 1967).

by Lukács and in defence of a far more liberal view of aesthetics. But none of them was in fact published at the time. Indeed the important essay 'Range and Variety of the Realist Style' had to wait for publication till 1954—after Stalin's death.

Benjamin's notes of his conversations with Brecht in 1934 also confirm my account of the reasons why Brecht rejected the idea of settling in the Soviet Union, even though there were strong material inducements to do so. He was far too keenly aware of the dangers threatening a non-conformist—in political as well as artistic matters—in Stalin's realm.

The collection of Brecht's narrative prose works which appeared in 1965 (Bertolt Brecht, *Prosa*, 5 vols., Frankfurt, Suhrkamp) is chiefly remarkable for the early short stories, many of which had been unpublished or available only in obscure periodicals, and for the first publication of a late and hitherto unknown work, *Me-ti, Buch der Wendungen* (*Me-ti, the Book of Twists and Turns*).

The early stories throw a good deal of light on Brecht's complex psychology (and confirm, at least in my view, the latter part of my analysis of Brecht's personal motivation). Thus the story *'Bargan lässt es sein'* (*Bargan Leaves Off*), which is clearly related to Brecht's most important early play, *Im Dickicht der Städte* (*In the Jungle of the Cities*), quite openly spells out the homosexual nature of the conflict in that play. Even more astonishing is the short story *'Brief über eine Dogge'* (*'Letter about a Bulldog'*, 1925), which describes an incident in the life of a hero, a young man totally alone in the world who lives in San Francisco and desperately tries to make friends with a bulldog belonging to a family inhabiting the same tenement. But the dog develops a deep aversion to the narrator, and when, during the great San Francisco earthquake, the narrator finds the dog half buried under debris and wants to rescue it, the animal snarls at him, preferring to die rather than to be touched by the narrator.

In other words, Brecht has here totally anticipated the situation between Jerry and the dog in Albee's *Zoo Story*. The

implications are obvious enough. Jerry as well as the narrator
of Brecht's story are outcasts of society, only dimly aware of
the nature of their psychological predicament, desperately
trying to make contact with other people, even if the only
way to establish such contact is violence. (In my analysis of
Brecht's attitude I quoted a good deal of material from his
own works and the observations of persons who knew him
in his early phase that seemed to me to indicate that it was a
deep feeling of inability to establish genuine human contact
that drove Brecht into the violent collectivism of his political
commitment.) The narrator of Brecht's story tries to analyze
why the dog rejected his offer of rescue:

> What was it that induced the animal to reject my helping hand?
> Is it my eye, the expression of which, as I have heard, has
> brought me success with some people, but repelled the more
> sensitive animal? . . . Ever since that animal displayed that
> attitude towards me I am incessantly pondering what kind of
> malformation—for there must be a malformation—it might be
> that distinguishes me from other human beings. Indeed, in the
> last few months I have started to believe that it might be inner,
> more deeply based malformations within me; and the worst of it
> is that, the more I try to investigate, the more deviations from
> the normal I detect in myself; adding one to the other, the
> more convinced I become that I shall never be able to discover
> the true reason; for it might, after all, be my mind that is
> abnormal and that cannot recognize the repellent as repellent.
> Without the least sympathy for such ridiculous phenomena as
> the Salvation Army with its cheap conversions, I can neverthe-
> less say that a deep transformation of my nature, whether for
> good or ill, can no longer be denied.

This is a revealing passage; it links a deeply felt conviction
of inability to make contact with other human beings directly
with a conversion experience along the lines of the Salvation
Army. The Salvation Army plays an immense part in
Brecht's *oeuvre* (*In the Jungle of the Cities*, *Happy End*, and
St Joan of the Stockyards) and it is clear that with its collectivism, military discipline, and religious fervour it shares a

good many features with the political party to which Brecht finally committed himself to escape the isolation of an individual deeply conscious of being unable to establish genuine personal contacts on an individual basis.

The late prose work, *Me-ti, the Book of Twists and Turns* (*Wendungen* means tactical evasive actions, turns in that sense), is a piece of chinoiserie, fables and meditations in a mock-Confucian style, greatly reminiscent of Brecht's earlier Keuner stories, but more radically *verfremdet* by the Chinese setting. According to the editor of the present edition, these fragments were written by Brecht between 1934 and 1956. As such they constitute a kind of spiritual autobiography and a record of his political attitudes and views on a number of subjects, from aesthetics to love.

There is too much in this fascinating work to allow quotation at length here. Suffice it to note that these fables and aphorisms, which are openly personal (a key to the names precedes the text and identifies Brecht as 'Kin, Kin-jeh, Ken-jeh, Kien-leh', which are all clearly derived from Keuner, his earlier alter ego) amply confirm the account of Brecht's political opinions and his moral attitude of enlightened self-interest contained in my own analysis. For example:

> Under Ni-En's [Stalin's] leadership industry was being constructed without exploiters and agriculture collectively organized in Su [the Soviet Union]. But the associations [parties] outside Su decayed. It was not the members who elected the secretaries, but the secretaries who elected the members. The political line was decreed by Su and the secretaries paid by Su. When mistakes were made, those who pointed them out were punished, but those who committed them remained in office. Thus they were soon no longer the best, merely the most compliant. . . . Those in authority in Su no longer learned any facts, because the secretaries no longer reported anything that might not be welcome. In view of these conditions the best [among the party members] were in despair. Me-ti deplored the decay of the great method [Marxism].

Or, as an expression of Schweikian ethics:

To earn one's supper one needs intelligence; it may consist in being obedient to those who are in authority. Intelligence of a different order may lead one to strive for the abolition of a system of people in authority and people under authority. But, for such an enterprise, one still needs intelligence of the first order; for, to carry out such an enterprise, one still has to eat one's supper.

The most important publication of hitherto unknown material by Brecht, however, has undoubtedly been the appearance of Volumes vi to ix of his collected poems. The method of publication has been an example of muddle, bad scholarship, and various attempts at suppression. Only after a vigorous campaign against the edition, originally announced as being in six volumes only, had caused violent controversy in West Germany, and the omission of vitally important material, which was known to exist, had been demonstrated beyond doubt, were the copyright holders induced to release additional poems. The material now available establishes Brecht as one of the greatest of German lyrical poets, with an *oeuvre* of surprising richness and variety. In particular the poems of his exile, and those written in East Berlin in the last few years of his life, reveal great delicacy of feeling, economy of expression, and, notably those of the very last phase, a deep melancholy.

That Brecht was a sad man in his last years in East Berlin, at the height of his fame, when he was a member of the privileged class of the East German establishment, must now be beyond any doubt:

> I was sad when I was young
> And am sad now I am old
> So when can I be gay for once?
> It had better be soon.

Brecht and the English Theatre

That future historians of English drama will describe the period since 1956 as an era of Brechtian influence is quite possible. If so, the phenomenon will be an illustration of the quirks and ironies of cultural diffusion between nations, for that Brechtian era had a great deal of talk and discussion *about* Brecht and what he was *thought* to stand for, but few valid productions of Brecht, little genuine knowledge about Brecht, and hence little evidence of any influence of Brecht's actual work and thought. The 'Brechtian' era in England stood under the aegis not of Brecht himself but of various secondhand ideas and concepts *about* Brecht, an image of Brecht created from misunderstandings and misconceptions. Yet, even though Columbus thought he had landed in Asia, he nevertheless discovered something; even though the idea of Greek tragedy on which the theatre of Racine and Corneille was based may have been wrong, the value of the work of these dramatists is undeniable; and whether the amalgam of ideas and heart-searchings that became known in England as the Brechtian influence was a true reflection of his work or not, in the last resort some interesting innovations resulted from it—and the British theatre will never be quite the same again.

Furthermore (and this is a measure of the English critics' inability to contribute to the artistic progress of the English stage) this undeniable influence of 'Brechtian' ideas established itself in the face of stubborn and often vicious attacks on Brecht by the vast majority of daily and weekly theatre reviewers, who not only dismissed a whole series of productions of Brecht's plays in English with contempt (which most of them fully deserved) but consistently denounced Brecht himself as a fraud and the inflated idol of faddists and perverse intellectuals.

The one exception among these critics, and the one whose merit—or fault—it was that Brecht's name suddenly achieved the currency of a cultural status symbol to be reckoned with among members of the theatrical profession and some sections of the public, was Kenneth Tynan. Tynan became drama critic of the *Observer* in 1954, and very soon made the name of Brecht his trademark, his yardstick of values, a symbol that could be thrown into any review of even the most mediocre local offering as a shining contrast, an example of excellence in playwriting, production, ideological commitment, care in rehearsal, dedication to the ideal of theatre as an art rather than as an after-dinner entertainment. Whether consciously and deliberately or by mere instinct, Tynan here repeated the device used by Shaw in the nineties, when he elevated Ibsen into the hero of the theatrical revolution of his time. That Tynan had been stirred by the Brecht productions he had seen is beyond a doubt. Yet as Tynan had only an Englishman's knowledge of German at the time, he was in no position to appreciate Brecht's first and decisive claim to greatness: his mastery of the German language, his stature as a major poet. Inevitably, this led to a certain deformation of the Brechtian image in English eyes: he came across to the readers of the *Observer* as, above all, a dramatist who was on the side of the angels ideologically, as a great director, and as an example of the potential of a theatre artist working effectively and experimentally within the framework of a wholly state-subsidized institution.

It is here that we touch on one of the most important reasons why discussion about Brecht became so widespread and excited at that particular moment in British theatre history: those were the years that preceded the decision to set up a state-subsidized National Theatre in England. For more than half a century the opponents of such an enterprise had argued very persuasively that state-subsidized theatres—one

had only to look at the Comédie Française!—inevitably became artistically sterile warrens of potbellied Hamlets and
post-climacteric civil-service-status Juliets on pensionable life
contracts, obeying the dictates of officials anxious to use the
theatre as a propaganda organ for outworn ideas of the most
suspect kind. These arguments could at last be effectively
silenced by pointing to the Berliner Ensemble, led by a great
artist, consisting of young, vigorous, and anti-establishment
actors and actresses, wholly experimental, overflowing with
new ideas—and state-subsidized to the hilt. So Brecht became
the focal point, the rallying cry of the younger generation of
theatrical artists who had realized that the future of the
theatre as a serious vehicle for ideas, enlightenment, and
beauty depended on the recognition that the commercial
system simply was no longer able to provide the basis for
viable drama.

By its very nature, its opposition to the purely commercial
aspects of theatre, its insistence on the rightness of public
financial support for an art, this movement was one of the
left. Brecht's status as a culture hero of Communist East
Germany further enhanced his appeal to these circles—and
correspondingly diminished his chances of ever pleasing the
artistic and political right wing. The year 1956 was the *annus
mirabilis* in the development of this left-wing movement. It
saw in April the opening of the Royal Court as a nursery of
angry young playwrights and in late August and early September the first visit of the Berliner Ensemble to the Palace
Theatre on Cambridge Circus. By a tragic coincidence Brecht
had died shortly before the date of the Ensemble's opening
performance; his note urging the members of the company
to play lightly and not too slowly to please an English
audience was one of his last public pronouncements.

The critical reaction to the three productions the Ensemble
brought to London (*Mother Courage, The Caucasian Chalk
Circle*, and an adaptation of Farquhar's *The Recruiting
Officer—Pauken und Trompeten*) was on the whole luke-
warm; but the impact on the theatrical profession all the

more profound. Ironically, however, because hardly anyone in the English theatre knows any German, this impact chiefly manifested itself in those spheres that remained unaffected by the language barrier: in stage design and lighting and in the use of music. Indeed, as far as design is concerned, one can safely say that practically *all* British stage design, outside the area of the most old-fashioned drawing-room comedy, today derives from the work of the main Brechtian designers, Neher, Otto, and von Appen. The principal lessons learned concerned the lightness of construction of Brecht's sets, their flexibility and mobility (Sean Kenny's vastly successful design for *Oliver!*, which was almost solely responsible for the great success of an otherwise thoroughly mediocre musical, is a good example) and above all their marvellous use of the texture of the materials employed.

The imitation of the use of songs and music in Brecht's work was less happy in its results. A rash of 'socially oriented' musicals with somewhat more astringent musical scores remained, on the whole, without lasting impact. John Osborne's *The World of Paul Slickey* (1959) was probably the most notable—and the most disastrous—of these. Joan Littlewood achieved the largest measure of success in this direction (*Make Me an Offer*, book by Wolf Mankowitz; *Fings Ain't What They Used t' Be*, book by Frank Norman) and she was also responsible for what must be regarded as the only really notable work that owed a debt to the Brechtian use of music in Britain in the period concerned: Brendan Behan's *The Hostage* (1959) with its many parallels to *The Threepenny Opera*.

To trace the influence of Brechtian theory and practice on directors and actors is far more difficult. How is one to tell which elements in Brecht a director *misunderstood* and then applied in his work? Brecht's theoretical writings were largely unavailable until the publication of John Willett's selection in 1964, and before then those directors who had no German (the large majority) had to rely on secondhand accounts of what Brecht had said. And even though there were a number of detailed works on Brecht's ideas available after 1959, the opportunities for misunderstanding were legion. And indeed, neither the critical accounts nor the texts themselves could serve any really useful purpose without a detailed knowledge of the German theatre in Brecht's time, *against* which he reacted in his theoretical writings. Brecht's constant insistence on emotional coolness in acting, on inhibiting the psychological processes of identification between actor and character, derives from the prevalent German style of acting, which aims at producing the maximum impression of emotional intensity by indulgence in hysterical outbursts and paroxysms of uncontrolled roaring and inarticulate anguish. These orgies of vocal excess and apoplectic breast beating had not been known in the English theatre since the days of Kean and perhaps Irving. Hence, the English style of acting already being cooler and more Brechtian than Brecht's own company's, most of his polemics against the heavy German style (and that after all is what his insistence on non-identification and alienation is really concerned with) are totally inapplicable to English conditions. Not knowing this, and thinking that Brecht was attacking the style currently prevalent in England as well as in Germany, some directors made desperate attempts to cool their actors down even further. As a result, for example, William Gaskill's production of *Mother Courage* at the National Theatre (1965) achieved an effect tantamount to miniaturization of the play and its characters. These wild and rambunctious figures, who should exude vitality, Rabelaisian appetite, lechery, and meanness, appeared cooled down into whispering dwarfs and bloodless spectres—an effect which became all the more eerie as the outward aspects of the production (design and lighting) were meticulously and almost photographically copied from the Berlin production, so that one seemed to be watching a play performed by zombies, re-enacting scenes from their lives after having been turned into lifeless puppets. On the other hand, William Gaskill also was responsible for what I regard as the most successful Brechtian production of the period: Farquhar's *The Recruiting Officer* (and the choice of play was obviously influenced by the fact that the Ensemble had brought Brecht's adaptation of this very play to London in 1956) at the National Theatre in December 1963. Here Robert Stephens, Colin Blakely, and Laurence Olivier did give performances that were larger than life and yet ironically detached, and the sets by René Allio (Planchon's brilliant Brechtian designer, imported from Lyons) were triumphantly light and flexible (and very reminiscent of von Appen's sets for *Pauken und Trompeten*). But then, in 1963, the translation of Brecht's theoretical writings had not yet appeared and Gaskill had perhaps not yet heard the news about the need to cool down the fervour of his actors! Peter Brook, the most gifted of the younger generation of British directors, has not yet tried his hand at Brecht. Yet he has probably assimilated the lesson of Brecht most consistently, most successfully, and most organically. Brook's great production of *King Lear* with Paul Scofield is frequently described as having absorbed the views of Jan Kott, who sees Lear in the light of Beckett. This is perfectly true; yet it concerns the interpretation of the text more than the actual technique of staging, which was most Brechtian both in the decor (a background of burnished copper—as in the Berliner Ensemble *Galileo*) and in the acting: unheroic, relaxed, free of ravings and rantings. Brook's *Marat/Sade*, generally regarded as an embodiment of the ideas of Artaud, also shows the clear and fruitful influence of Brecht (who, of course, also exercised a decisive influence on the playwright, Peter Weiss) in the use of music, nursery rhyme-type verse and delivery, and the multiple alienation effects produced by the convention of having the historical events acted out by the patients in a lunatic asylum.

Joan Littlewood's and Peter Brook's work on plays by other authors must, on the whole, be regarded as the most positive result of Brechtian influence on the art of stage directing in England. Hardly any of Brecht's plays themselves have received wholly satisfactory performances: Joan Littlewood's early attempt at *Mother Courage* (at Barnstaple in

June 1955) was a disaster, mainly because the Theatre Workshop company's resources were too feeble even to allow the music to be performed and so the songs (an essential element) had to be cut, and also because Joan Littlewood herself had to play the title role, an impossible feat for the director of so complex a play. *The Threepenny Opera*, directed by Sam Wanamaker in the Blitzstein version (spring 1956), emerged as far too cosy an attempt at turning this astringent work into a sugar-coated musical. George Devine's *The Good Woman of Szechwan* (autumn 1956) with Peggy Ashcroft in the leading part also failed, largely because it missed a truly Brechtian style and emerged as a somewhat *larmoyant* melodrama. But the performance had its moments: I remember Esmé Percy as one of the gods, gloriously camp and hence very much in Brecht's spirit (it must have been one of his last roles, he died the next summer) and John Osborne doubling a variety of bit parts. The Royal Shakespeare's production of *The Caucasian Chalk Circle* at the Aldwych (March 1962) came much nearer to success; under William Gaskill's devoted direction, Hugh Griffith gave a magnificent rendering of Azdak, and Patsy Byrne was very touching as Grusha, but the omission of the Dessau music and its substitution by a far sweeter score added a touch of sentimentality totally at variance with Brecht's intentions. Gaskill's production of *Baal* at the Phoenix Theatre (February 1963) provided a telling illustration of the idiocy of the Anglo-Saxon star system. It was Peter O'Toole's idea that the play should be performed because he wanted to play the title role. And so Peter O'Toole it had to be, although a Baal looking like a young god (even though slightly unshaven) made nonsense of the lines which indicate that he is meant to be a monster of ugliness, while Ekart, whom Brecht describes as a youth of angelic appearance, had, for contrast's sake, to be played by Harry Andrews, an excellent actor of heavy and ugly roughnecks. Add to this a translation that turned all the poetry (on which the play depends more than any other of Brecht's works) into jarring and incomprehensible prose and you get a measure of the failure of this particular production. An impossible translation also sealed the fate of *Schweik in the Second World War* at the Mermaid (June 1963) in spite of Frank Dunlop's very spirited direction and an excellent rendering of Eisler's music under Alexander Goehr. As the translator had failed to render the essence of the play—namely the fact that the Czechs speak a special Schweikian language—the actors had to fall back on a variety of local accents which completely confused the issue: Bernard Miles, an excellent comedian, made Schweik into a West Country yokel, while some of the other Czechs spoke standard English and the SS men Cockney. There could have been no surer way of misrepresenting Brecht's ideas of the class struggle. An earlier attempt at Brecht by the Mermaid Theatre, *The Life of Galileo* with Miles in the title role (June 1960), had been somewhat more successful, although the Mermaid's actors proved themselves largely inadequate to their tasks, and Miles himself, a fine comedian who yearns to play Hamlet, lacked the ultimate tragic stature, although he gave an extremely skilful and gallant reading of the part. Yet, in this case, the play itself triumphantly overcame the handicaps of acting and direction and emerged as a moving and thought-provoking *story*—that is, epic theatre in the true sense.

Tony Richardson, the most successful of the new directors produced by the Royal Court, tried his hand with Brecht in the summer of 1964 in a production of *St Joan of the Stockyards*. For sheer failure on the director's part to understand his text this beat all precedents; Richardson simply did not seem to realize that the heroic blank verse passages in the play are a *parody* of Shakespeare, Schiller, and Goethe. The production, beset as it was by other vicissitudes—Vanessa Redgrave, who had been cast as Joan, fell out at the last moment and was replaced by Siobhan McKenna—convinced most of the London critics (who seem unwilling to read anything about any play they see and therefore have to rely on what gets through to them in performance) that Brecht was after all a fad and a fraud. This led to a 'let's get rid of

Brecht!' movement among them which was further strengthened by Gaskill's *Mother Courage* at the National Theatre in the spring of 1965 and finally erupted into howls of triumph on the morning after the opening of Michel St Denis' *Puntila* at the Aldwych on 15 July 1965. Quite wrongly, for that production, though it had its faults, was on the whole true to Brecht's intentions. Perhaps too much so: for what really angered the critics this time was the propagandist content, the Communist tendency of the play, rather than any shortcomings of the performance. That this should have struck them as something new and unexpected is a measure of their ignorance of Brecht after so many years of intensive preoccupation with him. In any case, it seemed as though the end of Brecht had come at last in England.

But then, with a truly Brechtian touch of ironic paradox, the whole anti-Brecht movement collapsed within a few weeks. On 9 August 1965, the Berliner Ensemble opened its second season in London at the National Theatre with *Arturo Ui*—one of Brecht's most propagandist plays—and the critics began to rave about the precision, passion, acrobatic prowess, and general excellence of it all. Mercifully, as few of them understand German, they could not be put off by the actual content of this play and of those that followed it (Brecht's adaptation of *Coriolanus*, *The Threepenny Opera*, *The Days of the Commune* and, in a special private performance for the theatrical profession, the Ensemble's studio production of excerpts from *Mahagonny*, wrongly titled by them the *Little Mahagonny*, which in fact is a quite different work.) And so the verdict and final summing up of Brecht himself in England must be: if he is only seen without his words being heard, he is successful; if his texts are understood, he is a total failure.

Indeed, the only wholly satisfactory and successful production of Brecht in all these years was the performance of *Happy End* (first staged at the Edinburgh Festival of 1964, transferred to the Royal Court in the spring of 1965) which Michael Geliot directed under the auspices of the Traverse

Theatre. Here a director familiar with the original who had had a hand in the translation succeeded in re-creating the feel of the late twenties in Berlin, with the added charm that the period itself has now become encrusted with the patina of nostalgia. One must, however, also take into account that this is a play Brecht never wholly acknowledged, largely because it was a potboiler hurriedly put together to cash in on the success of *The Threepenny Opera* and is surely the most harmless and commercial of all of Brecht's works. Hence even the London critics could warm to its attractiveness.

So much for Brecht's impact on techniques of staging. There remains the question of Brecht's influence on the *writing* of plays. Here too his impact has been broad and superficial rather than deep. The new wave of dramatists had to acknowledge Kenneth Tynan as their prophet and so they were, willy-nilly, saddled with Brecht as a model, in spite of the fact that most of them had achieved their initial success in a strictly naturalistic—and therefore non-Brechtian—mode. As this largely autobiographical style was bound to yield to a law of diminishing returns, both John Osborne and Arnold Wesker were soon attracted by the possibilities of the epic form. Wesker used some vaguely Brechtian devices of story-telling in *Chips with Everything* (1962), more boldly in *Their Very Own and Golden City* (written 1964, first London performance 1966) where a social theme—the building of cities which are to be both beautiful and owned by their workers—is dealt with in a sequence of flash-forwards and flashbacks with compression of the time sequence and other epic devices. These, after all, amount to little more than the use of a cinematic technique of montage and cutting. Yet I am sure that without the example of Brecht such techniques might not have been so readily used by authors—and accepted by audiences.

Osborne went considerably further in the use of Brechtian devices than Wesker, not only in writing a satirical musical play (*Paul Slickey*) but above all in turning to historical subjects. Both *Luther* (1961) and *A Patriot for Me* (1965) aim at being epic drama with a Brechtian scope and Brechtian technique. In *Luther* the superficial impact of *Mother Courage* is particularly painfully obvious in the disastrously ill-written scene (Act III, Scene 2) of the Peasant War, which opens with a long narration by an anonymous Knight against a tableau of 'a small handcart . . . beside it the bloody bulk of a peasant's corpse.' Here Brecht's conception is present, but misunderstood as a kind of lantern lecture illustrated by charades. Yet this failure on Osborne's part is small compared to the much more fundamental mistake he made with *Luther*, namely the idea that one could embark on a great historical play without a deep understanding of the social, cultural, and political background of the period. *Luther* is in fact anything but epic theatre—it is an attempt to clothe personal psychological problems in the superficial garb of historical drama. The same is true of *A Patriot for Me*, which is a better play than *Luther* but equally inadequate as a serious portrait of the dying Austro-Hungarian Empire or an analysis of dying empires in general (with applications to present-day Britain). Osborne's understanding of the background is so sketchy, his inability to present whatever knowledge he may have acquired so total, that we are left with a Viennese operetta minus the music. And yet, when he is dealing with the real subject matter of the play, the problem of the homosexual in present-day English society, Osborne rises to considerable heights of eloquence. His mistake was to try to deal with the subject in a 'Brechtian' form.

Far more successful as a historical play is Robert Bolt's *A Man for all Seasons* (1960). Here Sir Thomas More's time and problems are presented with insight and a considerable knowledge of their background. But again the technique of 'epic drama' which the author quite openly adopted is no more than superficially related to Brechtian theory. There is a narrator, 'The Common Man', who goes through the play and appears also in various roles as ordinary people who remain passive in the face of the hero's sufferings. The story is told as a historical paradigm with applications to the

present, but in the last resort this is no more—and no less—
than the traditional English history play with moral uplift
and a patriotic afterglow, John Drinkwater or Clemence
Dane brought up to date.

At the other extreme we find the outright imitation of
Brecht—ideology, form, technique and all—notably in the
case of the gifted poet Christopher Logue (who spent some
time with the Berliner Ensemble studying its methods): the
musical play *The Lilywhite Boys* (of which he was part
author) achieved some success at the Royal Court but suffered
from being a pastiche of Brecht rather than original work
influenced by him.

Much more fruitful examples of inspiration from the epic
theatre are provided by two plays that were the direct result
of Peter Hall's conviction, when he decided that the Royal
Shakespeare Company under his management would have to
do more than just Shakespeare, that the future of contemporary drama lay in the field of the large-scale poetic and
epic play. Both John Whiting's *The Devils* (1961) and Peter
Shaffer's *The Royal Hunt of the Sun* (1964) were written at
Peter Hall's suggestion (although Shaffer's play was eventually produced under the auspices of the National Theatre).
The Devils makes excellent use of a narrative style of presentation and fluid non-realistic decor and deals with historical
facts in an illuminating manner. *The Royal Hunt of the Sun*
likewise presents a major problem—the contrast between
totalitarianism and laissez-faire societies—as well as making
a bitter statement about faith, and does so in a truly epic style.
What it lacks, however, is the ultimate consecration of poetry:
the language is efficient but smacks of purple passages in a
public speech.

The truest follower of Brecht—or at least of Brecht's
essential attitude—is undoubtedly John Arden. Arden has
frequently spoken of his admiration of Brecht, but stresses
that he is not aware of direct influence. It is more a case of
kindred poetical talents following common models in a more
distant tradition—Elizabethan drama, folk song, popular

theatre of all kinds. Yet whether the Brechtian influence is directly traceable or not, the fact that it was in the air during the period of Arden's first experiments as a playwright surely is not without significance. The linking of scenes by songs in *Live Like Pigs*, the use of folk song in *Serjeant Musgrave's Dance*, the masks in *Happy Haven* (not long after the Berliner Ensemble had used masks most tellingly in their 1956 appearance in *The Caucasian Chalk Circle*), the whole structure and technique of *The Workhouse Donkey* (with a narrator and copious musical interludes), the parable technique of *Armstrong's Last Goodnight*, all show a deep and genuine affinity with Brechtian concepts. Arden is left-wing in his personal politics, yet in his plays he is strictly neutral, morally as well as politically. In that sense he is at variance with Brecht. Yet Arden, like Brecht, is a major poet who uses drama as a vehicle for the special poetry of the stage. In this he embodies what is, in my opinion, the overwhelmingly important example provided by Brecht: that drama can be a medium for a major poet, that the quality of this particular type of poetic language and imagination transcends all theoretical and practical rules, devices and gimmicks, even commitment and ideology, and that this alone will produce truly great drama.

The Neurosis of the Neutrals:
Max Frisch

When German civilization collapsed in 1933—and it is a matter for argument whether the rise of Hitler was the cause of this collapse or merely its chief symptom—only one German-speaking area of Europe remained untouched by the calamity: German Switzerland. It is therefore no coincidence that some of the best writers now active in the German language are Swiss—members of the very generation that has remained totally sterile in Germany itself, the generation born between 1910 and 1920 whose formative years fell into the Nazi period. Among these Swiss writers, two, Friedrich Dürrenmatt and Max Frisch, have attained world fame.

Dürrenmatt is the scion of an old Bernese patrician family, Frisch the grandson of an Austrian immigrant. Yet it has rightly been pointed out that this makes Frisch the more typically Swiss; a higher percentage of present-day German Swiss citizens have an ancestry like Frisch's. While Dürrenmatt comes from a family of statesmen, professors, and parsons, Frisch has a background of artisans and 'artists'. He himself has described the artistic pretensions of his maternal great-grandfather, who 'called himself a painter, wore a considerable cravat which was much bolder than his drawings and paintings. . . . My mother, to see the great wide world, once worked as a governess in Czarist Russia; she has often told us about it. My father was an architect. Being the son of a saddler, he had not been able to afford a professional education and so it was his ambition to see his sons as university graduates.'[1] So Frisch has the more artistic background, yet he has striven much harder than Dürrenmatt to find a place

[1] Frisch, *Tagebuch 1946–1949* (Suhrkamp, 1950) p. 275.

in his society: as an architect he is a technologist and a very typical embodiment of our contemporary world, a world where construction and production play so decisive a part. In discussing his position with one foot in the camp of literature, the other in the camp of scientific technology, Frisch clearly reveals that he sympathises with some of the men he worked with who considered his writing as a somewhat crazy aberration: 'Having a dual profession as a writer and as an architect is, of course, not always easy, however many fruitful effects it may have. It is not so much a question of time as of strength. I find it a blessing to work every day with men who have nothing to do with literature; some of them may know that I write, but they don't hold it against me, so long as my other work is all right.'[1]

And yet for Frisch writing has always been a necessity, an almost compulsory activity, an effort at self-exploration. In a brief note, headed 'About Writing', in his published diary he gives a fascinating and ruthlessly sincere insight into the motives of his work as a writer:

> Years ago, in my capacity as an architect, I once visited one of those factories where our glorious watches are being made; my impression was more shattering than any I have ever received in a factory; and yet I have never succeeded in reproducing this experience, one of the strongest of my life, in conversation in such a way that it was relived by my interlocutor. Once it has been talked about, this experience always remains trivial or unreal, real only for the one who went through it, incommunicable like any personal experience—or rather: every experience remains basically incommunicable so long as we hope to express it through the real example that actually happened to us. Real expression can be found for me only through an example that is as far removed from my own self as from that of the person listening: that is, the fictional example. Communication is essentially possible only through the fictitious, transformed, re-shaped instance; and that is also why artistic failure is always accompanied by a feeling of suffocating loneliness.[2]

[1] *Ibid*, p. 282.   [2] *Ibid*, p. 411.

Frisch has enabled us to follow the process of transformation of his experience into fiction through a series of autobiographical writings, mainly journals and diaries, which are among the most remarkable writers' notebooks of our time. *Blätter aus dem Brotsack* (1940) is his diary of military service at the outbreak of war; *Tagebuch mit Marion* (1947) was later reprinted in the wider *Tagebuch 1946–49*.

His first novel *Jürg Reinhart*, which deals with a young man's attainment of maturity during a trip to Dalmatia, has a clearly autobiographical character. (Frisch travelled in south-eastern Europe before the war as a freelance journalist.) The delightful novella *Bin oder die Reise nach Peking*, which describes the lyrical musings of a young man who holds long conversations with Bin, his alter ego or second romantic self, on an imaginary journey to Peking, the ever unattainable goal of the German romantic tradition, also barely rises above the level of autobiographical statement. In Frisch's later plays and novels the transmutation of the material into truly fictional terms is far more complete, but the basic connection with the author's quest for his own self nevertheless always remains clear.

Frisch's origin and background account for some of the main themes of his writings: to be Swiss means to be a citizen of a relatively small, self-governing community with its inevitably petty local politics that tend to loom very large in the foreground even in times of world upheaval; the sensitive, artistic temperament tends to react against this by a violent yearning for the great, wide world: since his *Wanderjahre* in southeastern Europe before the war Frisch has travelled widely in the United States and Europe: the yearning for exotic climes, romantic distant islands is a recurring theme in his plays and novels; and so is scorn against the narrowness and pettiness, the complacency and arrogance of a small, self-contained community which feels itself free from the taints and crimes of other, less fortunate countries. To be Swiss also means to be the citizen of a country that has escaped two world wars. *Andorra*, Frisch's most widely performed play, is among other things an attack on this Swiss complacency. Andorra in the play is a small mountain country, proud of its freedom, proud of being better and morally superior; convinced that this moral superiority makes it immune to any foreign attack:

> As Perin, our great poet once said: Our weapon is our innocence. Or the other way round: our innocence is our weapon. Where else in the world is there a republic that can say this? I ask you: where? A nation like ourselves who as no other can appeal to the conscience of the world, a people without guilt. . . . Andorrans, I tell you: no nation on earth has ever been attacked without someone having been able to reproach them with a crime. What can they reproach us with? The only thing that could happen to Andorra would be an injustice, a gross and open injustice. And that they will not dare. Tomorrow even less than yesterday. Because the whole world would defend us. At one fell swoop. Because the conscience of the world is on our side.[1]

And yet Andorra is attacked, and the Andorrans sacrifice young Andri, whom they believe to be a Jew, to the anti-Semitic invaders. They have prided themselves on being free from the sins of those powerful neighbours, but they have carried the seeds of the same moral corruption within themselves all the time. They have been free from the crimes that great powers become guilty of only because, being a small power, they have never exercised any responsibility, they have never taken an active part in history; their innocence springs from their insignificance, from their pettiness, from their provincialism, from their bourgeois respectability. One of the impulses behind Frisch's writing is the passionate resolve *not* to feel himself free from the guilt and responsibilities of his age, to detect within himself the seeds of the crimes that sully the record of the great powers: in the plays *Nun singen sie wieder* (1945) and *Als der Krieg zu Ende war* (1949) as well as in *Andorra* (1961) he comes to grips with the problem

[1] *Andorra*, Scene 8 in Stücke II, pp. 258–59.

of the extermination of the Jews; in *Die chinesische Mauer* (1946) the problem of the atom bomb is boldly confronted: 'The flood can now be manufactured by man!' And the young poet, the 'contemporary man' (and thus undoubtedly an image of the author himself) who has come to inform the Emperor of China and all the great figures of history of this fact, reveals himself as not only unable to act to defend the suffering people; having delivered an impassioned plea against the bomb, having uttered a terrible warning to the Emperor, he is awarded a prize for fiction and ignored. Because he is helpless to change the course of history the poet, the intellectual, who knows the horrors to come and cannot act effectively, shares in the final guilt.

To be Swiss also means having been brought up to an ideal of bourgeois rectitude, having lived in a small community where neighbours know each other only too well and where one has to do one's utmost to maintain a façade of strict, puritanical respectability. This respectability is merely another aspect of the features of Swiss life against which a sensitive, artistic personality like Frisch is bound to react strongly: the narrowness of local politics, the righteous complacency of guiltless and petty neutrality will appear to such an individual as a refusal to face the world and human life as they really are, an escape from responsibility, from guilt, from temptation—and therefore from life itself. Such respectability is bought at a terrible price: by running away from any valid experience, by hiding behind barriers of timidity and moral cowardice.

This is one of the main themes of *Biedermann und die Brandstifter* (1957–58) (known in England as *Fire Raisers* and in the United States as *The Firebugs*). Biedermann (in German the name is also a generic term for a complacent, respectable citizen, a *faux bonhomme*) is a ruthless businessman, he has just driven an exploited employee to suicide; yet he prides himself on the fact that his daily life is amiable, well ordered, superficially that of a 'good man'. And that is why he cannot believe that the two sinister characters who have infiltrated themselves into his house can really be plotting to use the drums of gasoline and the bales of inflammable stuff they are hoarding in the attic to burn down Mr Biedermann's respectable house, and the whole respectable city he inhabits. For, after all, Biedermann manages to be on amiable conversational terms with them, he has invited them to dinner even; that shows he is human, friendly, benevolent, free from guilt and therefore he cannot, he will not be attacked (exactly as the citizens of Andorra are convinced that nobody can attack them because they are innocent of ever having furnished any good reason to be attacked). And so he even offers the incendiaries the match with which they will blow up his world. His false values, the inauthentic life and the lack of awareness, of consciousness they entail lead Biedermann directly to destruction.

Fire Raisers also has a direct political implication, quite different incidentally from that imposed upon it by a number of performances in Britain, notably Lindsay Anderson's production at the Royal Court. Far from being a play about the atomic bomb we have in our attic which will blow up our world, *Fire Raisers* deals—or dealt originally—with the Western world's inability to see through Communist tactics of infiltration. In Frisch's published diary for 1946–49 the idea for Biedermann is noted immediately after the entry about his consternation at the Communist takeover in Czechoslovakia. 'Worries about our friends. And to all this the glee of my acquaintances towards whom I have always presented Czechoslovakia as an example of a Socialist democracy; and all this topped by the general conceit: such a thing could not happen here!' These words are clearly the germ of the idea. Only if the fire raisers can be seen as revolutionaries threatening the bourgeois world will the play make sense. And it is significant that the other interpretation that will fit the play, at which Frisch hints in the Epilogue in Hell that he added after the success of the original radio version, refers to the inability of the German bourgeoisie to see the rise of Hitler in its true significance. Frisch despises the bourgeois precisely because, having forced himself into the image of *bonhomie* (which is a lie, for it is merely a mask for the cruelties of a system based on exploitation, merely a refusal to see the obvious hardships and sufferings of our world), having suppressed spontaneous human reactions by a dry, heartless, and calculating respectability, he has become incapable even of defending the values on which his well-being is founded.

How is one to react to bourgeois respectability and its dangers? The conventional reaction is to fall into bohemianism, so flaunt one's defiance of respectable values. Swiss cities like Zurich have their own brand of bohemian, artistic communities. And Frisch certainly frequented this world in his youth. But if anything these small enclaves of bohemianism are even narrower than the narrow bourgeois world they defy. Hence the Swiss nostalgia for the romantic, the exotic, and the far off. In Frisch's earliest published play *Santa Cruz* (1944) everything revolves around the conflict between the respectable and narrow circle of everyday lives and the mysterious pull of distant and exotic lands. The cavalry captain and his wife Elvira have lived together in a humdrum marriage for seventeen years. And all that time Elvira has been dreaming of the vagabond whom she once loved and who may be the father of her daughter; and all that time the captain has been dreaming of the friend with whom he once planned to roam the world and to visit the Southern Seas. Pelegrin the vagabond comes to visit them, as he is about to die, and the aging couple recognize that they have been dreaming of the same man, the same romantic ideal. But they also recognize that the real flaw of their lives was that each concealed his secret longing from the other. It is not the escape to remote romantic islands that is the solution, but the courage to be oneself and the courage to love. This question, the problem of identity, the problem of how man can find his true self, an authentic existence, is the central pivot around which most of Frisch's work revolves. It is also the main problem of existential philosophy and, although there is no evidence that Frisch has ever been preoccupied with the work of writers like Camus and Sartre, his approach to it coincides with many of their ideas.

Frisch is above all appalled by the influence that the opinions of other people have on our own identity:

> Some fixed opinion of our friends, our parents, our teachers . . . may weigh upon us like an ancient oracle. Half a lifetime may be blighted by the secret question: will it come true or will it not come true? . . . A teacher once said to my mother she would never learn how to knit. My mother often told us about this assertion; she never forgot, never forgave it; she became a passionate, extraordinarily skilful knitter; and all the stockings and knitted caps, all the gloves and pullovers I ever received, in the end I owe them to that objectionable oracle . . . ! To a certain extent we really are what others see in us, friends as well as enemies. And the other way round: we too are the *authors* of the others; in a mysterious and inescapable way we are responsible for the face they show us.[1]

We create the others in the image we ourselves make of them. And this for Frisch is the ultimate sin, the extinction of their authentic existence, the origin of all the troubles of our time. For the image that we thus make is a fixed, a dead thing, an imposition that can kill. If thus 'being-for-others' by fixing an image reduces human freedom, love that accepts a human personality as 'being-for-itself' creates freedom:

> Love frees from all images. That is the exciting, the adventurous, the truly suspenseful thing about love, that with those human beings we love we never reach an end: because we love them; as long as we love them. Listen to the poets when they are in love: they search for similes, as though they were drunk, they grasp for all the things in the universe, flowers, animals, clouds, stars, and oceans. Why? Just as the universe, God's inexhaustible spaciousness, is boundless, so boundless, pregnant with all possibilities, all mysteries, unfathomable is the human being we love. . . . If we think we know the other, that is the

[1] *Tagebuch*, pp. 33-34.

end of love, every time; but perhaps cause and effect are reversed . . . not because we know the other person is our love
coming to an end, but the other way round: because our love
is at an end, because its strength is exhausted, we have finished
with the other person. . . . We deny him the claim of all living
things, which must remain unfathomable, and at the same time
we are astonished and disappointed that our relationship is no
longer alive. 'You are not,' says the disappointed man or
woman, 'what I took you to be.' And what did one take the
other for? A mystery, that man, after all, is, an exciting riddle
we have become tired of. Now we make ourself an image. That
is the loss of love, the betrayal.[1]

This beautiful passage in Frisch's published diaries for the
years 1946–49, the most fruitful, formative period of his
creative life, certainly is the key to a great deal of his subsequent work. It defines the subject of his great novel *Stiller*
(1954: English title: *I'm Not Stiller*) and of a number of his
most interesting plays.

Anatol Ludwig Stiller, a successful sculptor at Zurich, had
disappeared without a trace for more than six years when a
man resembling him in all particulars was picked up at the
Swiss frontier because his passport, made out in the name of
White, was obviously not in order. Is the stranger Stiller?
He refuses to acknowledge his identity, any identity, and the
bulk of the novel is taken up by this unidentified man's
diaries in prison. He denies that he is Stiller and yet in the
end he has to accept the fact that he is Stiller. He wanted to
escape from the image that was constricting him, but the
world with all its powers of official and sentimental pressure
(through his wife, family, and friends) effectively puts a stop
to any such attempts. Seen from one angle, the hero of the
novel is a clinical case of split personality; seen from another,
he is a human being trying to assert his uniqueness, his freedom to choose himself (in Sartre's sense); he is also a legen-
dary hero, a Rip Van Winkle, who returns to his former
surroundings as a changed man. (Frisch has written a radio

[1] *Ibid*, pp. 31–32.

play on the theme of *Stiller* which has the title *Rip Van Winkle*.)

As a novel *Stiller* is a remarkable *tour de force*. We are made to witness the gradual rediscovery of his self by a man who has rejected not only the world's former image of his personality but his own image of himself. And at the end we feel with him that, although he must bow to the overwhelming evidence of his physical identity with Stiller, mentally and spiritually he remains as unconvinced as ever. He returns to his image as we slip back into an old suit we had discarded; the self the world imposes on Stiller is an alien, dead thing. He tried to discard his former self because he felt himself a failure as an artist and as a husband. Now he is pushed back into these roles, and he therefore must again end up as a failure.

Perhaps Stiller's failure is an even deeper one: he refused to accept the image of himself that society imposed on him, but he also could not make up his mind to be himself. As Stiller's wife lies dying, the public prosecutor who conducted the case and later became Stiller's friend tries to sum up the lesson of his life: 'As far as I know your life, you have again and again thrown everything away because you have been uncertain of yourself. You are not the truth. You are a human being and you have often been ready to abandon an untruth, to be uncertain. What else does this mean, Stiller, but that you do believe in a truth? A truth, that is, that we cannot alter and that we cannot even kill—which is life itself. . . . Again and again you have tried to accept yourself without accepting something like God. And that has turned out to be impossible. He is the power that can help you to accept yourself truly. All this you have experienced! And in spite of it you say that you cannot pray . . . you cling to your own powerlessness which you take for your personality; and yet you know your own powerlessness so well—and all this as though from stubbornness, only because you yourself are not the power. . . .'[1]

[1] Frisch, *Stiller* (Suhrkamp, 1958) p. 570.

Stiller himself makes no comment on these observations and the question remains open. We merely learn that Stiller's return to his wife, the renewal of his failed marriage, in the end killed the woman he loved and that after that he lived on as a broken man. And yet Stiller who refuses the world's image of himself, who is unable to accept his own image of himself, is himself a maker of images, a sculptor. (This is the subtlest turn in the labyrinthine complexity of this brilliantly conceived novel.) 'Whether there is not something inhuman in the mere attempt to make a picture of a living human being, that is a big question. It essentially concerns Stiller,' says the public prosecutor in his commentary that forms the final part of the book. Thus Stiller stands for the artist in general—and for his own creator, who, as a playwright and novelist, has also embarked on the dangerous and perhaps deadly pursuit of making images of human beings.

Stiller is a deeply serious, searching, and philosophical work. In a lighter and more ironical vein Frisch has dealt with the same subject in the play *Don Juan oder die Liebe zur Geometrie* (1953) which was written at almost the same time. Don Juan is here shown as a man whose ruthless determination to be true to himself creates a wholly false image. Far from being a seducer or voluptuary, he really is only interested in geometry. Betrothed to Donna Anna, and truly in love with her, he refuses to pronounce the marriage vows merely because he feels himself morally unable to pledge his future conduct so far ahead, for after all we can only know what our present self intends, never what may be the sincere feelings of our future selves. Having killed Donna Anna's father and having acquired the reputation of a wicked voluptuary as a result, he is so much sought after by the ladies that he finally decides to end it all by staging his own death in the most gruesome circumstances: the arrival of the dead Governor's statue and the swallowing up of Don Juan by the mouth of hell are elaborately stage-managed at his own expense in the presence of a multitude of his mistresses. It seems as though Don Juan, now believed to be in hell, could safely start a new life (just like Stiller after he had shed his old self) and devote himself to his true love, geometrical research. But one of the ladies who loves Don Juan knows his secret and so she can blackmail him into a life at her side —marriage and domesticity. This is boring and irritating, but at least Don Juan *has* shed his former image. But no—as the play ends a visitor arrives with a book, the newly published comedy about Don Juan, the seducer of Seville. The image has become immortal and will outlive the real Don Juan.

The problem of man's identity has other facets as well: it is not merely a question of the image that the outside world imposes on us. It is also a question of which of the multitudinous potentialities in ourselves is our real self. Are we what we appear to be in our self-controlled, conscious waking hours; or are we the wild wishes and violent desires of our dreams? In *Graf Oederland* (first version 1951, third and final version 1961) Frisch approaches this problem in a play that is probably his most intriguing virtuoso performance. An official of the utmost respectability, a public prosecutor, one day finds that he is identifying himself with the murderer whose trial he has been conducting in court—a humdrum little man who killed without motive, merely because he could not endure the deadly routine of a pointless existence. The public prosecutor helps the murderer to escape, takes to the woods, becomes the leader of a revolutionary force of outlaws which overthrows the legal government and thus the dictator of his country. Having entered the capital at the head of his victorious forces, he returns to his own house and finds himself there in exactly the same position and situation as at the moment when the whole fantastic sequence of events began. In a flash, and greatly relieved, he realizes that it has all been a nightmare, the wild fantasy of a man dreaming by the fireside at the end of a hard day in court. The public prosecutor, and the audience with him, can now see the whole violent sequence of events in all its extravagant improbability. Of course, it *was* all a dream! But then the maid asks: 'Do you want me to take off your muddy boots?' And the public prosecutor looks at his boots: the nightmare was reality after all. It was *not* a dream. Or is it merely part of the nightmare that we ask ourselves whether we are dreaming and still are so deeply immersed in the dream that we must answer that it is reality after all . . . ?

Frisch has here brilliantly succeeded in putting a most elusive human situation on the stage: the situation when we are going through some terrible event and hope it is a dream, or when we are dreaming and are hoping it is a dream and yet cannot but accept the dream as real. But beyond the mere virtuosity of re-creating such a highly ambivalent psychological state, Frisch here says something very important: dream or not, each human being really *is* what his hidden desires represent, as much as he really *is* the well-behaved and respectable shell that he presents to the outside world. The public prosecutor followed his *real* desires when he became an outlaw and it is therefore relatively irrelevant whether at the end of the play it all turns out to have been a fantasy or whether it all really happened; the violence was potentially present from the very beginning.

The public prosecutor's nightmare adventure merges into myth, the myth of Count Oederland, a fairy-tale figure that has been haunting the public prosecutor. And indeed our subconscious wishes and fantasies are closely akin to myth, in which the archetypal fears and desires of human beings have found lasting form. In the novel *Homo Faber* (1957) Frisch has attempted another *tour de force*—to re-create an ancient myth in the terms of our technological age. Walter Faber, the hero of this tale, which Frisch has subtitled 'A Report', is a technologist, an engineer. But he is also a modern Oedipus, a man fated to commit incest: he becomes the bridegroom of his own daughter. The role of the blind fate that drove Oedipus into guilt in the Greek myth is here played by the pitiless, impersonal directing force of our own lives: the workings of our mechanical civilization. Faber's fate is shaped by engine failures of aircraft, by a slight defect in his electric razor: if a bit of nylon thread had not stopped the razor he would not have been at home when the shipping line phoned to confirm his booking and would not have been able to take the boat on which he met the girl with whom he fell in love and who later turned out to be his own daughter. The engineer who prides himself on controlling machines is constantly controlled by the whims of minute pieces of machinery. What is more, the further we are removed from the true sources of human feeling, the more isolated we seem from the raw, primeval workings of humanity, the more certainly we are thrown back into the primeval human situation—subjected to the blind workings of an impersonal fate, involved in monstrous guilts. The image of Auschwitz, in which technological man could be seen as merely a more monstrous, because more powerful, repetition of the Stone Age savage, stands behind the subtle and delicate imagery of *Homo Faber*.

In *Andorra* Frisch returned to the problem of human identity, but he put it against the background of the terrible guilt of our age. The play is about anti-Semitism, but it also deals with the existential situation of man as the product of the opinions of his neighbours. Andri, the hero of the play, is the illegitimate son of an Andorran schoolmaster and a woman from beyond the borders of Andorra, 'the country of the Blacks'. Ashamed to confess his transgression to his wife, the schoolmaster has taken the boy into his home by pretending that he is a Jewish orphan, a victim of the anti-Semitic excesses of the Blacks. The schoolmaster is an idealist who wants to teach his countrymen a lesson about racialism. When the boy is grown up and generally accepted as a Jew he will reveal that he is his own son and no Jew and this will prove the fallacy of all racial prejudices and theories.

But Andri is not only regarded as a Jew; being looked at as a Jew imposes on him the patterns of Jewish character. The carpenter to whom he is apprenticed, for example, simply will not believe that he likes making furniture; he forces him to become a salesman because that suits his Jewish talents. Andri has fallen in love with Barblin, the schoolmaster's

daughter. When he asks his 'foster father' for her hand, he
meets a horrified refusal—and he is convinced that this is
due to his Jewishness. When the schoolmaster tells him the
real reason he simply cannot accept it. Having been seen as a
Jew by the others, he has now *become* a Jew and cannot but
be a Jew. And so he goes to his death as a Jew when the
Blacks invade Andorra and demand a scapegoat for the murder of a Black woman (who is none other than Andri's own
mother) at the hands of the xenophobic Andorrans. The
image we have made for ourselves has killed the real human
being, and now we kill the image *and* the man who bears it.

Andorra tells the story of Andri in retrospect. Each scene
is prefaced by the self-justification of one of 'the others' from
a witness box—or is it a dock?— at the side of the stage.
None of us wants to have been responsible afterwards, when
the consequences of our thoughtless actions have resulted in
tragedy.

Andorra not only became a major success in the theatre in
the German-speaking world and elsewhere (it was the first
contemporary foreign play to reach the stage of Britain's new
National Theatre in 1964), it also headed the best-seller lists
of books in Germany for a considerable period.

Frisch's next work, the novel *Mein Name sei Gantenbein*
(*Let My Name Be Gantenbein*, 1964) also became an almost
immediate best-seller. Here Frisch pushes his preoccupation
with identity a step farther: the novel consists of the un-
named narrator *imagining* himself in a number of different
identities—Enderlin, a scholar who has an affair with a woman he casually meets in a foreign city; Svoboda, that woman's betrayed husband; and Gantenbein, a man who
undergoes an eye operation and, when the bandage is taken
off, pretends that he has become blind, although his sight
has returned, and later marries a successful actress whose in-
fidelities he delights in observing as she neglects to conceal
the evidence from her 'blind' husband. We never learn who
the narrator actually is, but gradually the impression builds
up that he must himself be a betrayed husband, obsessed by

variations on the theme of his predicament. The scenes of love-making, adultery and its concealment are so vividly imagined in such meticulously convincing detail that the reader tends to forget he is merely following the day-dreams of the narrator and is repeatedly brought to confront this fact with a jolt. Images of incurable sickness and suicide, the melancholy dissolution of a household, the empty apartment, the loneliness of an abandoned spouse are interwoven like the musical strands of a symphonic poem. It all adds up to a kind of 'alienation effect'—a subtly intriguing puzzle which each reader is free to try to solve in the manner most congenial to his own personality, his own mood.

Yet, again, what it all adds up to is the impossibility of escaping the identity that the world, the environment, the blind chance of life, the 'others' impose upon the individual. The Gantenbein character of the narrator's imagination seems to come nearest to an escape—but only at the cost of maintaining the fiction of his own blindness, that is, by insisting that he does not notice, by refusing to accept that he is what he is, namely a cuckold. The title of the book seems to express the narrator's *desire* to attain this happy state of affairs, which could enable him to live with the woman he loves without having to act out the consequences of his position as a cuckolded husband. But the inference from the mood of the book must be that the narrator has, in fact, found it impossible to carry this out. But then, the detailed image of a suicide's body slowly drifting down the river through Zurich also turns out to be an unattainable dream of wish fulfilment, and the novel ends with the narrator emerging from his musings with the recognition that 'it is all as though it had never happened' and an acceptance of life as something that 'pleases me'. So, at the end, it seems, the narrator, having imagined the painful situation in all possible variations, has, by his imagination, healed his wound and emerged from his experience scarred but healed.

Mein Name sei Gantenbein is an impressive achievement, yet, in the light of Frisch's subsequent work, the play *Bio-*

grafie—ein Spiel (1967), the novel seems merely a preliminary experiment for the far more elegant, lucid and satisfying dramatic work. *Ein Spiel* could mean: A Play or A Game. But Frisch has insisted that the subtitle is more than just a generic description and that it must be seen as a definition of the play as a party game. The game derives from a remark made by Vershinin in Chekhov's *The Three Sisters:* 'I often think how it would be if one could live one's life once again, in full knowledge of the facts. How it would be if the life one has lived through were, so to speak, merely the first draft, and one's second attempt at life would be the clean copy. Each of us would then, I feel, try above all not to repeat himself. . . . If I were to start my life again, I should not get married . . . no, no.'

The hero Kürmann (which in German means, the man who has a choice) is in fact given this chance by a character called Registrator (i.e. the recorder of his fate). Kürmann's marriage to a young intellectual woman, Antoinette, has turned out disastrously. The Registrator gives him a completely free hand to re-live any situation he chooses in such a way as to *avoid* the disastrous course events have taken. But, try as he may, Kürmann cannot escape his fate—marriage to and painful betrayal by Antoinette. In the course of the play it gradually emerges that we are in fact inside Kürmann's own mind, while Kürmann lies in a hospital dying of cancer. Finally, when all attempts on Kürmann's part have failed to change the course of events which followed the night when Antoinette remained behind after a party in Kürmann's flat and had to spend the night there, the Registrator reverses the situation and gives Antoinette the free choice. She merely decides not to stay and leaves. If *that* had happened, Kürmann *would* have been free. But—would that have made that much difference in view of the fact that he was destined to die of cancer seven years later? The play's last words are the Registrator's: 'You are free—for seven years. . . .' The inference is clear: what would it have mattered in the end, in the face of the inevitability of death?

Biografie, however, is by no means a painful or tragic play. It is, as the subtitle implies, above all a *game*, a lightheartedly ironical examination of the hero's life and its turning points. Again and again Kürmann returns to that fateful chance meeting with an unknown woman, the coincidence that brought them together and transformed their lives. And it is clearly shown that, in fact, the development was well-nigh inevitable, that Kürmann's own character is his fate, that even with a different constellation of coincidences he would have involved himself in merely another set of equally unfortunate circumstances (his first marriage is shown to have gone wrong through his own passivity and weakness).

So light is Frisch's touch in this play, so great was its success with the public, that the more intellectual critics were tempted to dismiss it as a purely commercial product, a 'boulevard play'. This, surely, is a form of snobbery, contempt for success merely as a symptom of vulgarity. *Biografie* is a play of considerable insight and profundity, a subtle and only seemingly effortless distillation of the experience so painfully outlined in *Mein Name sei Gantenbein*.

Biografie continues the fluid argumentative style of plays like *Die Chinesische Mauer* or *Nun singen sie wieder*, which shows the influence of Thornton Wilder, whose *The Skin of Our Teeth* made such a tremendous impact when it was staged in Zurich towards the end of the war. But it also contains a good deal of Pirandello in its exploration of what might have been, the interaction of destiny and coincidence. *Andorra* with its rigidly didactic stance and its trial structure shows the impact of Brecht, with whom Frisch was linked by close ties of friendship during Brecht's stay in Zurich after his return to Europe from the United States and before his decision to settle in East Berlin (1947–49).

Frisch has left an unforgettable pen picture in his published diaries of Brecht at this period. But in spite of his admiration for Brecht as a man, an artist, and a champion of his political cause, Frisch did not follow him slavishly in his writing or in his stance as a public figure. In recent years he has increasingly taken part in the controversies of the day, notably in his polite but firm stand for modern literature in the debate provoked by a violent attack on the sordidness and lack of moral fibre of contemporary writers from the most revered traditional literary critic of Switzerland, Emil Staiger, which aroused a storm of protest and counter-protest in 1966. Although decidedly a man of the left, Frisch repudiates Stalinism and neo-Stalinism; he wrote the postscript to the German-language publication of Andrei Sakharov's important memorandum on 'Progress, Co-existence and Intellectual Freedom' —the daring attempt of a Soviet scientist to draw the attention of his leaders to the dangers of the degeneration of Soviet society into a rigid, Byzantine, conservative totalitarianism.

It is this ability to remain flexible and undogmatic that gives Frisch his irony in tackling a myth like the Don Juan legend in the spirit of Cocteau, Giraudoux, or Shaw. Frisch's existentialism also owes more to Kierkegaard than to the French or German schools of our own time. And it is in this easy mingling of European traditions that Frisch's essentially Swiss character emerges; indeed, in his preoccupation with the need for self-realization he shows the influence of the great Swiss novelist of the nineteenth century, Gottfried Keller, and his masterpiece *Der Grune Heinrich*.

But however eclectic Frisch might appear if he is thus summed up in terms of literary models and influences, he is, basically, a highly original and personal writer who has always strenuously refused to be classified or classed with any school or ideological grouping. This is precisely what singles him out among most German-speaking writers of his generation: where most of them indulge in wild generalizations, Frisch always remains concrete and direct; where they go in for *Weltanschauung*, Frisch remains ideologically uncommitted; where they are baroque and excessive in their style, Frisch is simple, direct, and yet full of lyrical power. Where they tend to offer panaceas and infallible solutions

Frisch merely wants to define some questions that ought to be asked:

> As a playwright I would consider my task to have been thoroughly fulfilled if one of my plays could succeed in so posing a question that from that moment on the audience could not go on living without an answer—without their own answer, which they can give only through their own lives. The general demand for an answer, a general answer, which is so often made so movingly, so reproachfully, perhaps after all it is not as honest as those who ask it believe. Every human answer as soon as it transcends a personal answer and pretends to general validity will be questionable, we know that all too well; and the satisfaction we find in disproving other people's answers makes us forget the question that bothers us; and that would mean: we do not really want answers, we merely want to forget the question. So as not to become responsible.[1]

[1] Frisch, *Tagebuch*, pp. 141–42.

The Neurosis of the Neutrals:
Friedrich Dürrenmatt

An interviewer once asked Friedrich Dürrenmatt to define what he understood by theatre. The Swiss dramatist hesitated a moment, then he said: 'Take, for example, two people who are drinking coffee. That's nothing. But if you knew that their cups contain poison, that might turn into drama.'

This definition certainly applies to Dürrenmatt's own theatre. This son of a Swiss Protestant clergyman, who is today recognized as one of the two most powerful dramatists now writing in German, is obsessed with murder, executions, and violence: hangmen climbing into the window to carry out clandestine executions, public prosecutors taking it upon themselves to execute adulterous wives; a horrifying ruin of a fabulously rich old woman arriving in a small town offering the citizens vast sums if they murder the seducer of her youth; a 'private bank' conducted on the principle that any depositor threatening to withdraw his funds is murdered —these are just a few of Dürrenmatt's subjects. He regards the crime story as the most appropriate art form for our age: 'How is the artist to survive in a world of "educated" people, of literates?' he has asked, and replied: 'It is a question that depresses me, to which I know no answer. Perhaps best by writing crime stories, by creating art where nobody suspects art. Literature will have to become so light again that it will weigh nothing on the scales of today's literary criticism. Only thus can it regain some weightiness.'

Like his countryman Max Frisch, Dürrenmatt is deeply preoccupied with the problem of guilt because, as a Swiss, he has not been afflicted with the hideous diseases of his time. For young men of spirit to sit idly on the sidelines while the world was being purged by fire and violence cannot have been but agonizing and frustrating beyond endurance. In Frisch's case it produced a violent, romantic yearning for the great wide world, a contemptuous dismissal of his own secure and complacent countrymen as fat, insensitive Biedermanns or as puny-minded Andorrans. In Dürrenmatt's case the 'neurosis of the neutrals' led to a relentless probing of the guilt, the murderous instincts behind the safe and bourgeois façade of his well-ordered world: the trains may be running on time, the patisserie may be exquisite, but there are murderers at work behind the well-scrubbed, well-curtained windows nevertheless. . . .

Dürrenmatt's writing owes much to the German tradition of grotesque fantasy: Kafka, E. T. A. Hoffmann, Büchner, and Wedekind are among his literary forebears. But there is an Anglo-Saxon streak in Dürrenmatt as well; he owes much to the English detective novel which also takes murder for granted in the most well-ordered of middle-class societies; and his vein of anachronistically ironic treatments of historical or mythological subjects is clearly based on Shaw.

An affluent, highly mechanized society, teeming as it may be with violence, cannot, in Dürrenmatt's view, give rise to tragedy because it is so mechanized that violence happens by remote control. There is no responsibility in an ant heap, and there can be no tragedy without responsibility: 'In the muddle of our century,' Dürrenmatt has said, 'there are no longer guilty or responsible human beings. Everybody claims that *he* is not to blame, that *he* did not want it to happen. And indeed, things would have happened without anyone in particular doing anything about making them happen. We are far too collectively guilty, far too collectively embedded in the sins of our fathers and of their fathers. We are merely the children of their children. That's our bad luck, not our guilt. Guilt presupposes personal action, a religious act. Only comedy can deal with *us*. Our world has led us into the realm of the grotesque, as it has led us to the atom bomb; just as the apocalyptic paintings of Hieronymus Bosch are also merely grotesque.'

If guilt and personal accountability for our actions are no longer possible, our misfortunes become like the pratfalls of people who stumble over banana skins. That is why the drama of our time has to be a drama of pratfalls—tragic farce. 'Fate,' Dürrenmatt says, 'has departed from our scene. . . . In the foreground of our stage everything is reduced to mere accident, disease, or crisis. Even war will become dependent on whether electronic brains predict its profitability. . . . Woe to us if someone tampered with our machines, interfered with our artificial brains. And even such possibilities would be less calamitous than the possibility that a screw might be loose somewhere, a coil entangled, a button out of order—the world might end because of a short circuit, a technical mishap. So we are no longer threatened by God, Justice, Destiny as we find it in Beethoven's Fifth Symphony, but by traffic accidents, a dam burst owing to faulty construction, explosions in atomic plants caused by an absent-minded apprentice. . . .'

So tragedy becomes impossible as a subject for drama. It is also impossible because there is no longer an audience for it: 'Tragedy presupposes a community, that is, a common shared view of the world and its purpose, and one cannot nowadays pretend without embarrassment that such a community exists; there is nothing more comic than to sit through the mystery plays of the anthroposophists without sharing their views.'

And yet, Dürrenmatt maintains, tragedy can enter through the back door; his grotesque farces may reveal it, in a flash, suddenly as a yawning abyss that opens up for a moment in the midst of grotesquely hilarious proceedings.

Nor, he says, are such tragic farces an expression of despair: 'True, he who realizes the meaninglessness, the hopelessness of this world may be led to despair; but this despair is not a consequence of the world being thus constituted, but an answer he gives to this world; and there could be another answer: his refusal to despair, his resolution to face this world, in which we often live like Gulliver among the giants. . . . It is still possible to show man as a being of courage. . . . The world, and therefore the stage which stands for the world, appears to me as something monstrous, an enigma made up of calamities that have to be accepted, but before which there must be no capitulation. . . . '

And so Dürrenmatt confronts his audiences with a world that may be horrifying and grotesque but that, he hopes, they will face with courage and a sense of humour. It is much to ask of a theatre public conditioned to after-dinner entertainment; but perhaps they will live up to this dramatist's high expectations.

A stout man of medium height, Dürrenmatt has the massive head of one of those Roman emperors' busts—a Claudius or Domitian—with dark, thick, horn-rimmed glasses. He speaks German with the characteristic guttural intonation of the Swiss. I met him the day before the London opening of *The Physicists* in January 1963. I started by asking him how the London production compared with the German ones he had seen.

'It's curious,' he replied, 'I had imagined the English actors would underplay much more than the Germans or the Swiss. But not at all. There are some passages where the German casts did more, there are others where the English are far more passionate and emphatic. In one of the best of the German productions, for example, the mad lady doctor made her revelations at the end sitting quietly on the sofa, using very little voice and emphasis. That gave it a marvellously mad effect. In Peter Brook's production there is a great deal of movement and vociferation. The London production is also the first I have seen that does not strictly adhere to the set as I described it in the stage directions. In Zurich, Berlin, Munich, and Hamburg they all followed my idea of a circular room with three doors leading to the physicists' rooms at the back. Here there is only one door. It is very effective, but I wonder how it will change the impact of the play. . . . '

I asked him how he reacted to England.

'It is very strange, more so than any European country I have been to, more strange even than America. I like it very much, although I am somewhat oppressed by all that politeness.'

We talked about his intention in *The Physicists*. 'It is not so much a play about the hydrogen bomb,' he said, 'as about science itself, and the impossibility of escaping the consequences of one's thinking. Once a scientist has followed a certain trend of thought he simply cannot run away from its consequences, its practical results. That is an act of cowardice.'

'Does that apply to individuals only or also to whole countries? For example, would you consider the suggestion made by some people in this country that Britain should opt out of having the hydrogen bomb as running away from the consequences of one's thinking?'

He pondered for a moment. 'No,' he said, 'that would be an act of courage, because it would be a political decision about an invention that is already in the public domain and that can be used rightly or wrongly; that is quite different from the case of a scientist who thinks he can suppress, or keep to himself, an invention he has made. But what prompted me to write *The Physicists* was not politics at all. I was interested in working out a situation, a situation that takes the worst possible turn; and also the workings of chance, which always fascinate me. In this case everything turns on the physicist who wants to escape into a lunatic asylum, having chosen the worst possible lunatic asylum to hide in; and on that choice, which is pure chance, the fate of the world may depend. In fact, in *The Physicists* I tried to write a modern version of the myth of Oedipus—a chain of events in which the hero goes to great lengths to avoid a disaster he fears and everything he does to prevent the disaster does in fact make it inevitable. In the episode with the Sphinx and his answering all her riddles Oedipus himself is somehow shown as a man of greatly superior intelligence, and yet that intelligence, as in the case of the scientist, the more he uses it, the more certainly it leads him to the conclusion he most wanted to avert. I am much concerned with logic and how its consequent application leads us into more and more diffi- cult paradoxes.'

I mentioned that I had been criticized for not including him among the authors discussed in *The Theatre of the Absurd*. 'No,' he replied, 'I don't think I am on the same lines as Beckett or Ionesco. I would call my own theatre a "theatre of paradox" because it is precisely the paradoxical results of strict logic that interest me. Ionesco and Beckett attack language and logic as means of thought and communi- cation. I am concerned with logical thought in its strictest application, so strict that it sets up its own internal contra- dictions. But this requires extreme rationality in structure and dialogue, in contrast to the Theatre of the Absurd in which language is shown in a state of disintegration.'

This led to the perennial question of literary forebears and influences. Was it true as had been said that Thornton Wilder and Brecht had been decisive in his case?

'Not really. Of course I read Thornton Wilder's *The Skin of Our Teeth*, but I did not see it at its performance in Zurich at the end of the war. I was not living in Zurich and was therefore also not, as has also been said, exposed to the great productions of Brecht at the *Schauspielhaus* during and just after the war. I only got to know Brecht's work around 1947, and by that time my own personality as a dramatist was already formed. Of course, it is impossible not to be influenced by a writer like Brecht, quite apart from the fact that he was very much of our time and dealt with the problems of our time in a manner most appropriate to our time; no one who tries to do the same can avoid touching on the same problems with similar methods. But the fact is that I came to the theatre fairly late. I specialized in classics at my school, and I was fascinated by Greek and Latin. I regard the great Greek tragedians and Aristophanes as the chief influences on my work. I grew up in towns that did not have very good theatres so I was not much exposed to drama. Of course, Shakespeare has influenced my thinking and so has Nestroy [the great Austrian comic dramatist of the first half of the nineteenth century, who also influenced Brecht]. But I did not set out to become a dramatist from the start. I was far more interested in philosophy, particularly in epistemology, in how we think; then I wanted to become a painter. And only when my realization that I had failed as a painter led to a really severe spiritual crisis did I finally turn to drama. . . .'

All this time Dürrenmatt had tried to light his massive pipe. But repeatedly just as he had lit the tobacco and was about to draw to make the flame take, the trend of the argument had led him to take it out of his mouth again so that it went out. Now there was a pause during which he puffed at his pipe and got it going.

I mentioned that of all his plays I personally liked *Romulus the Great* best. He smiled contentedly. 'I am glad about that.' It was quite clear that he also regarded this play, which deals ironically with imperialism and militarism, as one of his favourites. *Romulus the Great* has some pretty stinging things to say about German nationalism. 'This play was one of my most resounding failures in Germany. It flopped really monumentally. But Brecht liked it particularly. He wanted to put it on at his own theatre in East Berlin. But the authorities would not permit that. He was furious about it. So he suggested it to a producer he knew in West Berlin. But there too there were objections. Then there was an excellent production of this play, by far the best, at the Centre Dramatique de l'Est in France, just about the time De Gaulle took over in 1958. So that too had to come off because it was thought to refer to the situation by its satire on militarists and imperialists. But, I am glad to say, *Romulus the Great* is a tremendous success in Poland. It has been running in Warsaw for a long time, and there no objections are raised to it. I spent some time in Poland recently. That is a magnificently stimulating place today, you witness a tremendous upsurge in the wake of a spiritual liberation.'

The conversation turned to future plans: Dürrenmatt was

about to finish a new play, *Hercules in the Stables of Augeas*. I asked whether it was to be a stage version of a radio play of the same title which was published some time ago. 'Yes. But I have greatly developed and widened it for the stage. It is due to be staged at Zurich soon. Leonard Steckel, one of my favourite actors and producers, will direct it.'

Dürrenmatt's roots are, very deeply, in Switzerland. He deplored the action of a Swiss fellow writer who moved away from his home ground. 'And,' he added, 'Switzerland is a very good place for a writer to live nowadays. It is very useful to be able to survey the world scene from a vantage point that is not itself in the thick of the conflict. Moreover, while it is true that Switzerland is not a place for a bohemian style of life, in our world today a writer no longer has to lead that kind of life. He does not have to be, he can't be, a wild outsider. He is much more like a scientist, an observer and commentator who can and must live like other people. And Switzerland, which is becoming more and more highly technological, is a very good place for such a writer to observe the world around him.'

And Friedrich Dürrenmatt, the dramatist who uncovers the paradoxes of logic and displays the torrents of violence that rage underneath the surface of a well-ordered technological society, leaned back in his armchair, puffing at his massive pipe, looking very much like a comfortable Swiss businessman who had come to London to clinch some profitable export order. One could see what he meant: that the protective colouring of a respectable outsider might be of considerable advantage to a dispassionate and merciless observer of the shortcomings of our affluent, technological age.

Ionesco
and the Creative Dilemma

One of the principal and most persistent sources of error that tends to bedevil a considerable proportion of contemporary literary analysis is the implicit assumption that the writer's creative process is a wholly conscious and purposive type of activity. Few critics stop to inquire into the psychological basis and the mechanism of the creative process itself; hence their tendency to approach a work of art in terms of the author's intentions. The excellence of a work can then be deduced from an examination of the intentions in the mind of the writer (whether or not they are relevant and important) and of the degree to which these intentions have been realized. And even if the complexity of the creative process is recognized by a critic, once he has started to analyze, say, the imagery of a poem or play, the effect on the reader will tend to be an impression that the given author *deliberately* chose the metaphors or images concerned rather than following a semiconscious urge to express his intuition in these, and no other, terms.

Historically this attitude probably springs from the fact that criticism originated in schools of rhetoric that undertook to supply their pupils with rules that, if rightly applied, would guarantee the production of effective discourse; these rules could be deduced from the analysis of existing examples of excellent rhetoric and hence, by an extension of the idea to all literary work, rules of the correct construction of drama, correct prosody and imagery are implicitly assumed to be deducible from the study of recognized masterpieces in all fields. One often gains the impression that this is still the implicit and unconscious basis of much of the literary analysis of our own time.

And yet it is an empirical fact that great masterpieces are not produced by those who have most thoroughly mastered the principles of literary excellence arrived at by such methods. Indeed some of the best creative writers have themselves always placed an enormous weight on the concept of inspiration, that is, the mysterious workings of the creative process that are felt, by the writers themselves, to be to some extent outside their conscious control.

These considerations undoubtedly apply to lyrical poetry. A short poem is recognized as capable of being the product of an almost totally unconscious process, witness the case of *Kubla Khan*. To what extent, however, can this be the case when drama is concerned? Of all forms of literary activity the writing of plays undoubtedly appears as the most deliberate and rationally planned. A novel may ramble on and on; a play must be tautly constructed; a poem or a work of narrative fiction can be wholly subjective; a play, by the very fact that it is meant to come to life on the stage, independently and outside the mind of its creator, requires a high degree of objectivity, of abstraction from the purely subjective. Hence, it may well be argued, the playwright has to build his work with the almost mathematical rationality of an architect who assembles his materials, calculates the strength of his foundations and the tensions and stresses his creation will have to sustain. A play, like a building, has thus been traditionally required to be *well made* and the language of dramatic criticism has borrowed metaphor upon metaphor from that of architecture: a play has to have the right proportions, its design must be sound, its parts must be subtly and correctly interrelated; dialogue and characterization must be cleverly calculated and minutely judged.

These considerations undoubtedly apply to a great deal of the best in drama. Yet, of course, in even such brilliantly calculated masterpieces of dramatic architecture as the plays of Racine or Ibsen, the operations of subconscious forces outside the immediate rational control of their creators have played their important, their decisive part. The effect of *Phèdre* or *Ghosts* is based both on their impeccably calculated construction *and* on deep psychological undertones emanating from the depths of their authors' minds. Nevertheless the primacy of the element of construction and planned design has always been evident: if emotion nourished from subconscious sources gave drama its richness and flavour, firm design provided the skeleton to be clothed by the flesh of feeling and human ambiguity.

The emergence of a group of playwrights who maintain that their activity is based on processes akin to automatic writing and whose professed aim is the outward-projection of spontaneous visions springing directly from subconscious layers of the mind, however, reopens the whole question. The examination of such claims and an inquiry into the genesis of plays produced by playwrights of this persuasion should cast new light on the creative process of dramatic writing in general and enable us to gain a better understanding of the interaction of conscious and subconscious forces by which so complex a creation as a play is produced.

By far the most articulate and introspective of the playwrights in question is Eugène Ionesco, whose collection of autobiographical, theoretical, and polemical essays *Notes et Contre-Notes* contains much valuable material on his methods of work.

The clearest, though somewhat exaggerated, account of how Ionesco writes a play, however, is contained in an essay not collected in that volume, the preface to an adaptation of Dostoyevsky's *The Possessed* in which Ionesco himself made his debut as an actor:

It is obviously difficult to write a play: it requires considerable physical effort; one has to get out of bed, which is unpleasant, one has to sit down, at the very moment when one had got used to the idea of standing; one has to take up a pen, which is a very heavy object; one has to look for paper, which is always difficult to find; and one has to sit down at a table, which often collapses under the weight of one's elbows. . . . On the other hand it is relatively easy to create a play without writing it down. It is easy to imagine it, to dream it up, lying on a couch halfway between waking and sleeping. One only has to let oneself go, without moving, without trying to exercise control over events. A character emerges, one hardly knows whence, and evokes others. The first one begins to speak, the first exchange is established, the basic note has been struck, the rest of the dialogue emerges automatically. One stays passive, one listens, one 'watches' what is happening on the inner screen. Alas, my memory has lapses and I am obliged to take notes so as not to forget. The phantoms of the imagination often begin to sulk at such moments, for they don't like being interrupted, and they refuse to cooperate for a time, they shut up, they disappear. But these are, nevertheless, only accidents, that can be made good. One watches for their reappearance, and after a time, they do come back: the imaginary space is peopled by presences, that space has its soil, its sky, its logic, its own laws which derive, quite naturally, from itself. The play is ready, it remains only, as they say, to write it. The difficulty lies in being capable of not intervening in the unfolding of the daydream: to achieve the paradoxical impression of remaining outside it.[1]

Even if we make full allowance for humorous exaggeration, this is a remarkable description of the creative process, at least as far as Ionesco is concerned. The author here appears as the almost totally passive recipient of 'inspiration', his subconscious does all the work for him; from its depth characters and situations spring fully armed like Pallas Athene from the head of Zeus. As a theory of artistic creation this account stands at the extreme wing of romanticism: here subjectivity reigns supreme; and not merely subjectivity but spontaneity—the total disregard of rational rules of structure and composition. If we accept this account of the process of playwriting in Ionesco's case as correct, as indeed we are compelled to do, would it not follow that it would be quite

[1] Ionesco, Preface to *Les Possédés*, adapted for the stage by Akakia Viala and Nicolas Bataille (Paris, Editions Emile-Paul) pp. 9–10.

meaningless for a critic to inquire into why the author *chose* one type of construction rather than another, in what manner he *solved* this or that formal problem? For such a choice of terminology would imply that rational processes were involved.

On the other hand, it is by no means pointless to examine the formal and structural characteristics of plays produced in this way (and a far larger number of important works than one might suspect are, at least in substantial part, produced in this manner). After all, however subconscious a process of construction may be, it still is a process of construction and must therefore obey the *rules* of construction. Some plays produced by 'inspiration' are valid statements, others may be meaningless outpourings, precisely because they do not fulfil the criteria of the internal logic of their own construction.

Ionesco himself acknowledges this fact and stresses the importance of formal excellence. In the course of a polemic pursuing an entirely different target (the condemnation of 'committed literature', his chief bugbear) Ionesco makes the distinction between the intention, the *purpose*, of a piece of writing and its intrinsic value:

I may . . . want to write a letter, or a petition, and it may happen that, in spite of myself, it becomes a poem; I may intend an illustrated moral lesson, and it may turn into a comedy or a tragedy: it can well be the case that the profound, unconscious intention of the author is not in accord with his superficial, apparent intention.

An architect may construct a temple, a palace, or a cottage. A musician may compose a symphony. The intention, the architect tells us, is to give the faithful a place where they can pray, the King a dwelling large enough to receive important guests; to give the peasant shelter for himself, his family and his pig. And the symphony, the musician will tell us, expresses my feelings; it is a language.

But the architect is caught out: the faithful are dead, the religion has lost its power, but the temple still stands; and generations to come admire the disused temple, the empty palace, the old picturesque cottage which now only contains furniture or memories. As regards the symphony: it is the manner in which it is composed that above all excites the connoisseurs; the petty feelings of the composer have died with him.

The building, the symphony now only reveal the laws of architecture or the principles of that architecture in movement which is music. The building, the symphony have been restored to themselves, they are the pure expression of their own essence. . . .

A play is also a structure of the imagination which must also hang together from end to end; its quality consists in not being capable of confusion with a novel in dialogue form, or a sermon, or a lesson, or a piece of rhetoric or an ode; for, if it could be taken for any of these, it would cease to be a play and fall into the category of lesson, rhetoric, sermon etc.[1]

This seems as radical an expression of a classicist belief in 'pure form', structure as an end in itself, as the description of the spontaneous genesis of a play was one of extreme romantic subjectivism. How are these at first sight diametrically opposed points of view to be reconciled? How can we bring the demand for construction, analogous to the best classical architecture, into harmony with the claim that a work of the imagination must arise autonomously and almost automatically from the author's subconscious? If a play, like the symphony in the musical analogy, is to endure as a reflection of the eternal laws of dramatic construction, will it not, if it is the spontaneous product of the author's passive introspection, above all reflect his petty and ephemeral feelings?

There can be no doubt that for Ionesco himself these contradictions have no meaning. Speaking as he is only of his own experience, he can merely report what happens to him when he writes a play. And the fact is that for Ionesco, in

[1] Ionesco, *Communication pour une réunion d'écrivains français et allemands.* (*Message for the Assembly of French and German Writers*, 1961) in *Notes et Contre-Notes* (Paris, Gallimard) pp. 125–26.

his state of 'inspiration', the spontaneous creations of his sub-conscious emerge as ready-made formal structures of truly classical purity.

More than that, their very spontaneity, the very freedom with which he allows characters and situations to take shape, constitutes the basis and source of their purity of form: plays like *The Chairs* or *The Lesson* are enjoyed by their audiences as above all formal patterns of great simplicity and perfection. His own experience has convinced Ionesco that the spon-taneous reproduction of the *structures* of the subconscious imagination is bound to emerge in the form of structurally satisfying patterns. He is 'trying to be an objective witness to [his] own subjectivity' and 'the construction is merely the emergence of the internal structure which thus offers itself for discovery'. 'Just as a symphony, just as a building, a play is simply a monument, a living world; it is a combination of situations, of words, of characters; it is a dynamic structure the internal elements of which balance each other in their opposition to each other.' In other words, if a play represents the process by which the author's inner, subconscious conflicts are brought into the open and sublimated by being external-ized, the very fact that this externalization has taken place implies that the conflicts have reached a state of equilibrium and will therefore, necessarily, already appear in the shape of a balanced pattern that unifies the contradictions and as such has significant form. Or, to reverse the argument, we find satisfying a work of art that springs from its creator's having succeeded in resolving his inner conflicts; aesthetically satisfying form is satisfying precisely because in being an externalization of a conflict that has been solved it creates the precondition for a similar resolution of conflicts in our own mind—and this is felt as the *harmony* that is generally recognized as the source of aesthetic pleasure.

This, incidentally, gives us the key by which the work of the *artist* in this field can be separated from the outpourings of the neurotic, the distinction between the work of a van Gogh and that of so many schizophrenic mental patients who paint. And this, precisely, places an immense weight on the element of form in all art of this high degree of subjectivity. The more objective, the more representational a work of art, a piece of dramatic writing, the more clearly we can judge it against its model: truth of characterization, authenticity of language, verisimilitude of situation—all these help in enabling the critic to judge a realistic play. In work of complete subjectivity (as in that of Ionesco, Beckett, Genet, and their followers) we are deprived of all these criteria of judgment. And here it is the element of form, of structural balance, of the successful shaping of internal conflicts that takes the place of the objective standards of evaluation in realistic drama. The *psychological truth* of the works in question is an equally important touchstone (that is what Ionesco calls the *objectivity* with which he represents his own subjective vision) but it is through the balance, the formal pattern of its structure that we can best approach an assessment of this element of truth. For, if the author has reproduced his vision as an *organic growth* rather than a mechanical construction, it will, if Ionesco's experience has general validity, also be perceived as a satisfying, because genuinely balanced, pattern of form.

Here we can again see the close relationship between lyrical poetry and this contemporary type of non-narrative, nonobjective drama. In poetry also there is a correlation between the genuineness of the poet's experience and the quality of his imagery, the formal excellence of his statement. The stronger the emotions behind a poem, the more triumphant appears the poet's achievement in having given them a shape, a harmony. And so also in the most subjective form of drama, the wilder, the more chaotic the obsessions that tormented the playwright, the more liberating will be the effect on the audience if he is seen to have given them valid, organic, balanced shape. The theme of Beckett's *Waiting for Godot* is man's terror in the face of the total meaninglessness, total shapelessness of the universe and all the events of which it is composed. All the more liberating is the impact of the author's achievement in having given this feeling of the absence of shape a shape of deep balance and symmetry; for this shows the audience that in facing up to reality we can rise above reality. Liberty is the recognition of necessity. And catharsis is another name for the liberation that springs from the recognition of reality.

It is important to stress that Ionesco's statements about the process of creation are *not* a theory or an aesthetic, but an objective description of his own experience. No general rules for techniques of playwriting can be deduced from that experience, although it does shed light on the creative processes of other writers and is an indispensable tool for the critic who is trying to understand and to interpret the work of Ionesco and other writers whose creative processes resemble his.

It must also be recognized that a writer whose creative processes are so completely spontaneous is in many ways a tragic figure: if he is honest with himself and refuses to cheapen his own creative currency by the production of counterfeit works which are the product of deliberate, rational planning rather than spontaneous creativeness, he is utterly at the mercy of forces outside his own control. He cannot, like the realistic dramatist, sit down at his desk, pick out a subject from a newspaper or his own experience and dramatize it honestly and conscientiously. He has to wait for the moment of intuition when strange characters will spontaneously appear before his eyes, begin to speak and to enact mysterious events that are dictated by subconscious forces. What if the writer waits passively—and nothing happens? Lyrical poets whose creative processes are similarly based may dry up for years or even decades: Rimbaud's inspiration ceased altogether at an early age. Rilke waited many years for the creative outburst that produced the *Duino Elegies*. But the world of the theatre has more insistent demands than that of lyrical poetry. . . . For a playwright the periods of sterility produced by a drying up of the sources of 'inspiration' must be particularly painful.

There are indications that in Ionesco's own case the spontaneity of his creative process has in fact resulted in considerable problems of this type. The very long period of time that elapsed between the completion of *Rhinoceros* (written 1958) and *Le Piéton de l'air* (the manuscript of which is dated 'summer 1962') itself is an indication that his inspiration had lain dormant for a considerable period of time. Moreover, Bérenger, the hero of the new play as well as of *Rhinoceros*, is now openly described as a *playwright* (thus disclosing the autobiographical nature of the character). In *Le Piéton de l'air* Bérenger is asked by a journalist: 'When shall we be seeing a new masterpiece of yours on the stages of the world?' To which question Bérenger at first refuses to give an answer. But he eventually yields and says:

> People do things although there is no reason for them to do them. Nevertheless feeble spirits give themselves apparent reasons for their activities. They pretend that they believe in these. One has to do *something*, they say. I am not one of those. There used to be at one time an inexplicable force inside me that made me do things or write, in spite of a basic nihilism. Now I cannot go on. . . . For years I found some consolation in saying that there was nothing to say. Now I am too deeply convinced that this is so and this conviction is no longer merely intellectual, or psychological: it has become a deep physiological conviction which has penetrated into my flesh, my blood, my bones. It paralyzes me. Literary activity is no longer a game, can no longer be a game for me. It should be a passage towards something else. But it is not.

The journalist asks Ionesco/Bérenger whether it is true what some say, that fear of his rivals has led him to give up writing for the theatre. Bérenger replies:

> I rather think it is the need for an inner renewal. Shall I be able to arrive at such a renewal? In principle, yes, because I am not in agreement with the way events are going. Only he who does not approve the course of events can be new or rare. The truth is in a kind of neurosis. . . . It is not in health; the neurosis

is the truth, the truth of tomorrow against the truth of today.

If a writer of this type lived the life of a recluse (as indeed Beckett and Genet do to some extent) his reliance on his inspiration, on his neurosis would present him with fewer difficulties; long periods of silence would be accepted by the outside world without demur. In Ionesco's case, however, his own personality creates its own dilemma. Not only is he a gregarious person, unlike writers like Beckett or Genet he is highly articulate as a critic and likes to theorize. The temptation to bridge periods in which his inspiration—or neurosis—lies dormant by writing critical, self-explanatory articles is particularly great for a writer with Ionesco's facility and quick intelligence (which lies on a totally different plane and springs from sources quite different from those of his *creative* talent). The danger then is that his critical and polemical side will spill over into his creative work, or will tend to usurp the place of inspiration as a motive for his writing. Already in *Rhinoceros* there was evidence of this danger: the neurosis, the obsession which clearly lay at the basis of that play, was felt to be overlaid by a polemical element.

The pressures on a successful playwright in our time are immense: he is besieged by demands for new work. If his creative process demands obsession, inspiration, neurosis, will he not be tempted to nurse his own neurosis, make an effort of will to produce the spontaneity he needs to write? If he does so, he can hardly hope to succeed, particularly as the act of creation and the fact of worldly success will tend to obliterate the psychological sources of the neurosis. The act of writing is in itself an act of sublimation and a cure for the obsessions and inner conflicts that it dissolves into harmony. And, as I pointed out above, obsessions, dreams, and inspirations are almost impossible to counterfeit by clever construction or synthetic invention.

If the writer concerned possesses an acute critical intelligence, the situation becomes doubly complicated: he will then be able to analyze and watch his own creative process and its ebb and flow without being able, in full awareness of this fact, to do anything to help it along.

A masterly short story by Ionesco seems to be dealing with precisely this situation: *La Vase* (*Slime*) tells the story of a man whose life suddenly becomes stale and lustreless:

> Until then, my awakening in the morning had always been a triumph: I was reborn with each dawn. Becoming conscious that I was alive, in a universe that renewed itself each day, a deep joy rose in my entrails, in all my being, overflowed and carried me aloft; I jumped out of bed, opened my window impatiently upon a world that was inviolate and agleam with light. . . . Suddenly, one morning, which was followed by another and others still, I was compelled, before setting out, to seek the indispensable euphoria, the power of rebirth, the warmth that I needed to communicate to creation, in a small glass of alcohol. And even then, it was no longer the same.

Gradually the hero of the story gives up the habit of leaving his room, becomes inactive, tired, leaden. He still dreams of his work (which consists of *writing*, writing letters . . .) but stays in bed nevertheless. Everything around him decays. Finally in a last effort he rouses himself and goes out into the countryside; but he loses his way, stumbles into a ditch by the roadside and, unable to get up again, remains lying in the slime of the wet soil. His limbs detach themselves from his body, one by one. Finally nothing remains but the head, half sunk in the slime, with only one eye visible looking up into the sky. . . . 'I shall start afresh, I was still telling myself as I closed my eyelid. The mist had dispersed and it was with the blue image of a sky washed clean that I departed.'

An artist whose creativeness is wholly spontaneous, who is the passive recipient of intuitions however sublime, is always at the mercy of such a fate: he may strain his inner eye to the very last moment but the internal screen on which used to appear the characters that his intuition had projected may remain a total blank—a cyclorama that is a background to nothingness. . . .

Far from being a showman, a seeker of the limelight, a clown full of gimmicks, as he is so often represented in the popular press, which is characteristically apt to misunderstand and misinterpret the vagaries of a creative personality both difficult and complex, Ionesco thus appears as an artist of uncompromising purity who fully recognizes the precariousness of a creative personality dependent on the workings of forces outside his own control, and he boldly confronts this dilemma of the creative process.

'Truth' and Documentation
A conversation with Rolf Hochhuth

It is not often that a play, which most people, after all, regard as no more than a piece of ephemeral entertainment, can rock a great establishment. But Rolf Hochhuth, a German playwright born in 1931 and thus still under forty, has achieved this rare feat not once but twice.

In 1963 he shook the Vatican to its foundations with the presentation of *The Deputy*, in which he suggested that Pope Pius XII had put expediency before principle in refraining from intervening with Hitler on behalf of the German and European Jews during World War II. Four years later with *Soldiers*, in which he represents Winston Churchill as instigating the death in 1943 of General Sikorski, head of the Polish government-in-exile, he provoked heart-searching and controversy in establishment Britain.

Soldiers had its première in West Berlin in 1967, after the National Theatre refused to put it on in England. The allegation against Churchill made many people in Britain very angry indeed, but few as angry as Lord Chandos, chairman of the board of the National Theatre, who was a member of Churchill's wartime cabinet and hence, if Hochhuth's thesis is correct, co-responsible in this murder.

I spent an afternoon and evening with Hochhuth at his home, a modest apartment in a suburb of Basel, shortly after his return from the Berlin première. Hochhuth is a slight, dark young man with a lively flow of conversation, clearly someone obsessed with moral questions and overflowing with ideas. He speaks German with a mixture of Hessian and Thuringian accents. His features are handsome, but the left side of his face is less animated—he suffers from the after-effects of paralysis of the facial muscles. Although he has made a fortune from *The Deputy*, his style of life is utterly simple: within Basel he uses a bicycle rather than a car; his apartment occupies one floor of a typical Swiss suburban three-family house. But there are some fine original paintings on the walls, and innumerable books.

While his wife was putting his two young sons to bed, Hochhuth confessed to me that he had been by no means happy with the Berlin performance, which had been in general badly received by the hundred and fifty critics and forty-four radio and television reporters, and at which part of the audience had booed the author.

'But I don't want to blame anyone for this except myself. The play had to be cut down to about half the length of the printed text. And that this was necessary was my fault. For the most part I made the cuts together with my English translator, David Macdonald; but English is a faster language than German and so when the play was being done in German it turned out that it was still much too long. And when further cuts were made, unfortunate things happened. For example, in the second act, where Churchill directs the war from his bed, much of the serious political discussion was cut, while the witty remarks and jokes were left in—and so the seriousness, the tragedy of the situation, was lost and the scene acquired a false and unfortunate hilarity.'

Soldiers is subtitled 'Obituary for Geneva'. Originally the play's main theme was to be the policy of bombing civilian populations in World War II. Hochhuth described its genesis:

'The origin of it was an article by David Irving [the British author of a book on the Allied raid that destroyed Dresden] about Bishop Bell of Chichester [the English cleric who opposed the policy of mass raids on German towns in the House of Lords]. At that time I regarded Bell as a kind of Protestant counterpart to the Jesuit Riccardo [hero of *The Deputy*].

'But apart from that, the problem of the war in the air had long preoccupied me. I personally was not much affected by bombing—I lived in Eschwege, a small town in Hesse, and I was twelve years old when Kassel, the nearest large city, was bombed in 1943. I got an idea then, because my brother, who was fifteen, had to go with his youth group in the middle of the night to remove the corpses; I also had a friend who collapsed during this. All this gave me an idea of the air war.

'But above all, after the war, I realized that the war in the air was never dealt with in any of the war-crime trials. In not one of the Nuremberg trials was there an air force marshal among the defendants. Field Marshal Kesselring was not detained a single hour for the burning of Rotterdam. The Geneva Conventions operate today in such a way as not to protect Rotterdam, but to protect the man who destroyed Rotterdam. There is no international convention against the bombing of military targets, and that means that any town that some demented sergeant has decided to defend with one or two of his men can be bombed to smithereens quite legally.

'Today, I believe things like Auschwitz, or genocide by gassing, have been so totally discredited morally that nobody would ever dare to do anything of the sort ever again. Even Eichmann or Hoess did not defend *what* they had done, they only argued about their personal part in it. But the bombing of civilians is in no way outlawed, or discredited, today. We see that in Vietnam (even though I don't think there is area bombing there on the same lines as in World War II).

'That was the starting point for me in this case. Perhaps it might have been better if I had concentrated on that theme. But I soon noticed that it would have been a historical injustice to pin the bombing war on Churchill or the Allies. One can understand aerial warfare in World War II only if one asks: Why did they have to do this? And then one realizes: While the Russians were tying down a hundred and ninety German divisions, the British were engaging fifteen in the western desert. In 1942 and 1943, the British were not yet ready to open the second front that Stalin demanded. And so to show that they were doing something they had to go in for area bombing.

'While reading all this up I came across the correspondence between Churchill and Stalin, and the whole tragedy of Poland. And by pure chance I stumbled on a witness who told me about the circumstances of General Sikorski's death. I soon realized that it is very difficult for a playwright to dramatize the war in the air; it's too abstract, like submarine warfare. On the stage only human beings are effective; a problem that can't be personalized remains an intellectual puzzle. But the Polish tragedy *could* be personalized in the character of Sikorski, a very picturesque and knightly figure, the last cavalry general in history. That is how the death of Sikorski became one of the central points of my play.'

Hochhuth was well aware of the great difficulty of putting a war leader like Churchill and members of his entourage on stage while their memory was still fresh in the minds of people who had seen them in action, in newsreel films, and on television. So he devised a framework that would make it more plausible. The prologue and epilogue of *Soldiers* is set in Coventry in 1964, the centenary year of the original Geneva Convention which Hochhuth wants to reform by making air war against civilian populations illegal. A World War II bomber pilot named Dorland (after the author of the medieval morality play *Everyman*) has written and is staging the play in the ruins of Coventry Cathedral. Dorland, who had to bail out over Dresden, was so deeply shaken by the sufferings he saw there that he has become the champion of reform of the Geneva Conventions. So the tragedy about Churchill thus becomes a play within a play, and, Hochhuth believes, more believable to the audience since the actors concerned are portraying *actors* engaged in a kind of charity performance.

This play within a play is divided into three acts. Act I takes place on the battleship H.M.S. *Duke of York*. Churchill is travelling to Scapa Flow. With his advisers Lord Cherwell and Field Marshal Sir Alan Brooke he discusses the policy of mass bombing of civilians and the specific planned series of raids against Hamburg, referred to by the code name

'Gomorrah.' Brooke, the soldier, is against terror bombing; Cherwell, the scientist, is for it. Churchill—the words, in verse, are not his own but the style is based on his writings—sides with Cherwell:

> I should have expected, Chief of Staff, you would be with us.
> As you are not, I can justify Gomorrah politically:
> Make a million Huns homeless—that's a victory.
> It is not if you just destroy ten barrels of gasoline!

The decision to launch Operation Gomorrah is followed by a heated discussion between Churchill and General Sikorski about the future of Poland in which it becomes clear that Sikorski's attitude might wreck the alliance with Stalin. In Act II Churchill is conducting the war from his bed and is shown tacitly consenting to the plot of the airplane accident that leads to General Sikorski's death. In Act III, while discussing the ethics of terror bombing with Bishop Bell of Chichester, Churchill receives the news of Sikorski's death. The bishop remarks that Sikorski was Churchill's friend. Churchill replies:

> Men may be linked in friendship.
> Nations are linked only by interests.

The main theme of this play within a play is the tragedy of a war leader who must balance private against public morality. Churchill knows that he is fighting not only for his own country but for the future of civilization itself. He fears that the Russians might conclude a separate peace with the Nazis if they feel that the Western Allies are not pulling their weight or are plotting against them. So, unable to launch a second front, Churchill allows Lord Cherwell, whom Hochhuth portrays as something like his evil genius, to persuade him of the usefulness of mass bombing raids on civilians.

But, beyond that, Churchill sees his country and civilization threatened by the conflict between the Polish government-in-exile and the Russians. As Hochhuth sees it, the British had gone to war to defend the Poles against German aggression, but by 1943 it had become clear that if the Allies won the war the real danger to the Poles would come from the Russians, who were determined to get back the large territories in eastern Poland they had lost to the newly formed Polish state after World War I. The Poles, led by their highly respected leader, General Sikorski, were only too well aware of that danger. The British were anxious not to disturb relations between the Soviet government and the Polish government-in-exile, and were advising the Poles to consent even to losses of territory to the Russians.

Then, in the spring of 1943, a new issue arose between the Poles and the Russians. The Germans proclaimed to the world that they had uncovered a mass grave, near Katyn in western Russia, containing the bodies of some four thousand Polish officers. The German propaganda machine maintained that the officers concerned, prisoners of war of the Russians after Soviet troops had occupied eastern Poland in 1939, had been murdered in 1941, when the Germans were advancing into Russia and might have liberated them. The Russians replied that in fact these officers must have been murdered by the advancing Germans. Sikorski insisted that the Red Cross be called in to conduct an impartial investigation. The Russians replied by breaking off relations with the Polish government-in-exile and by forming their own Communist-led Polish National Committee. According to Hochhuth, Churchill was so anxious to prevent this disastrous development that he went so far as to engineer Sikorski's death.

Hochhuth insists that he *knows* this to be so. His witness has shown him proof, which is now locked in the vaults of a Swiss bank. But he adds: 'Until the day when I heard about this I had no idea about the whole question. But once I knew, I started looking for other evidence and I discovered such a mass of circumstantial evidence that it all became most convincing. This made me approach the one Englishman whom we Germans regard as the most prominent researcher in these matters of recent history, David Irving. I asked him to look into the matter.' But Irving's book, *Accident*, I pointed out, leaves the verdict open. Hochhuth answered that the British publishers did not include a final chapter, and that the full version of the book, which will be published outside Britain, will come down on the side of sabotage.

Hochhuth has written extensively about the circumstantial evidence involved, most of which he has put into the play itself—one of the reasons why it has become far too long to be performed without enormous cuts. I asked him whether he really felt that the material of the play must be *true*. After all, there are historical plays, regarded as classics, in which many of the incidents portrayed are known to be pure invention.

But Hochhuth will have none of that: 'I do not think that the author of historical plays is entitled to invent vital incidents. In fact, I think that in doing so he would ruin himself artistically. For example, in *The Maid of Orleans* Schiller made Joan die a heroic death on the battlefield instead of showing her real end at the stake. Shaw stuck to the facts, and I find his ending infinitely more moving. Indeed, there are many dramatists today who arbitrarily invent any incident that suits them just because they think it will be more amusing. I cannot understand this. I believe the opposite of art is not nature but arbitrariness. One should remember two sentences of Thomas Mann's. One of them says: "Do not just invent something, but make something out of reality." And the second one maintains: "All subject matter is boring if no ideas shine through it."'

Did this mean, I asked Hochhuth, that he believes in the Theatre of Fact, the Theatre of Documentation? He answered, 'No. I became the champion of "documentary theatre" quite unintentionally. I only noticed what had happened when Piscator [who directed the first production of *The Deputy*] wrote a programme note in which he used the term "documentary theatre". I am very unhappy about that catch phrase, for I believe it means very little. Pure documentation can never be more than a bunch of documents. Something must always be *added* to make a play.

'Those three acts in *Soldiers* which deal with Churchill, for example, are sheer invention as regards the places where the scenes are laid. I know that Sikorski did not travel to Scapa Flow on a battleship with Churchill in the spring of 1943. He once made a sea voyage with him, but that was much earlier. And the meeting between Churchill and Bishop Bell in the garden of Chequers is also invented, at least as far as that particular date is concerned. Any dramatist who ever wrote historical plays had to study the documents. Hence this catch phrase "documentary theatre" is meaningless.

'I must draw your attention to that quotation from Thomas Mann again: "All subject matter is boring if no ideas shine through it." I believe if one wants to write a historical play one has to find—I know it sounds pompous—some metaphysical relevance to it. If you read the third act of my play you will notice that there is something like a religious viewpoint in it, in the widest possible sense. I myself have never got beyond the Old Testament, the book of Ecclesiastes—man being as the grass, to wither under the scythe . . . . This is what interests me, why there should be wars, why people should rush to their perdition. I am not interested in documents so much; the documents are merely the raw material, the bricks with which one builds a play. One collects the bricks, but merely as a means to an end, in order to erect a structure.'

Yet, I asked, with a play like *Soldiers*, had he not a real aim in view, a practical objective: a reform of the international law about bombing? Did he not, like Schiller, regard the theatre as a moral forum?

'Yes,' Hochhuth replied, 'one must strive to achieve a real improvement in the world. But I must confess that I am deeply pessimistic about the feasibility of such improvements. But that does not mean one should not try.'

What then was his own ideological position?

'I am a humanist. In other words, I still maintain a belief in the autonomy of the individual and that the individual can make some impact on the world. I repeat: my belief in the power of the individual is small. But that does not mean that

one should not—without, I hope, in any way being a hypo-
crite—write plays about people who prove the opposite. I
don't agree with those dramatists like Dürrenmatt who pro-
claim the end of tragedy on the ground that the day of the
individual is past forever, that nobody can do anything, nobody is responsible any more. These people forget one thing:
the number of those individuals who *did* achieve something
has always been very, very small, throughout history.'

This then is the motivation behind the two plays that have
stirred up such intense excitement, so much bitter controversy. Hochhuth's aim is not primarily political. He is perhaps the most traditional, the most tradition-conscious, of
all modern dramatists, far less of a revolutionary than
Brecht, far less daring than Ionesco or Beckett. His models
are Schiller and Shaw. His aim is to explore the human
condition on the basis of verifiable human reality and to
penetrate to the tragic core of man's plight on earth.

The paradox of the situation is that Hochhuth himself
reveres Churchill as the saviour of civilization, that he introduced the episode of the 'murder' of Sikorski in order to
dramatize Churchill as a truly tragic figure. In a true tragedy,
according to Hegel, both parties to the conflict must be *right*.
Churchill was right in putting the interests of humanity
above those of a quixotic nation, or its quixotic leader, says
Hochhuth. But the Poles, led by Sikorski, were equally right
in insisting on justice for themselves. The war demanded area
bombing, so Churchill may have been right in sanctioning it;
but the women and children who were burned to death in
Hamburg had equally a right to live.

In trying to write his two tragedies of twentieth-century
man, Hochhuth has stirred up a series of gigantic wasps'
nests. In each case the wild rumours and debates that preceded the performances of his plays provided them with
publicity that must have been the envy of all public relations
men. In fact, this kind of controversy made it irrelevant—
from the commercial point of view—whether the plays were

good or bad. By the time they opened they were bound to run on sheer news value. I asked Hochuth if there had been any design in this on his part. He said, 'The surprise about this all has always been on my side. Both these themes—the Polish tragedy and the question of why the highest of all Christians never spoke out against Auschwitz—both of these themes were so obvious that it can only have been pure chance that I was the first to hit upon them.'

I have no doubt that Rolf Hochhuth's surprise is completely genuine. He is totally artless, an idealist and a scholarly, rather unworldly young man. He is too young to have been fully involved in World War II, yet having grown up in postwar Germany, he is consumed by deep moral indignation not only about the crimes committed by Hitler (he stresses that it is impossible to write a tragedy about Hitler because he was a psychopath, a medical case rather than a tragic hero) but equally about all the suffering caused by war on all sides.

He repudiated the suggestion one can hear in Britain and elsewhere that both *The Deputy* and *Soldiers* somehow aim at absolving the Germans from the guilt of their war crimes by shifting the blame on to the Catholic Church or Churchill. 'I was the first playwright,' he says, 'who wrote a scene with Adolf Eichmann in it, at a time when the Israelis had not even captured Eichmann. I was the first playwright to put Auschwitz on a stage. That should show that I was not trying to minimize German guilt. And secondly, in the whole of West Germany *The Deputy* has had half as many performances as in Paris alone, fewer than in New York. The play has not been performed in Germany in the last few years, but it is still being performed in Warsaw, in Prague, in Yugoslavia. That does not seem to me to indicate that the Germans regard the play as an apologia for themselves.'

As to *Soldiers*, the allegation that Churchill plotted the murder of a man who was his ally and friend is an exceedingly grave one. Having read Hochhuth's play and his articles about the evidence he has amassed, I personally remain un-convinced that he has proved his case. On the other hand, the tragic conflict he wanted to dramatize is a real one. There can hardly have been a major statesman who did not have to make decisions of this kind. Take John F. Kennedy and the Bay of Pigs. Or Churchill's and Roosevelt's decision to with-draw Allied support from General Mihajlovich and to trans-fer it to Mihajlovich's rival, Tito. All concerned knew that this decision meant the eventual execution of Mihajlovich, but here too the Allied leaders had to sacrifice an ally in the interests of winning the war.

Hochhuth himself is certain that an error in so essential a historical detail as the facts about the accident to Sikorski's aircraft would constitute not only a failure in historical re-search on his part but an artistic failure as well. I am not so sure. Since the documents that he maintains would prove or disprove his case will be locked away for another fifty years, it might follow that aesthetic and critical judgment on *Soldiers* would have to be suspended till then. But that is clearly absurd. The question is not whether the facts are as they are depicted in the play but whether, in the play, they are wholly *convincingly* depicted. Had Hochhuth concen-trated his tragic conflict on an event that is known to all— for example, the Mihajlovich tragedy—it would have been far easier for him to achieve this basic requirement. As it is, *Soldiers* is somewhat encumbered by the author's excessive need to provide documentation, and by the fact that the documentation can never be wholly conclusive.

Nevertheless, Hochhuth's achievement is already very con-siderable. He has written only two plays up to now, but he has created a larger immediate and visible impact than any other contemporary dramatist. This in itself must be regarded as a boon for the theatre as an institution and as an art form. For it proves that, even in the age of mass media (or especially in an age of mass media), the theatre still is a forum for the airing of moral problems, for intense political and social debate. He has also, in an age of experimentation and a multitude of fascinating but recondite eccentricities in the theatre, drawn attention to the fact that there is still a lot of life in the traditional mainstay of the stage: large-scale, historical tragedies in verse, basically of exactly the same type as Shakespeare, Strindberg, or Shaw. It would have been difficult, before Hochhuth came along, to believe that plays of such venerable lineage could start riots in the streets outside playhouses. To have shown that it is still possible is a very considerable, and very valuable, contribution. An institution that can arouse such indignation cannot be wholly dead.

There remains the question: How good a playwright is Hochuth? It is not easy to answer. Read in their (very long) entirety, these plays are most impressive. But both are far too long for the theatre and, cut down to size, are bound to become fragments. Each producer keeps different bits in, so each production becomes, in effect, a different play. This may have some advantages. It also has grave disadvantages.

But there can be no doubt that Hochhuth can create character, that he can even perform the very difficult feat of making 'great men' like Pius XII or Churchill wholly believable on the stage. His idealism, his savage indignation about the evils of his time, shine through Hochhuth's dialogues and give them real fire and poetic force. He is anything but a *documentary* playwright. He is a very impressive, traditional historical dramatist.

Up to this moment, that is. I asked him whether he was planning another historical blockbuster. 'No,' he replied. 'I am through with recent history. I am writing a social comedy. About the problem of twentieth-century slums.'

He opened a large cupboard to show me some of the documentation. The cupboard was crammed full of large envelopes, each of them bulging with press cuttings and other documents—material for dozens of highly explosive plays.

Eastern Absurdists:
Slawomir Mrozek—Poland

Strindberg, Proust, Kafka, Joyce—these are among the
literary models of the Absurdists. What have they in
common? Above all, the sense of the vanishing of firm
standards, the evanescence of human life, its extreme vulnerability, and, translated from the general to the individual
sphere, the precariousness of human personality, the elusive-
ness of reality itself. For Strindberg, who knew that he was
subject to periods of madness, the harshness of real life
merged into delusions of persecution, reality into dream;
Proust chronicled the relativity of human vision in time: the
remembrance of time past only emphasized for him the
unbridgeable gap between the pristine vision of the child
and the jaundiced eye of the grown man; Joyce progressed
from a meticulous chronicler of external reality to the mysterious half-light of the dreamer's shadow-world of coalescing
streams of language and symbol. And Kafka converted his
sense of guilt and helplessness in the face of reality into tersely
accurate descriptions of his own nightmarish struggles for
human contact and acceptance.

The drama of the Absurd which arose in Western Europe
after the end of World War II built on those foundations:
the playwrights in question were concerned, above all, in
dramatizing their sense of bewilderment at the collapse of
values, the debasement of language, the isolation of Western
man in a society which, with the collapse of religious as well
as political ideologies, went on working and producing an
abundance of goods, but without any sense of purpose or
idealism. The two bedraggled figures of Vladimir and
Estragon in Beckett's *Waiting for Godot* perfectly express

this image; they are alive, they are free to come or go, yet they have no sense of purpose. They vaguely feel that they may have an appointment with someone called Godot, but they are by no means convinced of it; so they just stand around and wait trying to pass the time of day. Their anxiety, the horror of their situation, is produced precisely by the absence of any directing force. They suffer, so to say, from a surfeit of freedom. Pozzo and Lucky, the second pair of characters in Beckett's play, try to escape from the same predicament by wild and senseless activity; their efforts are as vain—or even more so—as those of their more passive and contemplative brethren. The same is true of the characters in Ionesco's *The Bald Prima Donna* or *The Chairs*, or in Adamov's *La Parodie*. Whether active or passive, busy or idle, their lives are all equally futile and senseless. It is an existence in a moral vacuum in which the only regulating force is provided by habit—the 'great deadener' in Beckett's phrase—the empty routine which has taken the place of a sense of purpose.

In Eastern Europe, when at last—and in some countries briefly—the work of these writers could be shown, its impact was electrifying, but for quite different reasons from those which had ensured its success in the West. For a long time the public of the Eastern countries had been nourished on an unvarying diet of bland optimism; the doctrine of 'social realism' rigidly enforced by the Stalinists prevented any realistic description of things as they were; life under 'socialism' had to be depicted in the rosiest terms, the machinations of the West in the most hideous colours, yet always letting it be seen that the rule of the evil exploiters would not last long and was surely doomed. A play like *Waiting for Godot*, when it was performed in Poland came, for its very pessimism, as a breath of fresh air. For the futility it expressed was the same existential anguish that the Polish audience actually felt, but which it had never been allowed to show. No wonder that Beckett and Ionesco had a great political impact, especially in Poland and Czechoslovakia. No wonder that writers in these countries were tempted to try their hand in a similar vein.

Yet, the influence of the Absurdists in Eastern Europe produced a very different kind of drama. The absurdist playwrights in the West used the idiom of dream and symbol simply because they felt it was needed to express their emotions, their inner worlds. The East Europeans, who had immediately read political allegories into *Waiting for Godot* and *The Chairs* (Godot, who never comes although he always promises to come, struck the Poles as a symbol of the promised freedom which never came under Communism; the nonsense message at the end of *The Chairs* was received as an allegory of all the nonsensical speeches and proclamations of totalitarian progaganda), hastened to use the dreamlike, allegorical forms as a kind of 'Aesopian language' (to employ George Lukács's term), an idiom which, under the guise of grotesque nonsense, could be made to say, without undue danger, what could not openly be discussed. Slawomir Mrozek's first play *The Police* (1958), for example, takes place in a police state, where the state security organs have become so successful that only one single opponent of the regime remains, and even he, when the play opens, has decided to go over to the side of the dictator. Hence the police chief is terrified, for with the disappearance of political crime, the secret police itself seems doomed, his own job at an end. So the police are forced to organize political crime to keep themselves in business. Mrozek has carefully indicated that the play is to be acted in nineteenth-century costume, reminiscent of the Habsburg Empire. And he adds a little preface which insists that

> This play contains nothing beyond that which it contains; hence, no hints of anything and no metaphors. Between the lines there is nothing; to try and read between them, therefore, would be love's labour lost. The naked text is unequivocal; sentences and scenes have their logical sense—thus nothing has to be put into them. The play demands sufficient attention from the spectator anyway; if anything had to be added to that, it would, of necessity, be most tiring.

This deadpan air of innocence about the quite obvious political implications of a play like this in a society like Poland in 1958 not only adds to the fun of the audience, it genuinely puts the authorities into a dilemma: either to expose themselves to ridicule by admitting that they feel the satire is being aimed at them, or to sit idly by while the spectators laugh about a totalitarian government. The breakthrough of the absurdist style thus furnished playwrights in the East European countries—at least in periods of relative thaw—an idiom in which the real issues of the time could be ventilated and intelligently discussed in front of considerable numbers of people. Moreover, the very nature of the theatre helped it to become an area of relatively free speech; for the theatre, even in totalitarian countries, has its democratic aspect. Here people *can* still vote with their feet; they can stay away from plays which bore them; they can crowd into plays which strike them as relevant. And the effect of empty houses, when openly propagandist, pro-government work is being performed, is a most unfortunate one upon outside visitors, a most depressing one upon the members of any regime. This makes even totalitarian governments somewhat indulgent towards the theatre. They would rather have their theatres full than empty, so they will tolerate many a play which is not too openly hostile and brings in the crowds. Plays written in Aesopian language are at least not *openly* hostile. They may even serve as a relatively harmless outlet for the pent-up emotions which they convert into amusement and laughter, and even provide an illusion of relative freedom. In other words: even oppositional plays, so long as they are couched in allegorical terms, can serve their purpose as safety valves.

Such considerations were the basis for the rise of the East European absurdist playwright: Mrozek, Rózewicz, Broszkiewicz, Grochowiak, Herbert in Poland; Havel, Smoček, Klima, Uhde, Karvas in Czechoslovakia; Örkény in Hungary.

Of these Slawomir Mrozek is undoubtedly the most considerable in his achievement to date. Born in June 1930 he started life as a journalist and cartoonist. In recent years, after having achieved international fame, he has been living outside Poland (in Italy and now in France) although he did not in fact sever his connection with his native country. But his courageous condemnation of the Soviet invasion of Czechoslovakia in the summer of 1968 must inevitably mean that he has now become a political exile. His plays are now banned in Poland, and in other East European countries productions of *Tango* scheduled for the coming season are quietly being dropped or postponed.

The loss, surely, is Poland's. For without doubt Mrozek is one of the most considerable European dramatists of his generation, one of the most noteworthy in the long line of great Polish dramatists, which stretches back into the eighteenth century. The sources of Mrozek's style lie not only in the European absurdist tradition, but also in a very peculiarly Polish preoccupation with the grotesque in the theatre. Stanislaw Ignacy Witkiewicz (1885–1939), called Witkacy, who wrote more than thirty plays, was one of the first and foremost of European surrealists in painting as well as drama. And Witold Gombrowicz (1904–1969) must be regarded as one of the first to use the absurdist style in drama, well before the outbreak of World War II.

Witkacy's plays are more openly nonsensical, more extravagantly surrealist, Gombrowicz's more dreamlike than Mrozek's. Compared to these two forerunners Mrozek is a realist and a logician. He may be a caricaturist, but the likeness he draws is instantly recognizable and gives deep insight into the subject's real appearance, his real nature. The situations Mrozek puts before us may be fantastically crazy and grotesque; but, then, reality in Eastern Europe under the present regime is fantastically grotesque. If the West European absurdists introduced grotesque elements to point up the ordinariness of routine life in non-Communist Europe, Mrozek deals with a system of hypocrisy and doubletalk which is so weird that a realistic description of its outline will, by itself, appear as an absurd exaggeration. The case of

Mrozek's first play *The Police* fully illustrates this point. What could be more grotesquely absurdist than the notion of the police actually instigating political crime? Yet the history of the last fifty years in the Soviet Union provides an abundance of examples of just that very thing happening over and over again: Yagoda, Yezhov, and Beriya, three of Stalin's supreme police chiefs, were later accused of the organization of the most hideous political crimes.

Likewise, in the short play *Out at Sea* we find three castaways on a raft: the question arises, which one of them is to die to provide food for the two others, and thus perhaps a chance of ultimate rescue. One of these castaways is big and fat, one thin and small, and one of medium size. They try to determine the victim by a variety of processes: election, merit, the relative pleasure derived from their past lives. But, try as they may, the weakest of the three always emerges as the potential victim. ('How many divisions does the Pope command?' was Stalin's argument in a debate about the relative merits of Communism and Catholicism.) In the end the thin castaway accepts his fate, when it is pointed out to him that the individual's sacrifice is the noblest, most admirable, most meritorious, most glorious action that anyone can hope to achieve in life. The idea of such selfless sacrifice makes the little man happy. As he is about to be killed a tin of pork and beans is found at the bottom of the castaway's luggage. The castaway of middle stature is all for abandoning the thin one's execution. But the fat one is adamant: 'I don't want baked beans. And anyway . . . can't you see? He's happy as he is!' Again the diagnosis is utterly realistic. Again and again the little, suffering people in the Soviet sphere are assured that their suffering ennobles them, that they are far above such sordid considerations as thoughts of material affluence.

Where reality is based on a paradox, the absurdist playwright is the true realist, while it is the playwright of 'social realism' who deals in grotesque dreams. Because Mrozek's absurdist fables are essentially realistic, and because reality for a Pole of his generation—he was nine years old when the war started, fifteen when it ended, twenty-three when Stalin died—was shot through with violence, there is a streak of violence, even savagery, in his work, both as a dramatist and as a writer of short stories. The giant hand that strips two gentlemen, only too eager to co-operate with their despoiler, and finally crowns them with dunce-hats (in the play *Striptease*); the shooting of poor Peter Ohey, in whose bathroom his little son believes he has seen a tiger, by the hunting party arranged for the benefit of a visiting maharajah who insisted on going on a tiger hunt and had to be humoured by the local Foreign Ministry (in the play *The Martyrdom of Peter Ohey*); the sinister aristocrat who hunts snowmen by driving them too near fires in the story *The Eagle's Nest*; the brawl at a village wedding which is conducted with atomic bombs in the story *Wedding in the Atomic Village*; all these are powerful images of contemporary violence. Violence is closely related to power, the second of the twin poles around which Mrozek's images revolve. There can scarcely be a truer, or more terrifying metaphor of power than that in the short story *The Fate of Count N.* which tells of a powerful ruler who could only achieve an orgasm if, at the crucial moment, a regiment of soldiers could be heard marching by in the courtyard, a symphony orchestra played full blast, and a polar bear climbed atop the bedroom cupboard; hence in that ruler's country a large army was being maintained, a great symphony orchestra was lavishly subsidized and gave work to many artists, and a series of hunting expeditions to the Arctic were being organized. When a revolution finally overthrows the powerful Count N. and he is constrained to live in poverty, he can still be observed at times, watching the guards' regiment pass by on the parade ground, listening to orchestras at concerts, and standing, forlorn, outside the polar bear's cage in the zoo. Thus not only the grandiose folly of the powerful, who can indulge their fantasies to the full, is brilliantly captured in that brief tale (the relationship between sex and power there reminds one of Genet's treatment of the same theme in *The Balcony*) but also the way in which the modest habits of the poor reflect—in a reduced, attenuated form—the erotic power-fantasies of the rich and mighty. In another short story, *Siesta*, Mrozek takes us with equal incisiveness into another of the deeper regions of power: its deviousness. In a building lovingly described, and quite obviously the headquarters of a Communist party, an elderly aristocrat and a Catholic priest confront each other. They ask each other how it has come about that they, noble-man and priest, should be working for a Communist party, their natural enemy one might have thought. The nobleman works as a dancing-master and teacher of good manners, and that, as he can get no other employment, is fair enough. But the priest? Well, he confesses, he was approached to act as chaplain to the party. There are so many high functionaries of the party who still go to church and thus cause a public scandal. The party therefore decided to have its private chapel. And for that they needed a priest. 'I accepted because I was relying on my sermons. There was a missionary element in my decision.' So the priest went into the party's service, because he saw an opportunity to propagate his faith in the citadel of atheism. But, as an employee of the party, the priest also had to attend the compulsory training sessions in Marxism. As a result *he* was converted to Marxism. This, he tells the aristocrat, presented him with a moral dilemma: 'I went to see the secretary and explained to him openly that, as a result of my evolution towards Marxism, I could no longer perform the functions of Chaplain to the Committee.' But the secretary of the party refused to accept the priest's resignation. Precisely because he no longer believed in his religion, the priest had to stay in his post: 'You must realize,' the secretary explained, 'that not only is it necessary for you to stay at your post, but you have to work at it with even greater conviction to an even greater effect. You mustn't lose any of your high professional qualifications. Otherwise our comrades, having noticed a falling off in your form, may become dissatisfied and start going to church elsewhere, out-side the range of our direct influence. Just think of this responsibility and you'll understand how highly I value your devotion, conscientiousness, and fighting spirit. I appeal to your *conscience*.' Thus to lie and to deceive can—from the point of view of those in power—become a matter of deep moral import, a matter of conscience.

The relationships between violence, eroticism, power and moral equivocation also form the subject matter of Mrozek's most ambitious, and most successful play hitherto, *Tango*.

Ostensibly a farce about a crazy family—mad, artistic father and mother, dotty grandma, ex-cavalry officer great-uncle in shorts, loutish butler who sleeps with the mother, amoral girl cousin, intelligent, bewildered son—*Tango*, on deeper and different levels, is also a kind of modern *Hamlet* (the son suffering under the mother's amorality, trying to re-establish the moral order in the family, to put the times back into joint), as well as a brilliant examination of the dialectics of revolution. It is this last aspect that makes the play, which of course when first performed in Poland in 1965 was brim-ful with local and topical allusions, equally topical and relevant in the Western world, where talk of revolution is very much in the air—at least in student circles.

The usual order of things in the conflict of generations is reversed in *Tango*: it is the father and the mother who are revolutionaries, the son who longs for a conservative order. But, of course, this is only logical: the generation of the sons always rebels against the fathers; if the fathers have reached a stage of complete victory for all rebellion, then the only rebellion still possible is the rebellion against rebellion, i.e. the fight for the re-establishment of the order of things as it existed before the rebellion destroyed it.

What was the nature of the rebellion which Stomil and Eleonora, Arthur's father and mother, had fought for? It was, in the first place, a revolt against puritanism and repressive morals, a revolt against traditional standards also in the arts. In those days before the revolt succeeded, 'it was an act of courage just to dance the tango,' for so harmless a dance as the tango was considered too sensual, too obscene. 'You made love to me,' Eleonora recalls to her husband, 'in front of my mother and father, in the front row of the stalls during the première of *Tannhäuser* . . . It was a gesture of protest.' And Stomil fondly recalls 'the student demonstrations, way back in nineteen—whenever it was—yes, the really heroic ones refused to give up their seats to elderly passengers. We fought for those rights . . .'

The relationship between cultural and moral protest and political revolution is brilliantly brought out by Mrozek. The destruction of the political order, he argues, is directly linked with the erosion of artistic values and established behaviour patterns. A reactionary view, this, from the point of view of those who, like us in the West, are still fighting for the right to dance the tango! But remember that this view is voiced by a writer who was then living and working in a society which had passed through the phase of permissiveness and had landed in a period of much greater repression, political, artistic *and* moral. *How* this could have happened, *why* it had to happen, is precisely the question which Mrozek is about to pose. Young Arthur is fed up with the disorder, the lack of sense of occasion, the casualness of the permissive way of life. What sense of achievement can it give him to conquer the heart of his beloved cousin Ala, if she tells him that she is quite prepared to sleep with him, as with anyone else, at the drop of a hat. He despises his father's witless, and purely destructive, artistic experiments, and above all, suffers under his mother's promiscuous relationships with Eddie, the *lumpenproletarisch* butler, who typifies all the vulgarity and coarseness of humanity outside the circle of civilized values. Being young, Arthur *must* rebel; so he rebels against all this.

He seizes power by force, with the help of his old uncle Eugene, an ex-cavalry officer and gentleman of the old guard, and compels the family to dress neatly, to wear ties and stiff collars; he has the apartment cleaned up and forces Ala to consent to marry him in a white wedding ceremony;

he even bullies the grandmother into giving her blessing to him and his bride.

Everything seems set for the restoration of order. But when Arthur returns from a walk, just before the wedding, he is drunk, and he has changed. This is the most difficult moment for the producer of the play; the break in Arthur's character and behaviour is seemingly unmotivated; but only *seemingly*. What Arthur has realized in his drunken outing is a simple, but undoubted truth: that the old traditional order cannot be brought back by mere decree. The old ways are no longer alive; their substance has been destroyed. 'The old conventions won't bring back reality . . . . Convention must start from an idea. You were right, father, I'm just a pathetic formalist,' says Arthur. In other words, the old conventions of behaviour made sense because people believed in the philosophy that underlay them. That philosophy, and that faith, have been effectively destroyed. Arthur himself no longer believes in the ideas behind the old conventions. Gradually Arthur works out the only possible solution: 'If nothing exists and even rebellion is impossible, what is it that can be created out of nothing and given reality? I'll give you the answer: the only possible thing is power. Only power can be created out of nothing. Power can be, where nothing ever was.' For, where all rational, all ideological basis for a code of behaviour have been destroyed, only brute force can make people adhere to a pattern of any kind. So Arthur calls in Eddie as his henchman, the executor—i.e. the executioner—of his regime of naked power. He orders Eddie to kill Uncle Eugene and Eddie is about to obey, when, to distract Arthur's attention, cousin Ala, the girl he loves, cries out that she has been unfaithful to him with Eddie, the vulgar brute who was also the lover of Arthur's mother. Arthur, who after all is an idealist, a human being with sensitivities, is so deeply shaken, that he loses his grip. With a savage blow Eddie kills him. And over Arthur's dead body, Eddie, the vulgar *lumpen* proletarian, and Uncle Eugene, the gentleman of the old school, dance the tango, the symbol of the fight for permissiveness and the destruction of traditional moral values, which has now reached its logical, ultimate conclusion: the alliance of brute force, devoid of all culture, and all humanity, with the authoritarian trappings of a previous feudal order, where brute force also ruled under the thin veneer of good manners and aristocratic polish. (The nobleman who acts as dancing-master for the party in the story *Siesta* comes to mind here; he probably taught the party secretaries to dance the tango as well!)

Arthur has been defeated because while he was clever enough to evolve the theory of nihilism and the use of brute force as the last pillar of order in society, he lacked the ruthlessness, the brutality, the inhumanity to put his views into practice. The intellectual revolutionaries who, like Lenin, Trotsky, or Brecht, want to use force to establish their utopian ideals, are too squeamish for the ultimate consequences of their views. Their places are taken by Stalin, Beriya—and Eddie.

The form of *Tango* is reminiscent of Ionesco and his demented family groups in plays like *Jack, or the Submission* or *The Bald Prima Donna*. But the substance is grimly real, indeed, represents a piece of sustained political thought rarely rivalled in drama. One may disagree with Mrozek's analysis, but one has to admire the intellectual power, the relentless logic with which he carries it out, and, above all, the mastery with which he uses the conventions of drama, of absurdist drama, to serve as a genuine vehicle for political and social analysis. *Tango* is an exercise in dialectical thought. What Mrozek has shown is the ability of drama to serve as a vehicle for serious analysis of this kind. Drama with its high degree of concreteness is an ideal instrument of existential—as against abstract—thinking. That is why the great existentialists like Kierkegaard, Sartre, Camus, or Mrozek's countryman and contemporary Leszek Kolakowski (one of the most brilliant thinkers of our time) use drama or dramatic dialogue for some of their most important philosophical work. Slawomir Mrozek fully deserves a place beside these thinkers.

Eastern Absurdists:
Vaclav Havel—Czechoslovakia

Divadlo na Zabradli, the Theatre on the Balustrade, is one of the centres of the European avant garde today. Situated in the heart of the Old Town of Prague, a cramped small auditorium improvised in an ancient town house, it seats barely two hundred people and has a tiny stage. Here, in 1958, Ladislav Fialka established his troupe of mimes which has since become world-famous; in 1959 Jan Grossman, critic, director, theoretician of drama, and co-editor of the Czech edition of Brecht's plays, joined the theatre as artistic director of straight plays. In 1960 Grossman was joined by Vaclav Havel, a young man who at that time was just twenty-four years old, as *dramaturg* and resident playwright. And so one of the most remarkable teams now active in European drama was formed: Grossman, tall, about forty, serious, and at least in his outward appearance careworn; Havel, still looking no more than nineteen, short, cherubic, and outwardly cheerful, and around them a small band of devoted and immensely talented actors, designers, musicians, and an equally devoted public.

Havel's cheerfully beaming appearance is deceptive. His plays are very funny, certainly, but there is a core of deep pessimism, even despair in them. They are a mixture of political satire, absurdist images of the human condition, philosophical parables, and zany, black humour. Kafka and Hašek, the twin tutelary spirits of Prague, are equally present in them.

Franz Kafka's concern was the metaphysical anguish of man confronted with the vast mystery of existence; his inability ever to know where he has come from and where he is to go—and what obligations he will have to fulfil. It is not the burden of guilt carried by the religious believer who has transgressed against known and clearly definable ethical rules, but a more terrible burden: a definite consciousness of having transgressed without any clear knowledge of the rules that have been broken, a feeling that man's mere presence on the earth, his mere existence, already constitutes his original sin. Many other writers have tried to express this predicament of modern, secularized man. But Kafka found what was an almost ideal medium for expressing it—the peculiar atmosphere of Prague, that ancient, mysterious city with its dark winding streets and haunting legends of the Emperor who was an alchemist or the old rabbi who made an artificial man, a Golem, from a lump of clay; Prague, the seat of a vast and alien bureaucracy ruling a downtrodden population that did not know the meaning and purpose of the complicated rules and regulations it had to obey. From these elements Kafka built up a picture of human anguish in the face of the mysteries of existence that was both dreamlike and concrete, fantastic and real. Kafka's subject matter is the most universal, his imagery the most local; it owes everything to Prague, its atmosphere and history.

Hašek's *The Good Soldier Schweik* is also both local and universal. Here too we have the Czech's reaction against the incomprehensible, the blatantly idiotic rule of an alien and stupid militarist caste: Schweik reacts against the stupidity of his oppressors by taking their stupid orders at their face value and stupidly carrying them out to the last detail. He too, like Kafka's anguished and tormented heroes, finds himself in an absurd world, but he strives to end its absurdity by carrying it, *ad absurdum*, to the point where it must collapse because, at the back of his mind, he has a faint hope that the crash of the absurd order will leave room for a more rational one.

Schweik's hope has not been fulfilled: the Austro-Hungarian Empire collapsed, but after a brief interval of comparative sanity its place was taken by the even more sinister and absurd rule of Heydrich and Hitler; and after that there came Stalinism. In that succession of more and more absurd situations the Schweikian reaction of the Czech people was bound to become ever more dogged, ever more bitter, ever more Schweikian. In Havel's plays this attitude can be clearly discerned; in a wildly absurd world his characters conform to the apparent logic of absurdity by behaving in a wildly absurd yet logical manner. In *The Garden Party* they surrender to the logical dilemma that a government that asks the Office of Inauguration to abolish the Office of Liquidation cannot really abolish the Office of Liquidation because only the Office of Liquidation can carry out a liquidation, and therefore to carry out the liquidation of the Office of Liquidation you have to keep the Office of Liquidation un-liquidated. In *The Memorandum* we find the similar dilemma that the order for the introduction of a new official language, being written in that new official language, cannot be correctly interpreted because it is written in a language that the official charged with implementing the order cannot understand. These are Schweikian situations, but their implications on a deeper level of significance are truly Kafkaesque. It would be wrong to interpret Havel's Schweikian dilemmas as mere satire against the idiocy of a local bureaucracy. The bureaucracy depicted by Havel has profound metaphysical features; it also represents the inner, logical contradictions of existence itself, the dilemma inherent in the use of all language (and Havel's logico-linguistic antinomies have much in common with Wittgenstein's critique of language as a vehicle for logic), the antinomies inherent in all rules of conduct.

Havel's plays owe much to the atmosphere of experimentation and teamwork in the intimate little Theatre on the Balustrade. They owe an even greater debt to the presence of Jan Grossman as mentor and director and Havel's own deep involvement, as a member of the team, in the process of production. Havel and the Theatre on the Balustrade also owe an enormous debt to their public; there is in Eastern Europe a sense of isolation which produces an eagerness, a sense of occasion, a feeling about the urgency and importance of what is being done in an experimental theatre, that may be absent in the more blasé, more satiated atmosphere of Western Europe. In attending the performances of Havel's plays in their theatre of origin I was deeply moved and exhilarated not only by what I saw on the stage, but also by the involvement of the audience.

Günter Grass the Dramatist

If, almost a hundred years ago, Walter Pater could sum up the then prevailing trend in his famous epigram, 'All art constantly aspires towards the condition of music,' the dominant tendency of our own age might be described as an aspiration of all the arts to attain the condition of *images*. Even our music is said to be fully comprehensible only to those who, on hearing it, can *see* the symmetry and logic of its visual impact on the score; and certainly the contemporary novel tends toward a mosaic of strongly imagined snapshot images. So does the theatre of our day. Günter Grass, the novelist and the playwright, provides a perfect illustration of this tendency.

Grass, the grocer's son from Danzig, called to the colours at the age of seventeen, released from an American prisoner-of-war camp at nineteen, working as an agricultural labourer and potash miner at twenty, found his vocation when he decided to become a visual artist and sought entry to the Düsseldorf Academy of Fine Arts.

While waiting to gain admittance to that institution, he earned his living as a stonemason's apprentice and spent his time carving tombstones. He became a painter and sculptor of great promise and lived in Paris for some time among a cosmopolitan group of artists. As a writer Grass has remained a maker of images. His first published book, a slim volume of poems which appeared in 1956, is illustrated by his own spindly, fantasticated, semi-abstract drawings, and it is hard to tell whether the poems are there to illustrate the drawings, or the drawings to illustrate the poems.

Music has continuity, structure, harmony; that is why the

art of happier, more settled, more secure epochs could aspire
to the condition of music, a world with perfect transparency
of meaning, a world that made sense. But a child of our time
like Grass has seen the world move forward in a series of
grotesque jerks, the frenzies of nationalism collapsing into
national degradation, his native Danzig changing its status
three times within seven years, starvation obscenely alternat-
ing with affluence. To such a child life no longer moves
along as a harmonious and logical progression; for such an
observer the linking logical structure has departed and what
is left is a series of abruptly changing, grotesque, incongru-
ous, incoherent but painfully vivid images, sordid, sad, yet so
monstrous that one can only laugh about them.

> In our museum—we always go there on Sundays—
> they have opened a new department.
> Our aborted children, pale, serious embryos,
> sit there in plain glass jars
> and worry about their parents' future.

This short poem from his first collection sums up Grass's
world with its peculiar mixture of disgust and black humour,
compressed into the capsule of a highly concentrated
image.

His plays too are essentially images seen with the eyes of
a painter who is so obsessed with his images that they also
seek expression as poetic metaphors; a lyrical poet so eager
to see his metaphors come to life that he is compelled to write
for the stage. Or, to put it differently, so vivid were the
images in the painter's, the poet's mind that they had to start
to talk in dialogue.

Grass himself, when questioned some years ago about his
development as an artist, put it like this: 'Up to now I have
written poems, plays, and prose; all three types of writing
are, in my case, based on dialogue, even the poetry. And so
the transition from poetry to drama happened like this:
poems were written in dialogue form and then extended.
That was shortly after the war. Then slowly, gradually, stage

directions were added, and so, parallel with my main occupation at that time, sculpture, I evolved my first play. That is, in a relatively short time, between 1954 and 1957, I wrote four full-length and two one-act plays, which, just like my poems and my prose, contain fantastic and realistic elements; these fantastic and realistic elements rub against each other and keep each other in check. . . .'

The genesis of the plays from the poems can be seen in one or two cases from Grass's volumes of poetry. In his first collection there is a poem entitled 'Flood' that clearly contains the germ of the play of the same title:

> The cellar is submerged, we brought the crates up
> and are checking their contents against the list.
> So far nothing has been lost.
> Because the water is now certain to drop soon,
> we have begun to sew sunshades.
> It will be difficult to cross the square once more,
> distinct, with a shadow heavy as lead.
> We shall miss the curtain at first,
> and go into the cellar often
> to consider the mark
> which the water bequeathed us.

And in Grass's second volume of poems, published in 1960, there is a highly characteristic drawing of a cook swinging a spoon, which illustrates a poem about cooks and spoons:

> And some will say: a chef's a chef.
> All newly laundered, starched and spry
> in snowfall or against a wall
> that's whitewashed, chefs escape the eye
> and then the spoons they hold are all
> that stirs us, leaves us in no doubt:
> the things we eat, the chefs dish out.

Indeed in Grass's world cooks in their white uniforms play a part second only to that of the nuns in their black habits. No wonder that the cooks also carry a metaphysical significance. 'I like cooking,' Grass once confessed in an interview, 'I like cooking lentils, for example. Lentils and luck have a great deal in common for me.' And so the cooks, who feed us all, become images of man's quest for spiritual as well as physical nourishment.

There is an overwhelming, childlike directness and simplicity in the way in which the most earthy and concrete things—lentils, food, nourishment—are here equated with the sphere of the spiritual, the philosophical, the metaphysical abstraction—happiness, the meaning of life. It is the simplicity of the medieval craftsmen who carved the gargoyles that adorn the great cathedrals. And it is characteristic of Grass, the stone carver, the sculptor, the painter and maker of images. Grass's subject matter, the degradation of Germany in the time of Hitler and in the aftermath of war, is sordid in the extreme. And in his writings—poems, plays, and novels—he never tries to evade the most direct confrontation with these nauseating facts. But because he deals with them so directly, with the total lack of self-consciousness, the innocence of a child, the disgusting facts can be accepted without the physical reactions of disgust that would make them intolerable as the subject matter of an artist's vision. Brecht spoke of naïveté as one of the most precious of aesthetic categories; Grass possesses that innocence of vision to a degree unparalleled by any other writer of our time.

It is the vision of a Douanier Rousseau, a Paul Klee. And Grass's plays can best be seen as images from that sphere brought to life on a three-dimensional canvas: the house with its inmates and its rats with the waters rising and receding in *Flood* (*Hochwasser*, first performed in Frankfurt, 1957); the rusty engine stationary in an idyllic landscape, manned by a crew using nautical language, who delude themselves that they are driving along at top speed, in *Only Ten Minutes to Buffalo* (*Noch zehn Minuten bis Buffalo*, first performed in Berlin, 1959);[1] the series of images of the pedantic murderer

---

[1] The title of this play requires some explanation: *Und noch zehn Minuten bis Buffalo* is a line from a poem by Theodor Fontane (1819–98) entitled 'John Maynard'. This tells the story of a ship sailing from Detroit to Buffalo on Lake Erie, which burst into flame half an hour

Bollin, trying to fulfil his duty as a member of a murderous generation, and always foiled, in *Mister, Mister* (*Onkel, Onkel,* first performed in Cologne, 1958); and the image of the cooks—which Grass first used in a ballet, *Five Cooks* (*Fünf Köche,* performed at Aix-les-Bains and Bonn in 1959) —clinically white in their uniforms, professionals angry to see that the highest secret of their art eludes them, while an amateur gains effortless possession of it, in *The Wicked Cooks* (*Die bösen Köche,* first performed in Berlin, 1962).

None of these plays has, as yet, achieved a lasting success in the theatre. It has been said that Grass's dramatic works lack the documentary quality, the descriptive, autobiographical detail that he incorporates in his novels. But this, to me, seems to overlook the essential difference between the narrative and the dramatic form. If Grass wrote plays filled with details about his early years in Danzig he would be producing naturalist drama wholly at variance with his own artistic personality. In the novels it was possible to combine the most abundant autobiographical detail with the wildest flights of grotesque fantasy. There is no time in drama to preserve both of these elements. Yet, precisely because the dramatic form demands more conciseness, more concentration, because it makes Grass confine himself to a limited number of images in each of his plays, it brings out his lyrical quality, the quality of his vision as a carrier of images. Nor is it a coincidence that each of his long novels contains passages written in dialogue and, indeed, that these dialogue passages could be performed in the theatre: the episode of the nuns on the Atlantic Wall from *The Tin Drum* was staged in Düsseldorf, the discussion chapter from *Dog Years* at Munich.

Indeed, for a writer of Grass's chaotic and anarchic exuber-

---

before it is due to dock at Buffalo. Surrounded by flames, the heroic helmsman, John Maynard, remains at his post and steers the ship into port, saving the passengers' lives while he himself dies a hero's death. This poem, which is much read in German schools, is the German equivalent of 'Casabianca' and, for Grass, the epitome of bombastic nautical nonsense.

ance as a storyteller, the dramatic form provides a most salutary discipline; on the other hand, the dramatist is to a much greater degree in the hands of his directors and performers. His plays' relative lack of success in the theatre may well be due to the difficulty of finding the right style for their performance. Grass himself has criticized the timidity of German producers in tackling unusual works like his plays, and there certainly is some substance in these strictures. His play *The Plebeians Rehearse the Uprising* did indeed cause a stir, but here the more topical—and more sensational—subject matter played its part. For in this play Grass managed simultaneously to attack the sacred cows of Eastern and Western Germany, which is no mean feat.

In the play Grass showed a playwright and producer in East Berlin rehearsing *Coriolanus* on 17 June 1953, while the real rising is taking place in the streets outside the theatre. The identification of the playwright with Brecht is unmistakable; in the last years of his life Brecht was working on an adaptation of *Coriolanus*. Grass imagines him rehearsing the uprising of the Roman plebeians while the East German workers' uprising is raging outside. The revolutionary workers come into the theatre to ask Brecht to help them draft their manifesto. But Brecht, the Communist revolutionary, does not comply; instead he uses them as models for the staging of the scene in his play. And his arrogance in rejecting their demands is an exact parallel to the way in which Coriolanus in Shakespeare's play refuses to bow to the Roman plebeians.

In East Germany Brecht has become something like a Communist saint, as well he might, being one of the very few things Ulbricht's puppet state can boast about. And Grass's play shows him instead as a very fallible and problematic personality, an artist to whom the revolution is no more than a theme for his artistry, as convinced of his superiority over the crowd as Coriolanus, the proud patrician and Roman aristocrat. In West Germany, on the other hand, the workers' uprising of 17 June 1953 is regarded as a glorious page in

German history, and there have not been so many of them in this century to boast about; the heroic workers who rose on that day only to be crushed by Russian tanks are commemorated each year when a national holiday is proclaimed on the anniversary of the rising. Yet Grass has the temerity to suggest that, although they were heroic, they were also politically naïve and still displayed the German love of order that, even at the height of revolutionary excitement, made them respect the "Keep Off the Grass" signs in the public parks. No wonder Grass and his play were peppered with furious crossfire from both sides of the Berlin Wall! (Grass himself, I believe, was very pleased with this double denunciation, which proved that he had not been tarred with the brush of either of the two halves of a divided Germany and could thus regard himself as a spokesman for the conscience of the nation as a whole.)

Yet the real subject matter of the play lies at a far deeper level: Grass's concern was not to score a point against Brecht but to show the dilemma of the creative artist in his relationship with political authority; far from being an attack on Brecht, this is in fact a brilliant and moving statement of the tragedy of the exceptional man, the artist of genius who is a true aristocrat by virtue of his genius. Here again Grass found a powerful image which admirably summed up and compressed a complex state of affairs into a simple and telling metaphor.

Günter Grass is a committed writer; it is one of the most hopeful signs for the future of Germany that her leading literary figures have broken with a long-standing tradition that artists of all kinds should keep aloof from politics. However fantastic and unrealistic Grass's plays may appear at first sight, the social comment is present and very much to the fore: in *Flood* there is a powerful warning against any nostalgia for the times of calamity and *camaraderie*; the murderer in *Mister, Mister* and the murderous teen-agers have obvious implications for members of both generations in present-day Germany; in *The Wicked Cooks* there are clear reflections of power struggles and intrigues; even the slight, parodistic curtain-raiser *Only Ten Minutes to Buffalo* can, ultimately, be seen as an attack against illusions, a plea for realism in looking at the contemporary scene. There is thus no split between Grass the author of seemingly abstruse, absurdist plays, and Grass the indefatigable campaigner for the Social Democratic party in the German elections of 1965 and 1966.

> Whoever wishes
> to release, to breathe out
> that caries which long has lurked behind the toothpaste
> has no choice but to open his mouth.
>
> Now let us open our mouths,
> go to offices and hand in
> the bad gold teeth
> which we broke and plucked from the dead.
>
> Before you can hope to
> displace, to spew out fat fathers—
> now that we too are fathers and putting on fat—
> you've no choice but to open your mouths;
>
> just as our children in time will
> open their mouths, will displace,
> will spew out the great caries,
> the bad gold teeth, the fat fathers.[2]

Only if we understand that this is the impulse behind everything that Günter Grass writes are we in a position to appreciate his poems, his novels, and his plays.

[2] All the poetry above has been taken from *Selected Poems*, translated by Michael Hamburger and Christopher Middleton (New York and London, 1966).

Edward Bond's Three Plays

Nothing could have shown up the idiocy of British stage censorship in its declining phase better than the reaction of the public—and even the critics!—to the revival of *Saved* at the Royal Court. After the grotesque antics in which the moral tone of the nation was supposedly to be preserved by the imposition of a fine and the banning of the play, less than four years later it is staged, received with quiet respect and recognized to be a moral tract for the times, no less. Can anyone be proved to have been depraved or corrupted by it? Has it led to sadistic orgies? Or riots in the streets of Chelsea? Where then are all the arguments which maintained stage censorship in being for decades? 'Oh well, old boy, if you allowed that sort of thing, who knows what might happen?' Well, now we know the answer. Nothing—except that some people emerge from the theatre with a deeper insight, a greater compassion for the sufferings of some of their fellow human beings.

What a brilliant play *Saved* is, how well it has stood the test of time! Bond has succeeded in making the inarticulate, in their very inability to express themselves, become transparent before our eyes: their speechlessness becomes communication, we can look right inside their narrow, confined, limited and pathetic emotional world. This is the final step and the ultimate consummation of the linguistic revolution on the British stage: what a distance we have come from the over-explicit clichés of the flat well-mannered banter, the dehumanized upper-class voices of an epoch which now appears positively antediluvian—although its ghostlike remnants still haunt the auditoria around the Shaftesbury Avenue area.

Saved is a deeply moral play: the scene of the stoning of the baby which led to the first outcry about it, is one of the key points in its moral structure. Pam conceived the baby irresponsibly, without love; because she did not want it, she does not care for it; because she does not care for it the baby cries incessantly and gets on her nerves; because it gets on her nerves she drugs it with aspirin; and so, when, caring more for the man with whom she is infatuated than for her child, she leaves it alone in its pram, the baby does not respond to the first casual and quite well-meant attentions of the gang. Because it does not respond, they try to arouse it by other means, and that is how they gradually work up to greater and greater brutality, simply to make the mysteriously reactionless, drugged child show a sign of life. There could not be a more graphic illustration of the way in which lack of responsibility and lack of understanding, lack of intellectual and moral *intelligence*, lies at the root of the brutality of our age. The SS-man who kills a Jew just lacks the insight and imagination to picture his victim's feelings; the bomber pilot who drops bombs on civilians does not *see* his victims, and therefore does not trouble to think about them. The baby in the pram is neglected because his mother cannot picture him as a human being like herself; the boys of the gang kill him because having been made into an object without conscience they *treat* him like a mere object.

In his own note in the published version of the play, Bond himself calls it an optimistic piece, because of Len's loyalty to the girl who rejects him. It is true: Len is a touching character in his stubborn devotion to the girl. And yet I am not at all convinced that this is the main message of *Saved*. Why indeed is the play called *Saved*? As far as I can see the only direct reference to the title is in the scene when Pam is trying to win Fred, the murderer—and perhaps the father? —of her child, back to her after his release from prison. Len, who foresees that she will be rebuffed, has come with her to the café where the reunion is to take place. When Fred *does* reject her with contempt, Pam wants to believe that he is doing this because of Len's, a rival's, presence. She cries out: '*Somebody's got a save me from 'im.*' The irony of the title therefore seems to me to lie in the fact that Pam at the end has lost Fred and continues to live in the same home, the same household as Len, and that, although all speech has ceased in that house, she will inevitably go on living with him, in every sense of the word. So that, eventually, she has *not* been saved.

A thorough study of the text reveals many equally subtle and complex insights and ironies: the way in which, after the marvellous and horrifying scene where Len has to repair a ladder in the stocking of Pam's mother and is surprised in that compromising position by her husband, finally the two men find each other and establish a line of communication; the relationship between Len and his real rival, Fred; the brilliantly observed marital warfare between Pam's parents, etc.

At first glance there could be no greater contrast than that between *Saved* and *Narrow Road to the Deep North*. Here the dialect of the speechless, there the clarity of stylized poetic speech; here deepest London, there the farthest, most exotic orient. Yet, a closer look reveals the common ground. Here, as there, the problem of the disastrous influence of a morality based on an intellectually bankrupt religion, here as there the horror of violence which expresses itself in images of violence.

Written, very rapidly, to serve as a comment on a conference about city planning held in Coventry in June 1968, *Narrow Road* is a meditation on how to create a 'good city'. Laid in Japan at the time when the first Westerners had landed there, the play shows the creation of a city by Shogo an upstart who becomes a bloody tyrant and its capture by the forces of missionary English colonialism. We see the story mainly from the point of view of the old poet and priest Basho: on his way to the deep north, where he is seeking enlightenment in meditation, Basho finds an exposed baby, abandoned by his parents in a time of famine. Should he have saved it? He leaves it to its fate. When he returns thirty years later a city has been built on the spot, by Shogo, who may be that very baby who grew up resentful and evil because he had no love as a child (like Pam's baby in *Saved*). Shogo is overthrown, with Basho's help, by the Commodore and his bible-toting missionary sister—or concubine—Georgina. And when, in the ups and downs of battle, that Victorian harridan sob-sister is pressed to reveal the identity of the young legitimate heir to the throne, who is hidden among her pupils, she lets a whole form of children die, rather than betray that one child—and goes mad. And Kiro, who was refused as a pupil by Basho and has become a friend of the tyrant Shogo, finally, confronted with all these moral dilemmas, commits hara-kiri, just at the moment when a man who is drowning calls for his help. The man saves himself by his own exertions, Kiro dies. The message is clear: not in speculation about moral principles lies salvation, but in one man's active help for another: if Basho had given that abandoned baby his love and care, if he had taken Kiro as his pupil—could not so much bloodshed and evil have been averted. But Basho, the poet, preferred his meditation far up there in the deep north; it is up there that he met the Commodore and Georgina and told them about the more populous south; what would have happened if he had not selfishly devoted himself to poetry and meditation (which only led to the conclusion, after many years, that 'there was nothing to learn in the deep north')? What would have happened if the artist had not indulged in his selfish search for "enlightenment" and self-expression?

This is a beautiful parable play, very Brechtian in its mixture of orientalism (used as an 'alienation effect' to show familiar problems in an unexpected light) and moral didacticism. It is Brechtian also in the spareness and economy of its writing.

*

In Germany Bond's *Early Morning* is being performed in a translation with the title *Trauer Zu Früh*, which means, translated back, *Mourning too early* (*or too soon*). Whether the translator merely could not spell English, or whether there is a subtle pun here, which Bond himself intended, it shows how hard it is to make out this strange, significant and important play. Is it a play about death? Is it about the court of Queen Victoria and Prince Albert? Or, if neither of these, what *is* it about?

I think partly this confusion is due to the production the play has been receiving at the Royal Court, both during its brief and almost clandestine appearance last year, and again at its triumphant censor-free revival; partly also to the press publicity which again and again insisted on its being about Victorian England, when—in my humble opinion—it is, indeed, about nothing of the sort.

'The events of this play are true,' states Bond's own note on the first page of the printed text. Now, clearly, of the real Queen Victoria, the real Prince Albert, the real Florence Nightingale there is nothing that is historically true in the play. Prince Arthur and Prince George were not Siamese twins, Florence Nightingale was not engaged to one of them, there was no civil war in England in which Disraeli captured the Queen after she had murdered her husband and wanted to have her shot, etc, etc. Yet, the events of the play *are* true. They are true insofar as they mirror establishment politics and history as they might appear to a child exposed to the history teaching practised in most of our schools, where stereotypes and idiotic clichés of history are paraded before working class children who are barely able to understand the vocabulary of battles, civil and external wars, dynasties, and the whole panoply of terms in which politics and power are discussed.

But the events of the play are also true, perhaps even more so, in the way in which they portray the process by which out of this half-understood, and therefore already mythical, fairy tale material, a child would build up its private mythology, using the strange mythical beings it has been told about to express its subconscious fears and desires. Then the child's anxiety about the quarrels between his parents—and whose parents don't quarrel?—could easily be transmuted into civil wars between giant figures of authority, a Queen and her Consort; the image of the Siamese twins who hate each other's guts but are condemned to stick together through thick and thin is clearly a child's nightmare about being stuck with his brother with whom he shares a room or perhaps even a bed. And finally the strong emphasis on cannibalism which pervades the whole play, from the incident in the cinema queue in Kilburn (where a man and his girl-friend killed the chap in front of them because he had tried to jump the queue and ate him out of boredom) to the whole of the third act in Heaven, where the whole cast are reassembled after death to orgies of mutual cannibalism, simply because there is no pain and no death in heaven and it does not hurt to have one's limbs torn out and eaten, and anyway they grow again instantly.

The world of the establishment, therefore, mirrored in a child's consciousness, and in turn mirroring its subconscious sexuality (the oral phase of sexuality is, according to Freud, the earliest phase of the sex drive and leads to dreams about eating people) is the true theme of *Early Morning*. Hence, in my opinion also, the title, pointing to the fact that this is a picture of the world as it might appear in childhood, life's early morning.

Well, this is my theory, and I don't know whether it is correct. If it *is* correct, then it would explain why the first, short-lived, and almost improvised production seemed to me far more effective than the full-scale treatment that the play received at the Royal Court in 1969. In the earlier performance there was a minimum of scenery and costume, one could therefore try and picture the proceedings in one's mind's eye, almost as though one was witnessing a radio performance or a mere reading. In William Gaskill's 1969 production the scenery and costumes were more elaborate and forced one to see the play in their terms. And their terms were far too naturalistic, far too genuinely historical, and indeed far too sober; they therefore again and again inhibited the play from taking off into its own region, that of high, extravagant, childish fantasy. The historical characters being mere *Images d'Epinal* (primitive wood-cuts of historical figures sold at country fairs) they ought to *look* like such primitive images; there should be backdrops in the style of the Douanier Rousseau, or, indeed, of children's drawings. Likewise in the style of acting and production there ought to be a wilder vein of naïve fantasy. All this, of course, provided I am right about the true nature of the script—which I consider, in those terms, a masterly, profound and brilliantly conceived and constructed piece of work. It might be worth trying this approach in practice somewhere.

Be that as it may, the Royal Court's Bond Festival of 1969 has established him as a major figure in our contemporary dramatic Parnassus.

Peter Weiss:
Dramatist beyond Brecht and Beckett

The fact that Peter Weiss writes in German but lives in Stockholm and is a Swedish citizen is more than just an accident created by the storms and stresses of the period before the Second World War. Indeed, the peculiar standpoint and viewpoint of a German-speaking exile looking at the chaos and horrors of Europe from the vantage point of a neutral northern country explains a great deal of the character, the form, and the subject matter of Peter Weiss's work.

Peter Weiss was born in 1916 near Berlin. After Hitler came to power his family settled in Czechoslovakia; from there he anticipated the Nazi occupation by going first to Switzerland and finally to Sweden. In his two autobiographical novels *Abschied von den Eltern* (*Leavetaking*) and *Fluchtpunkt* (*Vanishing Point*) he has described some of the stages of this flight from country to country. In Sweden he worked as an artist, a director of documentary films, and a journalist. He also wrote, in Swedish, but with little immediate success. And then, after the war, he found his language. As he himself describes it in *Fluchtpunkt*, it happened in Paris:

> I stepped out into the stream of human beings, went along the Boulevard, among young, open faces, among laughing eyes, among the tall, proud figures of the Africans, went through the parks, in museums and libraries, sat on the terraces of cafés, and instead of winning something of this new life for myself, hour by hour I lost more of myself, until my own name became uncertain to me, until I no longer knew, sitting in a wicker chair at the edge of the roadway, in this babel of voices, which was the language that belonged to me. The language that had

been my environment during the last years seeped away, its words slipped from me, it was washed away here, in this crucible, it became clear how loosely it was tied to me, how little it meant for me, everything that was not firm, was not part of me, was sloughed off, all external structures crumbled, dropped away, ran off me. . . . People bent over me, stretched across me, called out words to me, talked over my head, laughter winged to and fro, and I was unable to reply, unable to take part, capable only of shouting out a few phrases I had picked up, *garçon, encore un café, l'addition, s'il vous plaît.* This was the moment of explosion, the moment I was hurled out into absolute freedom, the moment at which I was torn loose from my anchorage, any belonging, set apart from all nations, races, and human ties, the moment I had wished for, the moment in which the world lay before me. Now I could show who I was, what kind of I it had been that I had carried through the years of exile, that I had saved from being annihilated on the battlefield and in the gas chamber.

This is the basic experience of the refugee, the exile. And the exile is, I believe, the typical figure, the personification, the archetype of our century, which is a century of the culmination and the transcendence of nationalism. The exile, by the very fact that he is wrenched away from the traditional supports of human personality—tradition, custom, family solidarity—*must* in the end, if he survives the experience mentally and physically, find himself as himself, as a being for himself alone, in total freedom.

This freedom [says Peter Weiss] was absolute, I could lose myself in it, and I could find myself in it again; I was able to abandon all, all striving, all belonging, and I could start to speak again. And the language which now came to me was the language I had learned at the start of my life, the natural language which was my tool, which now belonged to me alone, and had nothing to do any more with the country where I had grown up. This language was present, whenever I wanted it and wherever I happened to be. I could live in Paris or in Stockholm, in London or New York, and I carried this language with me, the lightest of luggage. In this moment the war was overcome and the years of exile had been lived through. I was able to speak, able to say what I wanted to say, and perhaps someone was listening to me, perhaps others would speak to me and I would understand them.

This remarkable passage is not only perhaps the best statement of the relationship between language and human identity—for only when a human being finds *his* language, his style of thought, can he begin truly to be himself—in contemporary literature, it is also the key to the understanding of Peter Weiss. Weiss writes in German, but this language is *not* the German of present-day Germany, which has acquired all the sediment of its history, expressions and turns of phrase that originated in Nazi times, in the misery of the starvation of the immediate postwar period and the opulence of the economic miracle; it is the German he learned and spoke as a child, the German of a man who had to speak English, to speak and write Swedish for a living. No one else had exactly the same experience, no one else speaks exactly the same language. To have realized this, to have found his own language, and to have shown the courage to *speak* it, regardless of what others might think, is the secret of Peter Weiss's impact.

His *Marat/Sade* is written in doggerel verses, simple like those of some puppet play in Weiss's childhood, direct, cruel, primitive, infantile—and yet miraculously adapted to the subject matter, the argument of the play. But even more important than the language is the point of view; and this also emerges from the passage of autobiography we have just quoted. Absolute freedom, absolute detachment is the exile's stance. He stands *in* the cosmopolitan crowd on the Paris boulevard, but he is not *of* it, just as he watched the war from neutral Sweden, feeling helpless, unable to rescue even the few personal friends from Prague and Berlin who appealed to him from the death that awaited them at Auschwitz and Terezin. The awareness that human beings are conditioned by their viewpoint obtrudes itself for the observer who stands outside and above the horrors of his time.

In his first work to be published in Germany after he had found himself, the short novel *Der Schatten des Körpers des Kutschers* (*The Shadow of the Body of the Coachman*), Weiss describes this experience of alienation, of standing outside in a foreign environment. A series of events is described, not in the traditional manner of telling what the characters are thinking, what their motivations and emotions are, but simply by describing their outward appearance, the way they move, the gestures they make. This is how one experiences life in a country in which one is an alien, where one does not understand the native population's language and way of life. In such a situation the stranger is reduced to watching the shadows of bodies as they move across the lighted windows of the house; he stands outside and looks in. What is remarkable about this short but brilliantly conceived and written narrative is that it anticipates the French *nouveau roman* while following some of its most fundamental precepts. It is as though Peter Weiss from his own very personal experience had invented the *nouveau roman* for himself independently of Robbe-Grillet and Butor.

In *Marat/Sade* the basic concept is closely related to that of Weiss's novel. Here too we are shown a number of events which the audience is made to watch as outsiders: they are transported into the beginning of the nineteenth century (for the *whole theatre* is the asylum in Charenton) to watch a play dealing with events that happened years earlier in the French Revolution, enacted by lunatics. There are thus three alienation effects (in Brecht's sense) built into the play, which mutually point up the relativity of human viewpoints. We look at a performance with our own eyes, but we are forced to realize that we are in fact meant to look at it with the eyes of an audience on 13 July 1808, who are watching the 1808 version of 1793 events. At the same time however we also know that the actors are meant to be lunatics, some of whom do not even understand what they are saying, who are forced to act their parts; so that the actor playing Duperret, Corday's noble Platonic lover, is actually an erotomaniac who, while he is reciting a speech about the purity of his love, has to be forcibly restrained from assaulting the patient playing Charlotte Corday.

What Weiss is here pointing to is the fact that even in our own lives, and however sane we may seem, we may be playing a role imposed upon us by society and convention, while underneath we are actuated by subconscious impulses and desires over which we may have as little control as the lunatics in the play. And their actions will appear different to different audiences at different times in history. The play ends with an apotheosis of Napoleon in 1808, but we, the audience of the late 1960s, know what the audience of 1808 could not know, that Napoleon would be overthrown within seven years of that performance. As a further addition to the complex system of mutual relativities, we are told that de Sade, himself a man of violently eccentric views, has written the play, so that we also see history mirrored through a most peculiar mind. Again, we know that the de Sade of the play is a fiction and that the author of the play is of our own time, mirroring his view of de Sade's view of Marat and the Revolution. If we think all this out, we are made to realize the complexity of reality itself, which can be apprehended only through human minds, each of which is biased, ruled by subconscious motives as compelling as, if less obvious than, those that dictate the actions of lunatics. *The Persecution and Assassination of Marat as Performed by the Inmates of the Asylum at Charenton under the Direction of the Marquis de Sade* may be a very long title for a play, but it is also both accurate and necessary, anything but a mere gimmick to attract attention.

Moreover, at the very core of the play there is a philosophical argument of great subtlety and import: the debate between Marat and de Sade about the possibility of revolution. Marat defends the classic Marxist point of view: the world can be changed only if we impose a rational order by force. If we want to do good to our fellow men, we must start by being cruel to them at first. The Marquis de Sade's

standpoint, on the other hand, is that of the extreme indivi-
dualist:

> Before deciding what is wrong and what is right
> first we must find out what we are
> I
> do not know myself
> No sooner have I discovered something
> than I begin to doubt it
> and I have to destroy it again
> What we do is just a shadow of what we want to do
> and the only truths we can point to
> are the ever-changing truths of our own experience.

And indeed, in looking into himself, de Sade has uncovered
a vast world of violence and evil, a lust for torture, a wild
desire to impose suffering on fellow human beings. But when
the Revolution came and de Sade, released from prison, was
made a judge with the power of life and death over others,
he found that, having experienced the wild orgies of his
imagination, he had no urge to make others suffer and was
unable to impose the death sentence. That is why he was
removed from his office and put into an asylum by the
Revolutionary authorities. Thus we have the paradox that the
revolutionary who wants to do good ends up as the creator of
terror and mass executions, while the sadist who is prepared
to indulge the cruel aggressive impulses of his subconscious
emerges as the mild and non-violent sceptic who doubts the
efficacy of any action and refuses to raise a finger to harm
others.

It is a brilliant restatement of one of the main debates of
our time, the chief spokesmen of which in drama have been
Bertolt Brecht and Samuel Beckett. *Marat/Sade* may thus be
seen as a debate between Brecht and Beckett, in which it
seems that Beckett's standpoint wins, but which is conducted
in Brechtian terms—thirty-three short scenes or tableaux and
a multitude of alienation effects. The victory of the Beckettian
standpoint is, however, by no means certain. After all, the
text Marat speaks was written by de Sade; it is therefore only

to be expected that de Sade's position will prevail. We, the
audience, know that the argument was rigged and will therefore perhaps have to give the benefit of the doubt to Marat.
And, in fact, since he wrote the play Peter Weiss himself has
become a very vocal advocate of a Socialist—i.e., Marat's—
point of view.

In Weiss's dialogue *Das Gespräch der drei Gehenden* (*The
Conversation of Three Men Walking*) three men walk
through a landscape and tell us what they see. It is the same
landscape, but each of the three men sees totally different
things. How is one to escape from the relativity of human
viewpoints? How can one find what the world is really like?
In his work as a painter Weiss sought the answer in collage,
a technique that simply combines what others have seen into
an image in which the relativity of different viewpoints is
clearly indicated. Yet in his collages he likes using technical
illustrations, pictures from Victorian textbooks of anatomy
and engineering; they are as near as one can get to factual
objectivity.

Weiss adopted this same procedure in his play about the
trial of some Auschwitz guards at Frankfurt, *The Investigation*. Here we are back with the neutral observer who wants
to understand what is going on, the outsider who stands
aghast watching the horrors beyond the frontiers. Once more
Weiss refuses to moralize, to obtrude his own point of view.
He merely takes the proceedings of the trial and arranges
them in an order in which the facts can most easily be apprehended. Then he lets the facts speak. No, not the facts,
the *testimonies* of the accused and the witnesses, the speeches
of the prosecution and the defence.

Significantly the word 'Jew' is not mentioned in the play.
Precisely in order to de-emotionalize the issue Weiss omitted
the names, nationalities, and personal circumstances of
all the witnesses and used, when it was necessary, words
that were without any emotional undertones, although they
clearly stood for the things involved. Anyone who knows
enough German will immediately recognize that the word

Verfolgte (i.e., those under racial persecution) stands for Jews.

Whether *The Investigation* is an artistic success, whether the death camps *can* be dealt with by a mere factual, deadpan reporting of the evidence at a trial of minor concentration camp guards, is another matter. What concerns us here is that reality in this play is as complex and bewildering as the fantasy about the three men walking through the same landscape and describing different things, or reality and history mirrored in the minds of madmen. Are the concentration camp guards mad that they did such horrible things; the witnesses mad because they went through all this horror? They give completely different descriptions and interpretations of the same events. Weiss refuses to say where the true facts lie. Reality can be apprehended only as a system of contradictory accounts of the same event.

Weiss abandoned this objectivity in the plays that followed *The Investigation: Gesang vom lusitanischen Popanz (Song of the Lusitanian Bogeyman*, 1967) and *Diskurs über die Vorgeschichte und den Verlauf des lang andauernden Befreiungskrieges in Viet Nam als Beispiel für die Notwendigkeit des bewaffneten Kampfes der Unterdrückten gegen ihre Unterdrücker sowie über die Versuche der Vereinigten Staaten von Amerika die Grundlagen der Revolution zu vernichten (Discourse on the Antecedents and the Course of the Long-Lasting War of Liberation in Vietnam as an Example of the Necessity of the Armed Struggle of the Oppressed against Their Oppressors as Well as about the Attempts by the United States of America to Annihilate the Basis of the Revolution*, 1968).

Both these plays are examples of a highly effective theatre of agitation and special pleading. A group of performers, each playing a multitude of parts, stages a kind of review of political commercials: brief sketches alternate with slogans, songs, jingles, and passages of exposition and documentation. That this can be highly effective is beyond doubt. The production of the *Lusitanian Bogeyman* that Weiss and his wife, the designer Gunilla Palmstierna, supervised themselves in Stockholm was an exhilarating experience of total theatre. The *Vietnam Discourse* is beautifully written and inspired by the purest motives. Curiously enough, it is the quality of the writing, the highly stylized form of the presentation that seems to me to devalue the piece as *political* theatre; whether the facts are true or not, it is too obvious that they have been selected and angled, so that even the truest evidence loses its evidential character. Political theatre of this kind will preach only to those already converted to its point of view.

With his plays about Portuguese colonialism and Vietnam, Weiss had gained approval in East Germany and the Soviet bloc. It is a measure of his devotion to his own concept of socialism and to what he regards as the truth that his next play *Trotzki im Exil* (*Trotsky in Exile*, written between November 1968 and June 1969—i.e. after the Soviet aggression against Czechoslovakia—and first performed at Dusseldorf 20 January 1970) is bound to earn him active condemnation and a ban on the performance of his work in Eastern Europe.

At his desk in Mexico, immediately before his assassination, Trotsky re-lives his career, not chronologically but in a sequence of associative leaps: thus, for example, at the end of the scene of the October Revolution, in which he is shown as the effective leader, Soviet soldiers appear and announce his banishment as a counter-revolutionary; we are eleven years later. Here Weiss comes very near to an effective fusion of the strictly factual and informative function of post-Brechtian epic theatre with strong dramatic and poetic effects.

Weiss regretted that his Trotsky play, which should have had its first performance in Moscow, should have had to open in the centre of post-war German capitalism, Dusseldorf. By a further irony of fate, the dress rehearsal was brought to a halt by demonstrating left-wing students; while the first night itself took place all too quietly before an audience of stony-faced *bourgeois*. A more telling metaphor for the dilemma of the revolutionary artist in our time could hardly be imagined.

Pinter Translated

It is a cliché that the world is getting steadily smaller. Anyone who has anything to say, who is a success in London or New York has his books translated, his plays performed from Stockholm to Naples, from Brussels to Prague and Bucharest, if not to Vladivostok. Translations roll off the assembly lines like mass-produced cars. Yet how much do they convey of the originals, what use are they in making nation understand nation?

I was recently compelled, by some work I had undertaken, to read the German versions of Harold Pinter's plays, all of which have been performed in theatres up and down Western Germany. One does not often read authors one can read in the original in other languages. Hence my surprise at entering the strange world of Bottom's dream (Thou art translated!). In that enchanted wood howlers grow upon the trees in wild profusion.

In *The Birthday Party*, for example, the two terrorists Goldberg and McCann brainwash their victim, Stanley, by hurling all sorts of accusations at him—from 'You contaminate womankind' to 'You are a traitor to the cloth'. One of their more devastating questions is 'Who watered the wicket at Melbourne?' How does this reference to the British national sport fare in German.

Wer hat an das Stadttor von Melbourne gepinkelt? Which translated back into English reads: 'Who peed against the city gate of Melbourne?' How was this startling transformation of one sentence into another achieved? We can follow the trend of thought. Look up 'wicket' in the dictionary—it will lead to 'wicket gate'—'gate' at Melbourne?

Must be the gate of the city. Aha! And 'to water' then becomes almost obvious in its meaning!

Now, one howler of this sort would make little difference
—although the *range of references* in these accusations constitutes their dramatic point. Stanley is being accused of viola-
ting every possible law, even the laws of fair play and cricket.
But when a considerable number of this long sequence of
only *seemingly* nonsensical sentences turns out to have been
misunderstood, the basic idea of the scene simply disappears.
'What about Drogheda?' asks the Irishman McCann, thereby also fixing the blame for Cromwell's massacre of the
garrison and priests of that beleaguered town on our poor
little Englishman. The German version of the sentence is:
Was ist mit Stärkungsmitteln? (What about strengthening
drugs?) It is difficult to imagine how the learned translator
reached this result. My guess would be that he merely
assumed there must be some affinity between Drogheda and
the German word '*Droge*'—drug. 'What about the Albigen-
senist heresy?' ask the terrorists, and clearly the stress is on
heresy. *Was ist mit der Albigensenisten-Legende?* says the
German translation. The heresy has become a mere *legend*.
Why? I'd hazard the guess that the translator misread the
word heresy which he did not know for the word 'hearsay'
which he knew. Likewise the statement: 'You're a traitor to
the cloth' becomes: *Sie sind ein Verräter bis aufs Mark*
('You are a traitor to the marrow of your bones'): perhaps
the translator thought of the cloth of Stanley's underclothes?

Is it really coyness that makes McCann's threat 'I'll kick
the shit out of him!' into no more than: '*Ich werde ihm den
Schädel zu Brei schlagen.*' ('I'll smash his head to pulp')?
All these howlers can be found within a few pages of the
text picked at random. Yet, admittedly, a difficult text, with
lots of recondite allusions.

But then there are howlers in much simpler passages. A
few pages further on, Goldberg is telling the story of his
youth: 'I was very proud of my old greenhouse . . .'. In German: *Ich war sehr stolz auf mein Haus im Grünen . . .* ('I

was very proud of my house in the greenbelt'). Or, in another passage of Goldberg's nostalgic musings: 'Humming away I'd be, past the children's playground. I'd tip my hat to the toddlers.' The last sentence becomes in the German version: *Ich habe jeden Hausierer gegrüsst* . . . (i.e.: I greeted every *pedlar*). McCann sings a sentimental Irish melody:

> Oh the garden of Eden has vanished, they say,
> But I know the lie of it still . . . .

In German he makes a much more drastic statement:

> '*O, fuer uns ist verloren das Paradies*
> *so heisst es—*
> *doch ich weiss, das ist eine Lüge . . .*'
> (Oh Paradise is lost they say,
> But I know that is a lie . . .).

One last gem from the third act of *The Birthday Party*. Here Stanley has already been brainwashed, but he is subjected to a final orgy of intimidation. Goldberg and McCann hurl a list of phrases associated with illness and hospitals at him ('The stomach pump' 'The oxygen tent') and this also includes obvious references to the bones in his body which they are prepared to break—'The crutches' and 'The plaster of Paris'. The latter phrase in German has become *Das Pflaster von Paris* (The pavements of Paris).

It is one of the great difficulties of any reasoned review of a translation that one is inevitably tempted to pick out the more outrageously funny and extravagant mistakes. They alone, one feels, will be amusing enough to keep the interest of readers who don't know both languages. To make a list of the more humdrum, less outrageously funny mistranslations which abound in the German version of Pinter would be very boring. Yet these small mistakes, being so numerous, are probably even more damaging. 'Up till now' becomes 'since then', 'jam tart' turns into 'Sauce Tartare', 'anchovies' reappear as 'aniseed cakes' and in the end the flavour of the passage is as alien from the original as indeed jam tarts are from sauce tartare. 'A bloody liberty!' that archetypal phrase reappears in *The Dumb Waiter* as *Eine beschissene Freiheit!* (i.e. 'a shit-covered freedom'. And *Freiheit* means only political freedom! It cannot mean 'impertinence'—which in German is *Frechheit* a similar but very different sounding word). Whole passages suffer such strange sea-changes. Also in *The Dumb Waiter* one of the two hired murderers, Gus, complains about the difficulty of killing women. 'They don't seem to hold together like men, women. A looser texture, like. Didn't she spread, eh? She didn't half spread . . .'. The German version has Gus say: *Die können sich eben nicht so zusammennehmen wie Maenner, Frauen. Weicheres mate-rial, wahrscheinlich. Und was sie zusammengefaselt hat, was? Schoen was zurechtgefaselt* . . . (They can't pull them-selves together like men, women. Softer material, probably. And the nonsense she talked, eh? Talked proper non-sense . . .' (The dictionary probably said: 'to spread oneself' —'to talk at great length'!)

In *The Caretaker* Mick is talking about a man who re-sembled the tramp Davies. 'Had a funny habit of carrying his fiddle on his back, like a papoose. I think there was a bit of the Red Indian in him'. In the German version this man carries his fiddle on his back like *eine Schildkröte* (a tortoise). To get this result you only have to mix up *papoose* with *porpoise* and then to mix up *porpoise* with *tortoise* and —hey presto! Does Mick own the house where the play takes place? 'I got deeds to prove it' he says in Pinter's text. In German he exclaims: *Ich habe es durch Taten bewiesen* (I have proved it by my deeds [in the sense of actions]). And Mick has plans for the property: 'I could turn this place into a penthouse'. He is less ambitious in German: *Ich könnte aus diesem Haus eine Pension machen* (I could turn this house into a *boardinghouse*).

Yes, translation is a difficult business. You not only have to know two languages well, you must also know the topo-graphy and the way of life of the two cultures you want to put into communication. Pinter's German translator thinks that a 'detached house' (in *The Lover*) means *ein abgelegenes Haus* (a remote house). He makes Davies refer to the *Kensington* Oval, that well-known sports arena. He thinks that *The Nag's Head* is the name of an English city or village; and 'up near the Scrubs' becomes *oben am Park* (up at the Park)—scrubs—shrubs—greenery—park: it's a process of simple deduction. But then English gardens *have* their pitfalls. 'She's a common or garden slut' (in *The Lover*) turns into the far more graphic phrase: *Eine ganz alltägliche oder sogenannte Parkbank-Hure* (a quite ordinary or so-called park-bench whore). Here the English cliché has literally fired the translator's creative imagination.

Again, I am afraid, I have been unable to resist the lure of gaining easy laughs by parading the more outrageous type of howler.

The really serious deficiency of these translations, however, lies elsewhere. The point of Pinter is, to a considerable extent, his brilliant use of different levels of language. The vocabulary of the articulate is comically juxtaposed with that of the totally inarticulate, the way educated people use words, with the gropings of the half-educated. A translator who is unable to see even the dictionary meaning of so many terms, could not possibly grasp this higher linguistic level. Had he grasped it, it would still be very difficult to find an adequate rendering of these subtleties in German. Only a writer of great talent could accomplish that. Yet it could be done.

There is a third, and even more elevated level, of Pinter's linguistic skill—his use of rhythms and pauses. And his poetic ambiguity. That these are beyond the grasp of someone still lost in the difficulties of a Beginner's Course of English is only too obvious. Neither the social comedy of language in Pinter nor Pinter's poetic use of cadence and pause appears in the German version of the plays. What remains is something of the plot, something of the characters as revealed by their actions rather than their words. And that is precious little.

Yet such is the paradox of the cultural interchange in our

time, that these plays are stubbornly performed in German. The Lord knows what actors and producers think they are about. The majority of German critics keep on wondering what these strange primitive plays could mean. But such is the prestige of the mere fact of success in London or New York, that they also feel compelled to say that, after all, these are very *strange* plays, mysterious, disjointed, enigmatic, that in fact there surely must be something there.

So after all, the British, who simply ignore the bulk of foreign literature and who reject even a great poet like Brecht if the translations they are offered do not seem great poetry to them, *are* far, far wiser than the over-eager cosmopolitan Germans. Moreover, the British admit that they are not much good at foreign languages; the Germans tend to claim that all educated people in Germany *do* know foreign languages well, above all English. And yet—translations of a major dramatist like Pinter so full of elementary mistakes are commissioned by agents, printed by publishers, performed by theatres, accepted by audiences, without anyone pointing to the mistakes, or making a fuss about them. A little knowledge is a dangerous thing; to think that one knows a language can be a dangerous illusion. After all, wars have started over linguistic misunderstandings. . . .

Post Script: After this article appeared in the March 1968 issue of *Encounter*, Rowohlt, Pinter's German publisher commissioned a complete version of the translation in question. So these remarks no longer apply to Pinter's plays as they are now available in German. Yet—the general problem of translation remains as difficult as ever—and not only with regard to English texts translated into German.

The Future of the Theatre

Violence in Modern Drama

The connection between violence and drama is a very obvious one. It is one of the great clichés that all drama is conflict and that in a way, therefore, violence is built into drama. I do not entirely agree with this definition. There are many good plays that are purely lyrical and do not contain much conflict. But there is certainly an enormous element of violence in drama, and it is not, as in some other arts, extraneous, but something that is inherent in the form itself. In fact, the German dramatist Gerhart Hauptmann had the idea that all tragedy was founded in human sacrifice. There is no evidence for this at all, but there is, I think, a grain of truth in it, in the sense that drama does present pictures of human suffering to an audience that takes delight in them. In that sense drama is a human sacrifice of some sort. You can apply this not only to tragedy (as Hauptmann thought) but also to comedy; in comedy one laughs about the misfortunes of others, in tragedy one weeps about them.

In trying to deal with violence in modern drama as distinct from drama in general, it is useful to try to define the types of violence we find in theatre and then show how they work in modern drama. If one takes as one's principle of classification the recipients of the violence, the most obvious form is the violence that occurs *between the characters within the play*. That is, what one character in a play does to another, or equally what he does to himself, because in modern drama a kind of self-violence plays a particularly important part. This kind of violence is, as it were, within the world of the play itself. But this is not the only form violence can take. In fact, I think it is not the most important one. You can also have the violence *of the author or the director towards the characters.* You can have a rallying call for violence *from the stage to the spectators.* And this plays an enormous part in a great deal of the more objectionable modern drama. Fourthly, there is the violence that *the audience develops towards the characters on the stage.* This is an extremely interesting phenomenon and very relevant to the modern theatre. Fifthly, there is violence directed *by the author against the audience,* again a form that is particularly significant in modern drama.

Violence within the enclosed world of the play is the most traditional. If you look at Greek tragedy there are the murders in the *Oresteia,* the self-blinding of Oedipus. In the Elizabethan theatre there is also an enormous amount of violence of this type, and the Elizabethan theatre particularly is a theatre of fights, of violent clashes—all the history plays culminate in battle scenes. If you take the even wilder forms of violence you find in Webster and Tourneur, the romantic agony of the Jacobean theatre, you find veritable orgies of violence that the characters direct against each other. In comedy, this also appears— to give just one example among many—in episodes like the mocking of Malvolio in *Twelfth Night.*

In the modern theatre, that is, the modern theatre that is worth while from a literary point of view, this aspect of violence is not as important as it used traditionally to be in drama. The reason for this is a sociological one. With the rise of television, films, and radio it has become more and more difficult to produce effective fights or battles on the living stage. In the Elizabethan theatre the fights, the duels, were regarded by the audience as the high point of the acting. The actors even had a technique employing little bladders with bull's blood concealed underneath their costumes, and at the point when the hero finally killed the villain this bladder was struck and a spurt of blood went up into the air bespattering everybody. These skills were so popular that English actors were touring the whole of the Continent and

making a lot of money—from audiences who did not understand a word they were saying—simply because of this kind
of spectacle. In an age of photographic mass media this
does not work any more. I always feel embarrassed by fights
in the theatre, because I know all too well that the actors are
taking care not to hurt each other. I think, therefore, that
this most primitive aspect of the theatre has devolved almost
entirely onto the other media. This, of course, produces in
the modern theatre a need for very much more subtle forms
of violence, and if you look at this category of violence-
within-the-play you will find that physical violence has become a relatively unimportant part and that *psychological
violence* between the characters has become much more
important. Take, for example, what I consider to be a classical
example of violence in the modern theatre, Ionesco's *The
Lesson*. Although the play culminates in the professor plung-
ing the knife into the girl, the real violence is in the whole
play that precedes this simple act, which only, as it were,
consummates it. Consummates it in more senses than one,
namely the psychological domination of the pupil by the
professor, who gradually sucks out all her vitality so that by
the time she is killed this act has already been performed—
in a psychological or, you might say, in a linguistic manner,
because there is an equation between the use of language and
domination that is one of the forms in which violence appears
in the modern theatre. The fact that the girl is killed is in
itself not a very great shock to the audience and is really a
final symbolic coda to the event that has already been suggested in other ways. So that in fact you have a situation (and
this is very often the case when violence appears in this form
in modern drama) where the violence is one of psychological
domination or subjection that is then finally consummated—
or not consummated as the case may be—in such an overt act.

Another example from an opposite school comes from
Brecht, if you take a scene like the killing of the dumb girl
Katrin in *Mother Courage*. The girl has heard that the
soldiers want to attack a nearby town. She can't warn the

town that it has been surrounded, and she knows that all the children are going to be killed. She climbs up onto the roof of a shed. She can't cry out because she is dumb, but instead she takes a drum and begins to beat it. The soldiers threaten to shoot her unless she climbs down, but she refuses and the drum goes on and on and on until finally the soldiers shoot her down from the roof. There again is a situation in which the act of violence merely comes at the culmination of a really violent, heroic, brutal form of tension, which is produced by quite different psychological means.

There is, of course, in the contemporary theatre still a great deal of actual violence, of violence in the old Shakespearean sense. It is, however—if you take a writer like Tennessee Williams, for instance—one with strong erotic, sexual overtones. The rape at the climax of *A Streetcar Named Desire* is violence certainly, but not simply the violence of two people fighting and the audience saying how nicely they fight. The theme is always one of sexual domination and subjection. One recent American play, *The Brig* by Kenneth Brown, is one of the most violent plays I have ever seen in the theatre. This is a play that was done by the Living Theatre as a protest against the way prisoners are maltreated in a marine detention camp. A great deal of slugging goes on in the play. The poor inmates are continually being knocked around. But this doesn't come across as a terrifying experience—at least it did not to me. What is harrowing is the fact that the Living Theatre is rather like a large room. There is no stage as such, just the end of the room. This was screened off with wire mesh and behind it had been built an exact replica of a detention cell with about eighteen people and bunks in this tiny space. At intervals around the floor there were white lines. Every time a prisoner wants to cross a white line he has to ask permission from the guard. If a prisoner is ordered to get a bucket, for example, he has to stop at each white line and ask permission to cross. Half the play seemed to consist of the prisoners barking out requests to cross and the guards shouting 'Yes' or 'No.' This insistent repetition of these idiotic lines is far more violent and far more brutal than the fact that in front of you various people are being punched—which nobody believes, even though they do it very well. It may be a terrifying commentary on our time that, in the live theatre at least, real violence—to us who have seen so much—doesn't really have any effect. So it has to be buttressed by some kind of psychological violence.

The commonest form of aggression, of course, is verbal aggression, vituperation, the calling of names. I think this is the significance of a whole school of writers like the so-called Angry Young Men. The impact of Osborne's *Look Back in Anger* was, as everybody recognized, in the eloquence of its invective and the determination of its verbal aggression. It is this element that makes a writer like Osborne tick and it explains why if he doesn't write a play he writes a letter saying, 'I hate this country.' There is in this kind of theatre a violence of protest, a determination not to take the situation as it is lying down, which produces verbal aggression.

One type of violence that is much more true of the modern theatre than the classical is violence by the character against himself—an inner-directed, masochistic form of violence. In Brecht, for example, there are at least two examples of self-castration. The best-known one is in *Mann ist Mann*, where you have psychological violence driven to an absolute pitch of perfection—a man is changed through violence into a different personality—which is, after all, the greatest of all violences, the total eradication of the autonomy of a person. But in this play, which is, of course, sado-masochistic if ever a play was, you have a big, masculine army sergeant. He has, however, a weakness; he is hard as nails, but whenever it rains he cannot resist the lure of women. This has terrible consequences because he suddenly changes into a softy who begs to be treated kindly and disgraces the name of the army. It comes to the point where he knows he cannot go on because he will lose his reputation as a military man, so he takes out his revolver and castrates himself, shouting, 'Now it can rain as long as it likes.' In another Brecht play, *Der Hofmeister*

(*The Private Tutor*), there is a private tutor who always falls for the sisters of his pupils. He is thrown out of one house where he has made a girl pregnant and finds himself getting into the same situation in his next post. He castrates himself —and then happily marries the girl. Self-castration goes back, of course, to the *Bacchae* and Greek ritual, but this is a curious revival of it. And in one of the most violent of modern dramas you have the same thing—in Genet's *The Balcony*.

The second form of violence, the kind that the author uses against his own characters, you find wherever the characters are treated with really savage contempt by the writer. This happens in Ionesco's *The Bald Prima Donna*, where the characters are seen as lifeless puppets who have no human attributes left at all. But you can also see this in a writer who is much more profound than Ionesco, namely Beckett. In *Waiting for Godot*, for example, the author's ruthlessness towards his characters shows itself in the way in which he expends no sympathy on them at all, in the way in which he constantly pushes them into extreme situations where they are forever falling over. Somebody listed dozens of falls from the upright position, symbolizing the dignity of man. Another form of this, which Beckett also uses, is when the author readily mutilates his characters. This is related to masochism and is, I think, significant of the time we live in. There is a play by Adamov, *La Grande et la Petite Manoeuvre*, in which there is a man who, every time he shows some sort of weakness, loses a limb so that finally, having begun the play hale and hearty, he is a limbless cripple in a wheel chair—who is then pushed in front of a truck. Here is a form of masochism by the author, but also of aggression against his own characters whom he treats mercilessly. Another form is the use of masks, such as Brecht employed. If you give characters masks you also dehumanize them—rather like Ionesco in *The Bald Prima Donna*—and depersonalize them and say quite openly, 'These characters are not human—they are monsters.' This is an aspect of violence that is, on the whole, peculiar to our time—

a dramatist turning with such savage aggression against his own creatures.

Thirdly, there is the provocation of violence in plays designed to stir the audience into an attitude of violence. This brings us into the wide area of political propaganda. We have all seen many examples of this in our time. It certainly applies to Nazi plays about Jews. I have never seen any of the plays, although many were performed, but I have seen some of the films. During the war, in a little cinema underneath the Admiralty, we used to be shown German films that had been taken off blockade runners. The interest was in the calculated use of psychological techniques to provoke the audience into violence. I remember a film called *Jew Süss*, which was about an eighteenth-century Jewish court favourite who dominated the land and was portrayed as a highly sexed devourer of the virgins of the country. The heroine was as pure as driven snow and very beautiful and her husband was a lovely man and a poet. The culminating scene showed the woman being brought before the Jew. He makes advances and is, of course, indignantly refused. Thereupon he opens a door to reveal her husband, who is on some kind of a rack. He tells her that every time he waves his handkerchief the screws will be tightened. She still says 'No,' so he waves and the husband screams—this goes on for several minutes with the screams getting more and more bloodcurdling until finally she surrenders, and then there is a rather pornographic sequence of her undressing. It then cuts very quickly to a picture of her, totally dishevelled and running like mad for the river, where she drowns herself. The extraordinary thing was that you could see, you could measure, the atmosphere in that cinema after the film was over. Everyone there was an upright, liberal anti-Nazi, but at that moment they all seemed to be wanting to go out and kill the first Jew they found. This kind of thing was, and still is, of course, the normal technique used in patriotic war films. It still is the recognized technique in Soviet Russia. There are many plays in which the wicked imperialists are raping or killing for the sake of money and so on. All this is extremely relevant to our theme because it is calculated to create a feeling of aggression in the audience. All propaganda machines employ this technique, it is not a monopoly of any one country.

Fourthly, the audience may be provoked into violence against the characters on the stage. This may sound an odd classification but it is, of course, the case in all comedy, in all farce. You laugh from a sense of superiority. You are enjoying the misfortunes of other people, even in farce when someone slips on a banana skin. There, I think, the laughter is definitely an expression of engineered violence in the audience against the characters on the stage. This is, from the Keystone Kops to the Whitehall farces, an aspect of comedy that one should always be aware of. I don't think it is a very bad one—it releases feelings of violence in people in a harmless way. But laughter in much knockabout comedy or farce is of this kind. It is the release of one's own fears that shows itself in this kind of violence.

Finally, there is the author's violence against the audience itself. To go back to Ionesco, when he wrote his first play, *The Bald Prima Donna*, he originally planned that at the end of the play 'some people would cry "shame," whereupon the manager would come and try to calm the audience, but the audience would go on shouting, whereupon the manager would call the police, who would arrive with a machine gun, set it up on the stage and kill the audience.' When it was pointed out to Ionesco that this was too expensive a way of mounting the play, his second ending was that the author would walk on to the stage and, while the audience was still applauding, shower them with abuse. The management weren't keen on this either, and so finally they decided not to have any ending at all; they just went back to the beginning of the play which is, in fact, how the play now ends. This is a very clear expression of the feelings that the artist often has towards his audience. And I think it is a great tribute to Ionesco that he is so honest about this. The temptation to have people come to the theatre and then to insult them is very

great. Genet, as Sartre points out, and as is quite obvious from
everything he has written, has exactly the same attitude. It
has even been argued that the whole of Genet's theatre is a
revenge that Genet, an outcast from society, has devised
against the bourgeoisie—he gets them into the theatre, makes
them pay, and then showers scatological abuse on them. Indeed, if you look up the ending of *The Balcony*, where a
world of total falsity and vile sexual fantasy has been shown,
you find the last speech urges the audience to go back to their
own homes where everything is much more false than anything they have seen in this theatre. These are quite clear
cases of aggression against the audience, and the fact that
these plays are so successful shows that there must be a strong
element of violent masochism in audiences.

Most kinds of aggression on the stage have a shock effect,
and one often hears people say, 'Oh well, they are cheap
effects if they are shocks.' I would say, and here we come to
the core of the whole problem, shock effects are part of the
artistic experience itself. Ionesco once gave a lecture in London in which he made a very interesting point that I'm sure
is correct, yet it has never been so clearly put: if a writer is to
have an impact, obviously he cannot have it by saying what
has been said before—he would then be merely a parrot, not
a creative writer—therefore what he says must surprise or
appear novel to the audience. But if it does, it must act as a
kind of shock. It must be something that makes them sit up.
And so we come finally to the position that in fact all art that
is alive, while it is alive, must have shock effect. And if you
look at the history of art, whether it is Ibsen or Wagner or
whatever, this is precisely the impression that it makes. We
come near to a point where you can say that anything that
makes an impact is a form of violence. Certainly in the
theatre violence is an integral part of any kind of artistic
effect. There is no effect that is not, in some form, violence.
Of course, if you have audiences who don't really want art
but merely somnolence—what Brecht called a 'culinary
theatre' that you can consume and excrete without its leaving

any trace inside you—then you don't have these effects, but you don't have art either.   *fuckwit*

When the great French ~~prophet~~ of a new kind of drama, Antonin Artaud, coined the term 'the Theatre of Cruelty', this is the point he was making: you can have two kinds of theatre—the nice, easy kind for tired businessmen, or the kind where shocks are administered to you. And he believed that to have any kind of artistic effect you must make the audience sit up and, if possible, undergo a really harrowing experience because art is essentially a waking-up, not a putting-to-sleep process. The whole concept of the Theatre of Cruelty has been so misinterpreted lately that it is perhaps worth considering who Artaud was and what he meant by it.

Artaud (1896–1948) was an astonishing genius, an eccentric, a poet, an actor, and a director, who also spent considerable periods of his life in mental institutions. The son of a Marseilles shipowner, he began to write poetry while he was still in his teens. At the age of twenty-two he had to go into a mental institution where he stayed for two years, suffering from bouts of melancholy and mystical exaltation. Released, he went to Paris, where Lugné-Poë, the great director of the Théâtre de l'Oeuvre, was so struck by the expressiveness of his features when he encountered Artaud in the street that he offered him a small part in one of his plays.

So Artaud became an actor. Charles Dullin, another great French actor and director of that period, and a great teacher of acting, took him under his wing, not only as an actor but also as a designer of scenery. Artaud also acted in films: no real film lover will ever forget his ascetic face in the part of the monk who comes to confess the maid in Carl Dreyer's famous *La Passion de Jeanne d'Arc*, or in Abel Gance's *Napoleon* (in which, strangely enough, he played the part of Marat).

In 1924 Artaud became a member of the surrealist circle around André Breton, but broke his connection with this group in 1927, when Breton savagely attacked him for the sin of having contemplated something so sordidly commercial as starting a theatre. He went ahead with his stage project and ran for a time, together with Roger Vitrac, a venture called Théâtre Alfred Jarry (named after that grandfather of all modern avant-garde drama, the creator of the bourgeois caricature, King Ubu). This venture ending in failure, he supported himself as an actor, poet, and essayist.

His original output as a dramatist always remained small, for Artaud was a theoretician rather than a playwright. In 1931, at the Paris Colonial Exhibition, he saw a performance of Balinese dancers with their highly stylized ritual movements and strange music. This was a decisive influence on his thinking. From it there emerged the theory and doctrine of the Theatre of Cruelty which he developed in a number of essays and manifestoes published between 1932 and 1935. Having found some financial backing, he finally got his chance to demonstrate his ideas in practice: under the heading of Theatre of Cruelty, he staged his own production of *The Cenci*, a tragedy based on Shelley's play and Stendhal's story about the Roman patrician girl who was raped by her own father and murdered him in revenge. Artaud himself played the part of the father when this production opened on 6 May 1935 at the Théâtre des Folies-Wagram in Paris.

Of the phrase 'Theatre of Cruelty' Artaud has this to say:

> This Cruelty has nothing to do with Sadism or Blood. . . . I do not cultivate horror for its own sake. The term Cruelty must be understood in its widest sense, not in the material and rapacious sense which it is usually given. In doing so I claim the right of breaking the usual meaning of language . . . to return at last to the etymological origins of language which through abstract concepts always finally evoke concrete things. One can very well imagine a pure cruelty, without physical disruption. And, speaking in philosophical terms, what *is* cruelty? Spiritually cruelty means rigour, implacable application and decisiveness in an action, irreversible, absolute determination.
>
> It is wrong to give the word Cruelty a sense of bloody severity, of the pointless and disinterested pursuit of physical suffering. . . . There is in the exercise of cruelty a sort of

determinism of a higher order, to which the executer is himself subject. . . . Cruelty is, above all, lucid, a kind of rigid directedness, a submission to necessity. There is no Cruelty without consciousness, without a kind of applied consciousnesss. It is this which gives to each act of life its bloodcolour, its cruel nuance, because it is understood that Life is always the Death of someone.

Elsewhere Artaud added: 'The erotic Desire is Cruelty, because it burns of necessity; Death is Cruelty, the Resurrection is Cruelty, Transfiguration is Cruelty.' In other words, Artaud, who passed through phases of intense religious experience in the course of his stormy life, regarded Christ on the Cross and the re-enactment of the Last Supper in the Eucharist as supreme examples of what he understood by a Theatre of Cruelty. This surely is a far cry from the current practice of using Artaud's term to describe any play in which someone has his head bashed in.

Moreover, Artaud had very definite ideas about the *forms*, the artistic means he wanted to employ in his Theatre of Cruelty. Deeply influenced by oriental theatre, particularly by Balinese dancers and the rituals of Mexican Indians, he called for a return to magical devices in décor and sound effects, a hieratic poise in the actors, a delivery of the lines in an incantatory tone reminiscent of priests rather than naturalistic acting, and ultimately an abolition of the separation between actors and audience by placing the spectacle among the spectators themselves. The cruelty Artaud called for was thus tantamount to the demand that theatregoers should go through an experience that really *changed their lives* rather than a mere act of consumption.

Artaud's attempt to demonstrate his ideas in *The Cenci* proved a dismal failure, artistic as well as financial. Deeply disappointed and shaken, he embarked on a journey to Mexico, where he had been invited to lecture at the University of Mexico and where he wanted to study the life and rituals of an Indian tribe, the Tarahumara. When he returned to France in November 1936 he was at the end of his tether and behaved very strangely, brandishing a walking stick which he claimed had been St Patrick's own magical cane.

This led to a trip to Ireland, where he planned to study the magic of the Druids. Feeling ill and miserable, he tried to find help in a convent of French nuns in Dublin, but his intentions were misunderstood and he ended up in prison and was finally put aboard a ship to be taken back to France. After trying to jump into the sea, he continued to deteriorate and spent the years till 1946 in a succession of asylums. On his release he became the centre of a circle of admirers in Paris, gave some much-debated lectures, exhibited drawings, and recorded a radio programme which was eventually banned by the French authorities. On 4 March 1948 he died, aged fifty-two.

Artaud's influence on the French theatre has been, and still remains, immense. His book of collected essays, *The Theatre and Its Double* (the theatre's double being life itself), first published in 1938, remains the bible of the avant garde. Eugène Ionesco and Arthur Adamov among others were deeply affected by Artaud's ideas.

The methods used to achieve Artaud's ends are infinite, and they can be very drastic. The shock effects in Artaud's own work, for example, are violent colours and harsh sounds, but they can be simply that unexpected things happen. Artaud's friend Vitrac produced a marvellous shock effect in his play *Victor* by having a most exquisite and beautifully dressed lady walk on to the stage suffering from a terrible misfortune—she cannot contain her tendency to fart.

Another form of aggression quite near to this, which is also very prevalent, is the use of effects that the audience cannot help but become physically involved in. Obvious among these are pornographic or strongly erotic effects. Most of our modern theatre and particularly the *kitsch* theatre of television employs this form.

There is in the modern theatre, and in the theory behind it, a debate about this kind of effect. Should there be a direct assault upon the audience in hypnotic terms, or should one seek the non-identification of the audience with the characters in Brecht's sense, that is, the audience's aloofness and coolness? There is an interesting paradox in this. Because Brecht was a puritan at heart, he detested all forms of audience identification. Anything that increased the attention of the audience to such a degree that they lost the capacity to detach themselves from the characters he regarded as indecent, obscene. In a passage in his *Little Organon for the Theatre* he says that the most obscene sight you can see is to look at the audience and find everybody, as it were, totally disembodied, vicariously living through the experiences of the characters on the stage. Brecht believed that audiences should be protected against this because this was a form of aggression against them. So he evolved his theory of alienation—that you should keep the audience from identifying by constantly assuring them that what they see is not real. In that sense all effects that make you lose your sense of separateness and merge your experience with that of the characters are a form of violence—an aggression. The paradox is this: in order to prevent the natural tendency towards identification, which is a psychological archetype (you can't escape from it; if you watch a football match you are vicariously kicking the ball) Brecht used other forms of aggression against the audience. The devices used to snap the audience out of any normal tendency to get involved had to have a certain shock effect. This brings us back to the point that any genuine artistic approach involves a very considerable amount of aggression, violence, and shock in the audience.

What is involved in violence? What is its true nature? If I hit someone on the head, what have I done? I have deprived him of his autonomy as a human being—he wanted to go this way and I've knocked him that way. This seems to me the real essence of a genuinely violent act. Violence consists in depriving a person of his autonomy and of his freedom of choice. In this sense a good deal of the violence that is being used is, in fact, not true violence. It may be short-term violence, but it is not long-term violence. If Brecht counteracts the tendency towards identification he is stopping you from going in a certain direction. He puts a hand in front of you and says 'Stop!' In that sense he has used a short-term violence against you. But as his ultimate purpose, at least if you believe him, is to keep you free to come to your own conclusions about the situation, then in fact he is not using violence because he is trying to preserve your autonomy as an individual. On the other hand, the strip-tease artist or the political propagandist who is pushing you in a certain direction is perpetrating an act of real aggression because he is depriving you of your autonomy, of your free choice, and forcing you to act in a certain way. If the audience coming out of *Jew Süss* were, before they went in, harmless house-wives who then went home and said, 'We should kill all Jews', they had been turned into automata, into slaves of the manipulator who manipulated their psychological responses. To my mind this is the distinction between the legitimate and the illegitimate use of violence in the theatre.

If violence is used to heighten your sense of awareness of the world in such a way that the shock that has been administered to you makes you *more* capable of evaluating the reality of the situation you are in, then this violence has been rightly used and is ethically defensible. If the violence deprives you of your autonomy, forces you to act in ways that you would not otherwise want to, it is illegitimate. If Ionesco walks on to the stage and calls the audience '*Salauds*' it is a good thing because it might make them look a little closer at themselves to see if there could be any truth in it—particularly as the play that preceded it has exemplified all the faults of a conventional bourgeois way of life. This violence has been used to wake people up and has increased their sense of autonomy rather than decreased it. If, on the other hand, we are using empty forms of art in order to administer sedatives or sleeping pills, then we are in fact depriving people of their autonomy and committing an act of bad and reprehensible aggression. The most aggressive theatre is the one that has this kind of effect and covers up and prettifies the human situation—that pours a chocolate sauce of content-ment and complacency over people's lives. In that sense the most aggressive and the most immoral theatre is the ordinary entertainment theatre and the theatre of television and, up to a point, radio. This to my mind is the ultimate immoral use of violence.

In our particular situation we are faced with an age of mass media allowing the manipulation of human responses. Art, I think, being man's attempt to increase awareness of his own situation, has therefore the duty to shock people out of this. And if you look at the theatre as it is today the camps divide. On the one hand you have those artists who, however aggressive and violent and bitter their lesson may sound, try to shock people into a genuine awareness of reality. On the other hand you have the vast apparatus of mass media using the outward forms of art for a form of hypnosis, which is, in fact, a denial of art. And this is the form of violence that I most deplore.

Nudity: Barely the Beginning?

At the highly respectable, not to say staid, Shakespeare Memorial Theatre at Stratford-on-Avon in 1968, history was made when, in Marlowe's *Doctor Faustus*, the audience was shown not only the face that launched a thousand ships but the breasts and buttocks as well. This vision of Helen of Troy appeared clothed only in a tiara.

More and more, nudity seems to be invading the theatre in our time. Is that a good thing or a bad thing for art? Is it a symptom of declining morals? A sign of social decadence? One might well ask these questions, for one thing is certain: the new permissiveness in the theatre is a significant development.

Of course, there has always been nudity in the theatre. The art of stripping is one of the liveliest and oldest of folk arts. But it used to be confined to burlesque houses. What we have now is nudity in 'artistically serious' drama: be it the nude scene in an avant-garde musical like *Hair* or the nearly forty-five minutes that Sally Kirkland was nude in Terrence McNally's off-Broadway play, *Sweet Eros*. Off-Broadway, there was also Rochelle Owens's *Futz* and another play by Miss Owens, *Belch*, with infinite expanses of skin. In London, there were the nude *males* in John Herbert's play about homosexuality in a prison, *Fortune and Men's Eyes*.

In trying to assess the significance of all this, we must clear our mind of some widespread misconceptions. Above all: the naked human body on a stage is *not* in itself erotically stimulating. On the contrary, anybody who has visited a nudist colony knows that complete nakedness, particularly in the mass, is positively anti-erotic in effect. The nude scene in

Hair, for example, is *touching* rather than titillating; it reveals the vulnerability, the helplessness of the young people in the play, and arouses compassion rather than lust.

Nudity *can* be made stimulating, but then the whole trend of the play must work towards it, by creating a *situation* in which the nude body will appear as the culmination of erotic fantasy and desire. But once all this effort to build up a situation of this kind has been expended, the effect would be just as erotic, indeed more erotic, if the man or woman in question were *not* completely nude.

Indeed, partial nudity, by setting off the audience's imagination, can be more stimulating than complete nakedness. I firmly believe that the strong taboo against complete nudity on the stage, which is now in the process of crumbling, was based more on the audience's embarrassment, its fear of witnessing the confusion and shame of performers on the stage, than on any real fear that nudity would overexcite the spectators. To see an actress who looks beautiful in a lovely costume revealed as spindly legged or otherwise imperfect in figure is, after all, as embarrassing as seeing her forget her lines, or slipping on a banana skin during a sentimental scene. And the same is even more true of male performers: a pot-bellied hero would be ridiculous. How many good actors are there who could withstand that kind of ordeal?

What is it, then, that seems now to have weakened these resistances and taboos? Undoubtedly, the complete disappearance of legal restraints on the frank discussion and description of sexual matters in literature has been a decisive factor. If one can *read* all the physical and anatomical details on love affairs in books like *My Secret Life* or John Updike's *Couples*, it clearly becomes rather silly not to have them enacted or presented on the stage as well. Moreover, in the age of the bikini and the topless waitress, life itself has preceded the theatre. Nudity, or near-nudity, has become commonplace. We have become inured to nude scenes in the cinema, in advertisements, in magazines. Why should, how *could*, the theatre lag behind? It was only the lingering after-effect of puritanism, which always regarded the live theatre with special fear and surrounded it with especially severe legislation in the Anglo-Saxon countries, that could possibly have delayed the blossoming of nudity on stage as long as it has.

And now that the inhibition seems to be going, what effect will it have on the art of drama? My guess would be: not much. The theatre has always contained a strong and healthy element of exhibitionism and voyeurism. We simply would not go to the theatre if we did not have a desire to see beautiful human beings in the flesh. Beautiful people alluringly dressed never left much to the imagination. To see them in the nude will not give us much more beyond informing us of the exact shade of the colour of their pubic hair. And this, in some cases, might be disillusioning.

And what about the sexual act? Kenneth Tynan was asked some time ago whether he would allow intercourse to be performed on stage. And he quite correctly replied: Yes, if it were artistically necessary. What he forgot to mention is, of course, that the sexual act *has* often been shown on stage. Take the bedroom scene in *Romeo and Juliet* where the lovers discuss whether the bird they heard was the nightingale or the lark. They are in bed, we know that it is their marriage night. What difference does it make that we are not actually getting the physical aspect of the act in close-up? Seeing it would add nothing to the erotic atmosphere of the scene; on the contrary, it might destroy the illusion. And that is just one example: how many Feydeau farces are there where people are seen in bed! The actual physical detail, here too, is unimportant.

Where the enactment of sex *does* have a value is precisely in plays like Michael McClure's *The Beard*, which played to full houses in London. Here it is not the sexual act, but the *unorthodox* sexual act—cunnilingus—which matters. The public display of a practice that many members of the audience indulge in themselves, but which they regard as deviant or especially sinful, must have a reassuring effect. If it can be shown publicly, it may not be quite as horrifically sinful as they had, in their tortured minds, believed it to be.

This also is the attraction—and therapeutic value—of the present spate of plays about homosexuality. If art can relieve guilt feelings, can relieve a sense of belonging to an outcast minority, this, in my opinion, is wholly to the good. For that, after all, is what art is about: to make us aware of the common humanity that unites us all, to establish genuine communication between human beings at the deepest level, that of shared emotion.

So, ultimately, the appearance of nudity on the stage in serious drama is merely one, and a fairly belated, symptom of the sexual revolution of our time—which may well be a revolution as important and decisive as any political or social revolution of past ages.

It is, after all, not the wickedness of the times that has led to a situation like the present confused state of permissiveness mixed up with remnants of puritanism, but rather the breakdown of the iron rules of the past (which, incidentally, were always more honoured in the breach than the observance). Modern psychology, modern medical knowledge, the rise of science, the loss of faith in rigid ethical rules of all kinds—these are the real causes of the crumbling of ancient taboos.

What is needed is a new, humane, enlightened, rational system of sexual ethics, without fear of hell-fire, without guilt and shame. To evolve such a code we need, above all, free discussion and the maximum of knowledge. The various experiments of the artists, whether writers, painters, actors or directors, must be seen as attempts—however modest, however foolish, however misguided, however adolescent they may appear—towards that surely very necessary and desirable end.

The Theatre of the Absurd
Reconsidered

Having, to coin a phrase, 'coined a phrase', I am in two minds about whether I should feel a thrill of pride every time I read a reference to the Theatre of the Absurd in a newspaper or a book, or whether I should not rather hide my head in shame; for what I intended as a generic concept, a working hypothesis for the understanding of a large number of extremely varied and elusive phenomena, has assumed for many people, including some drama critics, a reality as concrete and specific as a branded product of the detergent industry.

When I wrote my book I had been struck by the fact that the work of dramatists writing quite independently of one another in different countries had certain fundamental features in common. I was excited and moved by writers like Beckett, Ionesco, and Harold Pinter. So I thought it would be useful to isolate and describe what was the common factor that made their plays so difficult to follow. Shortly after the book was published, the very different and individual writers were immediately asked by officious journalists, 'Do you agree with Martin Esslin that you belong to the school of the Theatre of the Absurd?' Which is an absurd question. You might as well ask an African tribesman who carves masks whether he agrees that he is a member of the cubist school. Neither the primitive sculptor nor the most sophisticated modern playwright is, in his creative activity, concerned with anything but his own vision, his own impulse.

A concept like the Theatre of the Absurd concentrates on certain important elements in individual works containing a multitude of other elements that make them, in other

respects, quite different from one another. It is a basic mistake
to assume that all the works that somehow come under this
label are the same, or even very similar; and it is nonsense to
try to attach a value judgment to the whole category. If the
common factor among the absurdists were an ideology, then
the category could be rejected en bloc. If one disagrees with
Stalinism, one can reject all art that embodies strictly Stalin-
ist precepts. But—and I thought I went to great lengths in
my book to make this clear—what these writers express is
not an ideological position but rather their bewilderment at
the absence of a coherent and generally accepted integrating
principle, ideology, ethical system, call it what you will, in
our world. And the lack of such a unifying force, an individual's sense that it is lacking, is not an ideological position;
it is a matter of fact. If Ionesco feels unsatisfied by Catholicism or Communism or any other ism, that is his own very
personal affair which is not really susceptible to argument.
As it happens, one writer covered in *The Theatre of the
Absurd*, Adamov, in the course of his development has
managed to find a firm ideological foundation for his work—
and has therefore ceased to come under the heading of the
Absurd.

What is far more important to the concept of the Theatre
of the Absurd is the *form* in which this sense of bewilderment and mystery expresses itself: the devaluation or even
downright dissolution of language, the disintegration of plot,
characterization, and final solution which had hitherto been
the hallmark of drama, and the substitution of new elements
of form—concrete stage imagery, repetition or intensification,
a whole new stage language.

Innovations in form can be judged only in particular contexts. It would be silly to say that the five-act play is a better
form than the three- or one-act play, that the circle is a more
satisfying shape than the square. The Theatre of the Absurd
is above all a new form of the theatre that says some very
important things about our time. And what it says is not
necessarily, as is sometimes claimed, totally nihilistic, totally

negative. As I have tried to point out in my book, the recognition that there is no simple explanation for all the mysteries of the world, that all previous systems have been oversimplified and therefore were bound to fail, will appear to be a source of despair only to those who still feel that such a simplified system *can* provide an answer. The moment we realize that we may have to live without any final truths the situation changes; we may have to readjust ourselves to living with less exalted aims and by doing so become more humble, more receptive, less exposed to violent disappointments and crises of conscience—and therefore in the last resort happier and better-adjusted people, simply because we then live in closer accord with reality.

This open world view, humble and without preconceived notions, is, as I tried to point out in the last chapter of my book, complementary to the scientific attitude—science concentrates on the area of light about nature and the world, which it tries to extend by patient probing; the attitude of the artists of the Theatre of the Absurd concentrates on the area of darkness that surrounds the patch of light of science. To be well adjusted to reality we have to be as aware of the one as of the other.

I am often asked whether I agree with those who say that the Theatre of the Absurd has now said what it could say and that drama will henceforth develop in other directions. What I feel is that the writers I have grouped in that category have developed a whole new vocabulary of theatrical forms that has enriched the stage's possibilities of expression immensely and added a new dimension to the art of the theatre. The innovations and new devices introduced by the absurdists will, I am convinced, continue to be used and will eventually be absorbed into the mainstream of the tradition.

Which are the innovations of the absurdists, the new modes they have contributed to the vocabulary and syntax of the theatre? Above all they have demonstrated that poetry in the theatre is not merely a matter of language but that the theatre itself is a form of poetry: concretized metaphor, complex imagery on multiple planes of meaning and association, from the most earthily concrete to the most esoterically abstract.

To illustrate what I mean, in *The Theatre of the Absurd* I described the reaction of the convicts of San Quentin to a performance of *Waiting for Godot* by Herbert Blau's and Jules Irving's Theatre Workshop: they unhesitatingly interpreted Godot as the freedom they were waiting for. At a meeting of theatre personalities from east and west of the Iron Curtain held in Vienna in March 1965 Jean Duvignaud, the French critic who used to teach at Tunis, reported on a performance of *Waiting for Godot* in Algeria when that country was still a French possession: the audience of landless fellaheen had no doubt that Godot referred to the long-awaited but never forthcoming distribution of land to the peasants. A Polish delegate countered by pointing out that in Warsaw in 1956 the same play had been enthusiastically received as a parable of the ever promised but never forthcoming national independence of Poland from the Russians. Everyone knows the interpretation according to which Godot stands for salvation in a Christian sense. How can all these totally contradictory interpretations be true? asked some literal-minded participant in Vienna.

The answer, of course, is that the play is so powerful a poetic metaphor, so archetypal an image, that all these interpretations are not only equally acceptable, they all equally *impose* themselves; the play provides an existential reconstruction of one of the basic human emotions and situations—it is a poetic image of the *act of waiting* itself. No wonder everyone immediately thinks of whatever it is that he has been vainly waiting for in his own personal, spiritual, or political life. Of course, the theatre has always been able to provide such basic poetic archetypes: the encounter of Romeo and Juliet stands as an image of all nascent love, Lear's lonely ravings on the storm-tossed heath for all the loss of aging and death. It is the special achievement of the absurdists, however, to have demonstrated that such archetypal images need not be accidental by-products of conventional plot but are capable of being put on the stage as the very centre and essence of a play; that the poetic image is not just an illustration but the centre of the dramatic experience. In doing so they have liberated the stage from the tedious and long-winded necessities of conventional exposition and the even more tedious tying up of plots at the end of plays. Just as lyrical poetry is far more compressed and economical a form than the realistic novel, a poetic theatre of this kind is far more compressed and economical of time than a naturalistic theatre.

The absurdists have further demonstrated the theatre's ability to deal not only with external reality in providing a a concrete and photographically correct reconstruction of real life but also, and much more interestingly, with the vast field of *internal* reality—the fantasies, dreams, hallucinations, secret longings, and fears of mankind. This too represents an eruption of the poetical into the theatre in both subject matter and technique: archetypal situations in associative sequence, rather than strictly photographic situations in rigidly chronological order. Here again the absurdists have merely enlarged a long-established practice: the ghosts of Hamlet's father, Banquo and Caesar, to name but the most obvious examples, also concretize inner visions of the Prince of Denmark, Macbeth, and Brutus. What the absurdists have done is liberate this kind of internal reality from the necessity of having to emerge from an external plot situation with neat transitions from reality to dream, from nature to hallucination.

The Theatre of the Absurd, having conditioned audiences to accept happenings on the stage as expressions of internal, psychic reality, has added an additional element of suspense to the theatre: the action can now often be seen *both* as reality and as dream, as natural and as hallucinatory at one and the same time, an ambivalence and ambiguity that is in itself of the essence of poetry. Hamm and Clov in *Endgame*, for example, are acceptable as human beings living in a kind of science-fiction reality of a post catastrophic age; they can at the same time be regarded as archetypes, components of a single dreamer's mind. In Harold Pinter's theatre the external reality of the characters in plays like *The Caretaker* and *The Homecoming* is completely convincing, their speech almost terrifyingly real. Yet at the same time *The Caretaker* works most forcefully as a dream, a myth of the expulsion of the Father by the Sons, while in *The Homecoming* the weird situation of a father and two younger brothers turning the elder brother's wife into a prostitute is presented in such a way that the play can be seen both as a completely realistic piece of near pornography and as a dramatization of the archetype of the sons' dream of taking over a mother image as an object of sexual enjoyment (the elder brother then appears as a reduplication of the father image, his wife as a reduplication of the mother—and here Pinter has brilliantly suggested that the dead mother in the play may also have been a prostitute, while the elder brother's wife, like the mother, is shown as having three sons, and the play ends with the old father begging the reincarnation of his wife for some scraps of her sexual favours now bestowed upon the two younger sons). In this kind of theatre reality co-exists with myth, the audience can experience the mythical character of reality as well as the reality of mythical situations.

Another important achievement of the absurdists has been the destruction of the concept of drama as no more than another literary form: they have re-emphasized the *physical* nature of the theatre, its intimate links with ballet, slapstick, acrobatics, and the magical physical actions of ritual. In some senses this has amounted to a *devaluation* of language; it has enabled the playwright to use inarticulate sounds, meaningless clichés, or language that is openly belied by the action. It can also be argued that this has made language more rather than less important in the theatre. After all in lyrical poetry, too, language is freed from the dry utilitarian function of merely conveying factual information. By placing the main burden of the action on the physical happenings on the stage, the absurdists have increased the *poetical* potential of language in the theatre; its rhythm, sound, tonal quality again become important autonomous elements.

Precisely because the action in *Waiting for Godot* consists in the absence of anything happening and because the dialogue has been freed from any storytelling function, we are enabled to see the language in Beckett's masterpiece as an infinitely rich symphony of poetic sound and subtly varied rhythmical patterns. Yet these poetic patterns and rhythms are not just arias or superimposed ornamentation, they *are* the patterns and rhythms of the action of the play itself. The same applies, *mutatis mutandis*, to such poetic masterpieces as Genet's *The Blacks*, Ionesco's *The Chairs*, Pinter's *The Dumb Waiter*, or—to take an example from a completely different sphere—Tadeusz Rozewicz's brilliant play *The Witnesses*, in which the horror of our time is expressed by such devices as a dialogue between a married couple, in the whimsically bantering tones of cheap romantic love fiction, from which it gradually emerges that they are watching a kitten being brutally blinded and buried alive by children outside their window. Once again the language is not just a straight expression of the content it relates, it is in a dialectical relationship to that content and emphasizes its horror by seemingly denying it.

It may appear paradoxical but is nevertheless true that the absurdists have also greatly re-emphasized the *importance of form* in the theatre. One frequently finds the notion that the Theatre of the Absurd has made the craft of playwriting too easy by allowing anyone to turn the most spontaneous and formless whims of his imagination into drama. This conception is on a par with the idea that expressionist and abstract painting is on the level of the childish scribblings of infants and equally easy. On the contrary, the greater the fluidity of the subject matter, the more associative rather than chronological the sequence of events in a play, the *greater* becomes the need for formal control, for shape and structure. This is again analogous to the case of lyrical poetry where ideas and images are presented in a non-narrative, associative pattern and devices such as rhyme, rhythm, and fixed patterns of repetition impose themselves. In a novel or short story it is the chronology and logical sequence of events that enables the reader to keep pace with the contents; in a poem it is the formal pattern that serves this purpose by arranging the imagery in an aesthetically satisfying order. Exactly the same is the case in a theatre of concretized poetic images in associative sequence. An examination of any of the really successful works of the Theatre of the Absurd will confirm this rule: the symmetry of Acts I and II of *Waiting for Godot*, the rigid ritual structure of *The Blacks*, the movement from repose to paroxysm and back to repose in *The Bald Prima Donna*, the inexorable accumulation of empty chairs in *The Chairs*, the strophic form of the duologues in *The Dumb Waiter*, are cases in point. Each play of this type has to find its *own*, rigidly formal pattern, which must inevitably arise from and express the *basic conception* of the play. Much of the tension and suspense in this kind of drama lies in the gradual unfolding of its formal pattern. Hence its formal pattern must embody the very essence of the action. And so, in the Theatre of the Absurd, form and content not only match, they are inseparable from each other.

In its rebellion agaainst the naturalistic convention the Theatre of the Absurd entered the consciousness of its audiences as an *anti*-theatre, a completely new beginning, a total breach with the conventions of the past. Now that the first and delicious shock effects have worn off, we can see that the absurdists merely emphasized hitherto neglected aspects, stressed some forgotten technical devices, and discarded some unduly inflated aspects of a long-existing tradition of drama. Far from being anti-theatre, they were in the very centre of the mainstream of its development, just as revolutionary movements of the past—Ibsen, Strindberg, Shaw, or the Expressionists—that were regarded as the grave-diggers of tradition can now be seen as its main and decisive representatives. Indeed, seen from the vantage point of today, it is the brief episode of photographic realism in the theatre that stands out as a deviation from the mainstream of the development of drama. It is the achievement of the Absurdists together with the Brechtians to have brought the theatre back to the full richness of its traditional vocabulary, to have freed it from the narrow restrictionism of pretending to be reality observed through a missing fourth wall, which made it impossible for actors to be aware of and to address their audience, forbade them to reveal their inner lives directly through monologue, confined them in the strait-jacket of the actual time of action (with endless pouring out of coffee and lighting of cigarettes) and banished all the delicious world of the dreamlike, the supernatural, and its stage machinery from the theatre.

Epic Theatre, the Absurd and the Future

Today's vanguard of drama has more than just one spear-head. In the Anglo-Saxon countries and in France one wing of the avant garde represents a trend that goes back to the early 1930s and Brecht's epic theatre, which could make its full impact felt only after the downfall of Hitler (whose accession to power thirty years ago put an end to any creative experiment in Germany). The other main wing of today's avant garde, the Theatre of the Absurd, is the culmination of a movement that, in surrealist painting or in the writings of Kafka and Joyce, reaches back into the 1920s. In Britain some years ago the avant garde also included the practitioners of a neo-naturalistic school whose main achievement, though it appeared revolutionary in a British context, was to have introduced working- and lower-middle-class vernaculars on to a stage that had hitherto been mainly reserved for a stylized upper-middle-class idiom. But this was an achieve-ment the naturalists in Germany and France had accom-plished sixty years ago, and that, in the United States, might be dated from O'Neill's *The Hairy Ape*, written in 1921. In France a turning toward poetic drama, which had petered out in Britain in spite of some successful work by Christopher Fry and T. S. Eliot, still shows signs of vitality in the works of writers like Shehadé or Pichette, but is probably not strong enough to constitute a trend. So, after all, we are left with just two main spearheads of today's avant garde: a socially committed, left-wing, epic theatre on the one hand, and an introspective, non-political, grotesque drama on the other.

In France, where the logical implications of issues are always faced most boldly, these two wings of today's avant garde of drama are engaged in intermittent but nonetheless explosive polemics. The Brechtians in their organ, the lively periodical *Théâtre Populaire*, violently attack the exponents of the Theatre of the Absurd whose main spokesman, Ionesco, counterattacks from every possible platform, including that of his own plays. The point at issue between the contending parties concerns the validity of the claim each makes to be truly avant-garde, truly non-conformist, truly anti-bourgeois. The Brechtians reproach Ionesco and those who write in a similar vein that their work is iconoclastic and anti-bourgeois in appearance only: the bourgeoisie is presented as a collection of puppets spouting fossilized clichés; man is shown as threatened by isolation, cut off from his fellow beings by the difficulties of communication; action is futile, the human condition is irremediable. But, if the caricature of the bourgeoisie appears savage, the very pessimism of the general outlook of the plays of the Theatre of the Absurd (so the followers of Brecht contend) also makes any effective action against the bourgeoisie and its atrophied way of life pointless. Hence, in the end, the bourgeoisie is left undisturbed. This is why, it is argued, the plays of the Theatre of the Absurd have become commercial successes with bourgeois audiences; they give them the illusion of having undergone a process of ruthless self-examination without requiring them to do anything about their own shortcomings.

Ionesco's counterattack against these arguments, on the other hand, maintains that the anti-bourgeois attitude of the political left in the theatre represents a conformism every whit as deadly as that of the bourgeoisie, based as it is on collective virtues that are indistinguishable from the patriotic and moral virtues of the middle class. Ionesco argues that true art cannot merely serve as a vehicle for the propagation of political, social, or, for that matter, philosophical theories (as do the plays of Sartre) because, by definition, a work of art is self-explanatory, self-contained, and the perfect expression of itself. It cannot therefore be a mere statement of theories or ideologies that are already in existence and thus *must* have been more adequately expressed already. Art can communicate only individual experience and therefore cannot serve as a vehicle for collective plans of action.

It is significant that this debate, which has been waged with a great expenditure of energy and hot tempers, never really touches on questions of *artistic method* and remains almost wholly confined to the *aims* and *purposes* of theatre and their ideological implications. And, on the whole, I believe this concentration on questions of ideology has tended to create the not entirely accurate impression that there are also great and insuperable differences in artistic method. Of course it is quite true that the political left demands, and up to a point practises, realism and shuns the fantastical and irrational, while the writers grouped under the heading of the Theatre of the Absurd allow surreal elements to intrude into their work. Yet it is my contention that, far from being contradictory and mutually exclusive methods, these two styles are complementary and could well be fused in the future. And it is here that I see at least a possibility for a new and exciting step forward for the avant garde of drama.

In any case these two movements have a great deal in common. It is no coincidence that Brecht's starting point lay in very close proximity to that of the German Dadaists, that some of his early plays are in the direct line of development towards Beckett and Ionesco, or that a playwright like Adamov developed from the Absurd towards Brechtian realism. Moreover, isn't it striking that Brechtian realism itself is anything but identical with the naturalistic realism of a Chekhov or Stanislavsky? Brecht's theatre contains elements of Expressionism (a deliberate heightening of emphasis in the interests of didactic purpose, the insertion of songs and comment on the action) and the grotesque (Hitler and his minions conceived as gigantic marionettes in *Arturo Ui* are near neighbours to the bourgeois marionettes of *The Bald Prima Donna*, to give but one example out of so many). Brechtian realism makes use of clowning and those broad comic effects that the Theatre of the Absurd derives from the silent film and the music hall (the wedding scene in *The Caucasian Chalk Circle*). Admittedly, on a deeper level, the difference in approach is very great, for Brecht and his followers use all these devices in order to depict a social, *external reality*, whereas the Theatre of the Absurd is mainly concerned with the outward projection of a *psychological reality*; in the Brechtian theatre the main emphasis is on the play as *narrative*; in the Theatre of the Absurd the main stress is on the play as a *poetic image*. But, great as these differences in approach may be, they are not mutually exclusive. External and internal reality are, after all, merely different aspects of the same reality; there is no reason why a playwright should not move from one to the other within the same play, as, indeed, Brecht himself has done in a minor but important work, *The Visions of Simone Machard*, where the same set of characters appears both in cold daylight and in the fantasies of the patriotic little French girl. In this play Brecht indicates the dream atmosphere by his use of language: Simone hears her figures of fantasy speak an idiom that sounds like intelligible speech but is, in fact, nonsensical.

Realism and the absurd are fused in a different way in the work of so professed a follower of Beckett and Kafka as Harold Pinter. Here it is the exactness of the transcription of the speech of ordinary people that brings the dialogue from the utmost realism into the realm of nonsensical gibberish, simply because real people, particularly those who are unlettered and inarticulate, do speak a language devoid of logic, grammar, and sense. This, in Pinter's case, applies to his plots as well where the strictest application of realism produces a feeling of the fantastic and the absurd. The real events we watch are bound to be far more puzzling, mysterious, and obscure than the well-constructed plots of what had hitherto been regarded as the most naturalistic plays in today's modern theatre. The more rigorously we exclude the interpretative patterns that our own minds impose on reality, the more genuinely we concentrate on reality itself, the more illogical and dreamlike it tends to become, the more arbitrary, the more *absurd*. The dividing line between the external and the internal (psychological) aspects of reality itself will thus gradually dissolve; for, as in physics so in the observation of ordinary life, the presence of an observer is itself part of the reality the observer wants to observe and cannot, therefore, be validly excluded. All art is reality seen through a human temperament; in the theatre, which inevitably gives the illusion of an objective representation of a three-dimensional reality, this fact may be overlooked, but it is present nevertheless. And in so openly subjective a picture of the world as that presented by the Theatre of the Absurd, it is at least freely admitted rather than concealed by implication, as it is in a seemingly 'objective' theatre. Professed subjectivity may thus be both more honest and more true to reality than apparent objectivity. If the Brechtian theatre in its external realism and the Theatre of the Absurd in its subjective realism each depict merely one half of reality, could not a fusion of both styles around an attempt to comprehend both sides of the coin represent a higher stage in the age-old attempt of the theatre to find a satisfactory solution to the problem of depicting reality?

The starting point for such a development is indeed more than favourable. Both wings of the avant garde are agreed in their negative purpose—the destruction of the shackles of the naturalistic conventions that imposed on the stage limitations almost as stringent as the three unities of French classical drama. Any theatre that springs from a fusion of the epic and the absurd will be a *liberated* theatre in the sense of the word in which Tairov, one of its first pioneers, used that term; a theatre in which no holds are barred and in which everything is possible; where realistic décor can alternate with the most fantastic, verse with prose, spoken dialogue with song, musical numbers, and even mime; where the audience can be kept at a distance or drawn into the action, etc.

The far greater potential realism of the mass media logically forces the theatre to fall back on to ground where the

Such then is the outline of the theatre that might emerge
from a fusion of the two main wings of the dramatic avant
garde of our time: a fluid, theatrical kind of drama that uses
the stage with the utmost freedom and is able to move from
realism to a heightened expressionist, stylized version of
external reality, and from there to an internal reality of introspection, dream, nightmare, and obsession; a theatre that
would be able to combine direct statement and direct address
to the audience with all the Brechtian techniques of *distantia-
tion*; a theatre that would rely on the poetry of the stage
image as much as on the freest possible use of language—
from the verbal brilliance of a Harold Pinter or a Beckett to
the total breakdown of language in some of Ionesco's most
impressive works; a theatre that would be able to range from
the most tender to the most grotesque, but that, in its essence,
would always, basically, remain tragicomic.

But is such a forecast not merely a hodge-podge made up of
a mechanical summation of the characteristics of some of the
most interesting contemporary dramatists rather than a
feasible, practical call for possible future action? Are the in-
gredients not mutually incompatible and, therefore, is not
any attempt to mix them foredoomed to ridiculous failure?

I should like, in all humility, to suggest that, provided playwrights bold enough and talented enough appear, the
possibility of such a development is indeed very realistic,
practical, and theoretically well founded. In fact, some of
the best and most promising work in contemporary drama is
on these lines. Harold Pinter's most mature plays combine
the thematic preoccupations of Beckett and the Absurd with
a technique that is, outwardly, both realistic and poetic, and
he uses the stage with a freedom comparable to that of
Brecht's approach. *The Collection* is a case in point. It is a
play as lacking in motivation and exposition as any of the
Theatre of the Absurd, its dialogue is almost that of clinical
realism, and it is set in a four-fold composite décor. *The
Collection* is a small-scale work, admittedly, but it does
point to the future. Or, in a different cultural climate, there

is the whole *oeuvre* of Max Frisch and Friedrich Dürrenmatt. Both these very considerable dramatists acknowledge Brecht's influence while being free from his political commitment and his Marxist aesthetics; both have a view of the world, and occasionally use techniques, clearly akin to the Theatre of the Absurd. Frisch's *Fire Raisers* is reminiscent of Brecht and of Ionesco at one and the same time. The relentlessness of the action, the grotesque caricature of the dehumanized bourgeois, are akin to *The Bald Prima Donna*, the parodistic Greek chorus of firemen comes straight from Brecht. Dürrenmatt's grotesque opera *Frank the Fifth* has echoes of Brecht's *Threepenny Opera* (a bank that operates by theft and murder) but the view of the world underlying it is absurdist rather than Marxist. And the same is true of a great deal of Dürrenmatt's other work.

One of the most promising young playwrights now active in the English language, John Arden, also seems to be preoccupied with themes and techniques that suggest an analogous line of development. *Serjeant Musgrave's Dance* is Brechtian in its fable and its use of folksong and picaresque incident, but the final scene in which the Cromwellian deserter Musgrave confronts the people of the town with the skeleton of one of their fellow citizens killed in a colonial war and then threatens to revenge the iniquities of such wars by firing his gun into the crowd has all the obsessiveness, the nightmarish psychological reality of the Theatre of the Absurd—without ever leaving the plane of external realism. In another and far less successful play, *The Happy Haven*, Arden is right inside the techniques and preoccupations of the Theatre of the Absurd, among the half-demented inmates of an old-age home who are about to be given an elixir of youth and end up by administering an overdose of that medicine to their doctor, reducing him to babyhood.

Arden is a writer of tremendous potential; the fact that he has experimented in both techniques indicates that he may well bring about a more effective fusion of the two styles. In the United States Edward Albee may be on a similar road:

from the near pastiche of Ionesco to a style outwardly more realistic but charged with all the obsessive and grotesque over- and undertones of the absurd. In Poland some of the dramatists who have come to the fore after the cultural revolution caused by the political upheaval of October 1956—and they are undoubtedly among the most interesting playwrights now active in Europe—have naturally developed techniques drawing on both traditions: Slawomir Mrozek in *The Police* and *Out at Sea* uses satire that is political and realistic in a Brechtian sense but at the same time fantastic and grotesque: three men on a raft debating which of them should be eaten; the secret police, in a totalitarian state where all members of the opposition have been converted into staunch supporters of the regime, desperately trying to persuade the last oppositionist to remain steadfast, as otherwise the staff of all prisons and concentration camps, all secret agents would lose their jobs. Tadeusz Rozewicz in a brilliant play, *The Witnesses* or *The Little Stabilization*, presents lyrical variations on a single theme, the precariousness of the liberalization in Poland (or for that matter the thin crust on which the Western affluent society stands) in a succession of stage images clearly derived from the Theatre of the Absurd, but in a Brechtian technique of the montage of contrasting moods. These are only a few examples quoted almost at random; the list could be made much longer.

What I should like, with all due caution, to suggest is that playwrights will feel increasingly free to use devices and methods from both the main wings of today's avant garde as though they formed part of the same, unified vocabulary, and that they will be able to do so without being in danger of appearing to mix styles or create monstrosities of fashionable eclecticism. That this is already happening should, I hope, have emerged from the examples of actual plays I have given above. And so should the reason why this is possible, because, however different the premises may be from which the various branches of the experimental avant garde have started, however different the ideological positions they represent, however different the methods they employ, basically they spring from common roots and from common soil which is no less than the general cultural and spiritual situation of our age.

Every age has a common aspect which makes the most divergent elements of the epoch instantly recognizable as stemming from it: a Baroque Jesuit may have been at daggers drawn against a Baroque Protestant or a Baroque free-thinker, yet their style, their mode of thinking, their whole attitude will be instantly recognizable to us as having a common basis. They may represent opposing extremes of the debate of that time, but they nonetheless *belong* to the debate of that time and are thus part of a unified mode of thinking. Karl Marx has more in common in that sense with a Victorian exponent of capitalist thinking than with a present-day Soviet propagandist.

And indeed if we look at the ideological and philosophical premises of the two opposing wings of today's avant garde we will find a great many common concepts. Brechtian leftism, Sartrean existentialism, and the philosophical basis of the Theatre of the Absurd, for example, spring from a common root: they are reactions to the collapse of former systems of ethics based on supernatural sanctions. The Brechtian conception of human character is the outcome of the dissolution of the age-old idea that every human being is a divinely created, essentially immutable and eternal essence. Brecht sees man as malleable, human personality as infinitely changeable because there is no such thing as an eternal soul and therefore man is merely the product of his social environment; change the environment and you get a totally different character. The Theatre of the Absurd also starts from the postulate that man's identity—the answer to the question, 'Who am I?'—is an insoluble problem. For Beckett as for Ionesco, human character is infinitely evanescent and questionable; and character, the conception of character, is the very basis of all drama. Like human character, reality itself has become a relative concept. For the Brechtians reality changes with external circumstance; for the absurdists external and internal reality are interchangeable. The same applies to the concept of language. In the classical tradition, language was, through the Platonic idea and classical logic, an expression of a solid, immutable reality of Being which stood behind it. For the Brechtians language has become a very questionable tool of communication; there is a vast field in which what people say does not express any real meaning at all. For example, a capitalist who tells a working-class girl he loves her may well be speaking the truth subjectively, but objectively his words are meaningless, because, as a member of the exploiting class, he is objectively her mortal enemy and, in that sense, cannot really say he loves her. The Theatre of the Absurd also questions the validity of language as a means of communication, as an instrument for breaking the existential barrier between individuals. Seen from this angle, there is a great deal in common between Marxists, existentialists, and the followers of Wittgenstein.

And these, being the main issues of our age, are the main subject matters of contemporary drama and will undoubtedly remain so in the immediate future. The seemingly divergent, bitterly opposed strands of the avant garde are, seen from this angle, different approaches to the same problems; no wonder that ultimately they may well merge and mingle in a multitude of combinations.

The Happening

In Xanadu did Kubla Khan
A stately pleasure dome decree

. . . .

So twice five miles of fertile ground
With walls and towers were girdled
    round:
And here were gardens bright with
    sinuous rills
Where blossomed many an incense-
    bearing tree;
And here were forests ancient as the
    hills,
Enfolding sunny spots of greenery.
But oh! that deep romantic chasm
    which slanted
Down the green hill athwart a cedarn
    cover!
A savage place!

Coleridge's pleasure dome anticipated those reformers of
the theatre who compose new and magical environments, the
creators of 'Happenings'. Wandering through those forests
and gardens, where sunny spots of greenery dramatically gave
way to savage chasms, while 'ancestral voices prophesying
war' were heard from the distance, visitors to Kubla Khan's
pleasure dome enjoyed what the audiences at some of the
best Happenings were to experience, albeit perhaps on a less
grand and less satisfying scale: a *real* adventure, magical and
poetical enough to alter their perception of everyday reality,
a poetic vision lived through in three-dimensional space and

biological time—'Poetry which has been torn away from the cemetery of the printed page; painting liberated from its daubed and commercialized canvas; psychodrama removed from the brain-washing factories,' to quote Jean-Jacques Lebel, the Franco-American painter and one of the leaders of the Happenings movement.

In the era of the mass media the theatre has entered an age of transition. Many of the time-honoured assumptions about its function and its aesthetic structure will have to be re-examined, radically thought out anew and some, perhaps, completely discarded.

The theatre had its origin in ritual, religious and secular. In this ritual, whether it was a war dance or a hunting dance or a fertility rite or a human sacrifice designed to placate the angry gods, the whole tribe participated. Men, women, and children danced and sang and there was no separation into performers and spectators. It was only later that the secular spectacle was divorced from the religious ritual and the performer from the audience.

The idea of theatre bequeathed to our generation by the nineteenth century—of the stage as a segment of real life watched, as it were, through a pane of glass like the antics of animals in a zoo or fish in an aquarium—is a very special and untypical form of theatre. This 'Theatre of Illusion' is now radically threatened by the mass media. In the cinema and on the television screen the illusion is much stronger, much more convincing, because there we watch segments of photographed reality; they really *are* magic windows into the lives of other people. Confronted with such overwhelming competition, the live theatre must seek to establish areas of experience its audience cannot get in the mechanical, photographic mass media. And these areas of experience *must* lie in the region suggested by the adjective 'live'.

Since World War I the theatre has been struggling to free itself from the shackles of illusion. The expressionists and Brecht re-established the idea that the stage was not for the slavish reproduction of real life, but was a platform for the direct revelation of human emotion from actor to audience. It could be a lecture hall for the teaching of socially useful knowledge or a laboratory for the discussion of ideas and experimentation with actual human behaviour.

The Theatre of the Absurd used the stage to represent a reality outside the scope of the photographic process, which, after all, can only mirror the surface of life. It peopled the stage with images of an inner reality of subconscious dream images. In doing so, the dramatists of the absurd used theatrical forms of the era before the illusionist stage became predominant: circus and music-hall clowning, *commedia dell' arte* types, mime and burlesque.

Another movement concentrated on the element of spontaneity—improvisation and direct audience participation. Solo performers like the ad-libbing satirists of the Lenny Bruce and Mort Sahl school and groups like The Second City belong in this category.

What have all these movements in common?

They concentrate on abolishing the idea that what happens on the stage is an illusion of real life. They no longer try to hypnotize their audience into thinking that the actor playing Lear really *is* Lear. By letting the audience into the secret that the actor playing Lear is, in reality, Joe Snooks, they are confronting the audience with *more* reality than before, for Joe Snooks *is* more real, more flesh and blood, than Lear.

The audience at one of the absurdist plays is also, albeit in a quite different way, more deeply and more really involved than the audience at an illusionist play. It is confronted with a spectacle that, in itself, could not be a reproduction of surface reality but that is all the more obviously the expression of the actual anguish of its author. The audience is taken right inside the mind of a Beckett or Ionesco and therefore put into the most intimate contact with a very frightening reality, a reality made up of symbols and images which each member of the audience must interpret and work out for himself. In that sense the play invades the spectator's mind, his subconscious.

The alienation effect, both in the theatre of Brecht and in the Theatre of the Absurd, therefore postulates an active involvement of the audience at a deeper level than the mere identification process in the Illusionist theatre.

This is the point from which the avant garde of today starts out: How can the spectator be even *more* actively involved? How can his experience become even more direct, even more real? Clearly it can happen only if the barriers between spectator and performer are broken down even more completely. The spectator must be drawn right inside the dramatic experience (whether this is still to be described as a play or not). He must become part of a new reality, at least *as* real as, and perhaps *more* real than, the ordinary workaday world he inhabits.

Antonin Artaud spoke as early as the mid-1930s of the need to tear down the barriers between actor and audience. Various movements for the reform of stage design have tried to solve this problem by arena stages or theatre in the round. These have drawn the audience more deeply into the play by placing it nearer to the actors, and also by drawing the audience into the décor, as it were. From every angle in theatre in the round, the audience forms the background to the actors, and it is often more fascinating to study the faces of the spectators opposite than to watch the actors themselves. Yet, ultimately, this is not a change of fundamentals. The play remains the play, the actors remain actors, and the audience remains an audience.

One of the most fascinating young experimental directors in Europe, the Pole, Jerzy Grotowski, directs the Theatre of Thirteen Rows on the top floor of an ancient reconstructed building on the market place of the city of Wroclaw. His novel solution to the problem is to design a fresh *space* for the audience in each production so that it becomes part of the action. A play that takes place in a prison, for example, is performed in a network of cells enclosed by wire mesh. The audience is led into these cells and watches the action of the play taking place in another cell, centrally placed so that it can be seen from the others.

For a production of Marlowe's *Doctor Faustus* Grotowski filled his theatre with a long horseshoe-shaped medieval dining table. As the audience came into the theatre they were led to seats at this table, at which Faustus was already seated, praying. Grotowski had reshaped the text in such a manner that the play became a flashback inside Faustus' last great monologue. The spectators thus became the dinner guests at Faustus' last supper (and the religious analogy was certainly intentional).

The play opened at the point when Faustus began his last speech, and the flashback action took place on the table at which the audience sat.

But even here, although the spectator is drawn so closely into the action that the impact becomes frighteningly intense and intimate, there still is a *play*, a preordained sequence of events with a beginning and a foreseeable, and foreseen, outcome. And this still is a diminution of the reality of the experience the spectators undergo.

The next step is the Happening.

What is a Happening? How can it be defined?

So far as can be ascertained, the term was coined and first used in 1959 by Allen Kaprow. Born in 1927 in Atlantic City, he is a painter by profession and at the time was teaching art history at Rutgers University. In the literary review, *The Anthologist*, published by Rutgers, there appeared an article by Kaprow proclaiming the need for a really new art. This was followed by a text, which at first glance could have been taken for a poem. It was headed *Something to Take Place: A Happening*, and was, in fact, the blueprint for a kind of theatrical performance.

It called, for example, for an area with groups of chairs placed at random, and went on: 'People will sit in the chairs whose arrangement causes them to face in different directions. Some are dressed in winter coats—others nude—others quite everydayish (visitors will be given numbers of seats where they will go upon entry—they will find themselves seated next to nudes, coats and bums, who will be placed amongst the seats).'

Later the same year, in October 1959, Kaprow produced his *18 Happenings in 6 Parts* at the Reuben Gallery in New York City, and so the term 'Happening' entered the language. Other artists working on similar lines had tried to find other names for the new form, but Happening stuck to them all in the end, whether their creators agreed with the term or not. Hence it does not describe a narrowly definable art form, but rather a spectrum of different creations ranging from a static, three-dimensional image—sometimes called an 'environment'—to fairly elaborate performances that are almost, if not quite, plays. What all these events have in common is that the rigid time structure of a play, which follows a meticulously prescribed course, is abandoned; that much more is left to chance and improvisation; that boundaries between stage and auditorium, between illusion and reality, are far less clearly defined. The Happening is an open-ended image with which the spectator has to come to terms by himself.

Indeed, in doing so, he ceases to be a mere spectator, he becomes part and parcel of the image. He is sucked into it, as though it were possible, in walking through an art gallery, to be sucked right into a painting by Breughel or Bosch. Thus, in Kaprow's *Eat* (1964), the participants were introduced into a network of caves (once occupied by a brewery) and confronted with a variety of situations in which food was dangled before them in bizarre circumstances. In Claus Oldenburg's *Injun* (1962), the participants were led through a group of derelict buildings filled with strange things and even stranger human beings. And at the famous Happening at the Edinburgh international drama conference of 1963, devised by Ken Dewey, the staid proceedings of one of the conventional international conferences suddenly dissolved into a sequence of mad but highly significant events: a nude girl passing across the back of the platform; a famous film star suddenly darting from the platform into the audience, jumping across the rows of seats to fall into the arms of a bearded man in the back row; a bagpiper in Highland dress parading around the gallery, and the recorded voices of speakers at previous days of the conference echoing from all sides in snippets of cliché.

Each of these examples is very different in its own way. In the first, the participant was taken into a new environment to which he had to adjust. In the second, he was led through an adventure. In the third, the familiar environment and context were suddenly undermined, crumbling away into grotesque distortions of themselves. But in each of these instances (chosen very much at random) the onus lay on the spectator-participant (or however he should be correctly described) to adapt himself to a new environmental situation of peculiar significance and psychological relevance to himself. He was no longer in the position of a mere voyeur who watches a play and decides for himself to what extent he can get himself involved from his safe distance. In these Happenings, the spectator experiences something himself, whether he likes it or not—and many of the good people of Edinburgh at that Happening did not like their experience in the least!

They had been drawn into the Happening against their will, unaware at first that they were faced with a planned artifact rather than with reality. For a moment they must have felt that they had gone mad, that their innermost secret wishes (yearnings for a nude girl) or their secretly voiced and repressed feelings about the drama conference ('All this stuff is really nonsense!') had suddenly materialized in the form of hallucinations. To them it was as though the solid ground of predictable reality were dissolving beneath their feet. No wonder many of them were deeply outraged; no wonder the organizers of the conference were sued in the Scottish courts for causing a public outrage (they were acquitted).

Such an experience is very different from that of the spectator of a play who, however deeply he may feel involved with the fate of the characters on the stage, always remains aware that those events are an illusion.

Happenings are written, composed, and planned as plays are written, or ballets sketched out on paper by the choreographer. Some are very rigidly worked out in advance; in others, a considerable latitude is given for change and improvisation. As Allen Kaprow has said: 'I try to plan for different degrees of flexibility within parameters of an otherwise strictly controlled imagery. For example, a part may consist of sweeping thirty square yards of paper in a "slow, unhurried way". One could sweep it this way or that way, with a brown broom or a pink broom—in any fashion that one wishes, if it is generally done in that slow, ritualized way. Or: a riot is called for. Everybody exchanges clothes; a complete orgy is taking place. Who exchanges clothes with whom makes no difference at that point as long as one just keeps exchanging clothes. In these cases I will permit almost any flexibility. But there are other stricter limits of variability. . . .'

So Happenings can be staged more than once, following an identical pattern and yet each performance differing in numerous details from its predecessors. The degree of involvement of the audience also varies. Some authors of Happenings will prescribe certain actions to the participants, giving them an active role; others will merely let them watch the events that take place around them and might engulf them at any moment without ever actually doing so.

Happenings, three-dimensional poetic images that envelop the participants, are therefore anti-literary theatre of the most extreme kind—if they are theatre at all. In this respect they are a direct continuation of the tendency already manifested in the Theatre of the Absurd, which diminished the importance of the narrative line, character, plot, and dialogue in favour of the presentation of concretized poetical imagery.

Put the spectator right inside such a poetic image and you have a Happening. The importance of the image is thus immensely enhanced. Indeed, the Happening owes a great deal to and is a direct continuation of similar tendencies in modern painting and sculpture.

In action painting, for example, the *action* of painting became almost as important as the image it produced. Action painters gave *performances*, and thus there came a point at which theatre and painting met. In collage and modern sculpture using *objets trouvés* (found and ready-made objects) the real world and painting intersect. A lavatory bowl or an old bicycle pump may assume a new and poetical significance if incorporated into a work of painting or sculpture. Pop painters like Robert Rauschenberg go further—their paintings tend to reach out into three-dimensional space. The Happening, as a three-dimensional environment in which people are introduced as an additional element of ready-made reality, is merely a logical continuation of this process. Indeed, many of the best practitioners of the Happening, like Lebel and Kaprow, are painters who have taken this logical step forward.

But composers and dancers have also contributed. John Cage, the avant-garde composer and musical director of the Merce Cunningham Dance Company, is rightly regarded as a founding father of Happenings. Cage is deeply concerned with the entire world of sound and considers any kind of noise as a form of music. He would even consider an occasion at which the orchestra sat silently on the platform as a concert. In the context of a concert, with the audience straining to hear something, chance noises from the outside, or the slight rustle of programmes or shuffling of feet in the auditorium would *become* music—and at the same time theatre. For Cage defines theatre simply as 'something which engages both the eye and the ear'.

Seen from this angle, 'one could view everyday life itself as theatre'. This sounds paradoxical, but is anything but nonsensical.

What Cage is saying is that the attitude of the perceiver is the essential element. To a creative imagination, which looks at the world with the awareness of an artist or mystic, every incident of life, even the most insignificant, carries the impact of poetry—the buzzing of a bee, the way an old man crosses the road.

What the fully structured and organized theatre does is to bring this home to an audience whose senses in everyday life have become blunted. They are made to feel sentimental by a sunset evoked on a backdrop by spotlights with red filters—yet they fail to notice the real sunset outside their windows. What Cage and his followers are saying is: Let's put a frame around reality. Let people come and look through it at reality *with a sense of occasion* and they will suddenly see reality as they have never seen it before—which, after all, is the true function of art.

The German Pop artist and Happenings practitioner, Wolf Vostell, arranged a Happening for the citizens of the town of Ulm in 1964 which consisted in their being taken in buses to see the airfield, a car-washing plant, a garage, a swimming pool, a refuse dump, an abattoir, and a number of other everyday sights which, however, were somewhat heightened by strange announcements coming over the buses' intercom systems and by unforeseen details, such as the fact that the car-washing plant was decorated with a curtain of raw meat and that, in the swimming pool, the water suddenly started to go up in flames. The tour lasted some six strenuous hours, and the participants certainly learned to see their own home town with new eyes.

There can be no doubt that such Happenings, whether they confront their participants with artificially enhanced or actual chunks of reality, produce the effects usually postulated from an artistic experience—they make us see the world more intensely, with more emotion and insight. They provide us with a life-enhancing adventure. But the question arises: Is that still theatre?

My own opinion is that this is really a somewhat futile

exercise in semantics. It all depends on one's definition of theatre, which, let us remember, arose from ritual—another way of presenting reality in an enhanced context. The ritualistic element in Happenings must not be underestimated.

The history of theatre is rich in examples of events that were theatrical but nearer to the present-day Happening than to our conventional idea of drama. There were the medieval mystery plays, performed on a number of simultaneous mansion stages, and the *triomfi* of the Renaissance, sumptuous processions with elaborate floats. In modern times there are the three-ring circus, the carnival parade, the Haunted House at Coney Island, the roller coaster that produces violent emotions of fear and relief as it hurtles over its steep course and makes the girl grip her boy friend tightly. All these are examples of a real situation poetically enhanced and structured after the manner of the Happening.

Even the restaurant with a Venetian or Spanish décor, the Playboy Club with its Bunnies, or the movie house built like a Chinese pagoda make use of the same procedures, at however attenuated and vulgarized a level. They attempt to introduce poetry into our everyday life by artistic means, by putting us into an environment that is both real *and* artistically structured and enhanced.

And what of political rallies and conventions, bullfights, baseball games, heavyweight prize fights, military parades, and presidential inaugurations? Here, too, artifice and chance event are mingled in a new poetically structured reality that essentially serves the purpose of providing the audience with an enhanced experience of life through elements of ritual *and* theatre—costume, décor, music, lighting, and so on.

In other words, much of our life *is* theatrical—and by no means the least significant or enjoyable part. The dividing lines between fiction, artificially enhanced reality, and ordinary reality are extremely tenuous and exceedingly difficult to define. The part played by truly religious ritual in our world is diminishing, and it is only natural that the perpetual human hunger for significant occasions should be met in new and different ways.

A good many Happenings have been primitive and inexpert. Others have produced poetic images of great power and have enhanced the lives of those who took part in them. I have little doubt that the potentialities of this form of art—call it theatre or not—are immense. We are moving into a period of automation and undreamed-of amounts of leisure time for human beings in the industrialized societies of the world. The era of the Pleasure Domes is therefore bound to come. And Happenings are the modest germs of deeply felt, frightening or pleasurable experiences as yet unimagined: total theatre, concretized poetry, magically structured human experience.

Varieties of Dramatic Criticism

'I found it tedious, positively tedious, a boring play. And I've said so in my review!' He was a well-known London critic, talking about a performance of some play by Brecht. 'I think you are a little unfair to the play,' I retorted, 'It is a brilliant play. But I agree with you: the performance was very poor and made it *look* boring. Could you not have done justice to a great work of dramatic literature, while condemning the performance?'—'But you are asking the impossible. How on earth *was* I to tell the performance apart from the text? Quite impossible!'

A true story. And all too typical. Quite apart from the fact that the text of the play in question had long been available in a good translation, a critic who does not have the ability to listen to a performance in such a way that he can not only hear the words as they are actually spoken, but can also imagine how they *should* be spoken, simply has no claim to the title of critic. Critic, after all, comes from the Greek verb κρίνειν which basically means to distinguish, discern, differentiate and hence to judge, to form an opinion, to evaluate —on the grounds precisely of the ability to distinguish between the different elements that make up a complex whole like a work of art, the ability to tell the good from the bad, to analyze.

I am convinced the lack of a sufficient body of sound critical appreciation is one of the causes for the present malaise of the theatre in the English-speaking world. And this applies to the daily and weekly reviewers (who have a very important function, apart from the fact that they influence the commercial success of all theatrical ventures) as much as it does to the more serious monthly and quarterly reviewers in avant-garde and highbrow periodicals (from the late-lamented *Encore* to the ever flourishing TDR), and the academic critics of drama who appear in the pages of the same periodicals as well as in their own learned and weighty tomes. I don't think the trouble lies in a lack of intelligence, understanding or even insufficient factual knowledge (although in this respect the short-term journalistic reviewers are much at fault) so much as in a lack of clarity, in the minds both of the critics themselves and in those of their readers, concerning the functions and objectives of dramatic criticism, or rather the functions and objectives of the many different *kinds* of dramatic criticism. For there surely are many different, and often equally legitimate, types of critical writing on drama. There is nothing wrong with such a multitude of genres, provided that writers and readers are aware at all times with *which* genre they are, at any given moment, confronted, what the implicit underlying assumption—the editorial brief—behind the review or essay in question really is. Otherwise chaos reigns in a truly Babylonian confusion of tongues.

Look at the assembled motley crowd of critics at any first night in London or New York: you barely find two among the Butchers of Broadway, the Fops of Fleet Street, who are after the same thing. Mr A may regard it as his function to tell his readers whether the show is suitable for one's mother-in-law or teen-age daughter: he sees the critic as a sales adviser, a consumer's counsellor; and bases his assessment on the concept of *entertainment* value.

Mr B at the same time may be watching the proceedings with an eye hungry for some acting performance which will enable him to add another charming cameo to a growing gallery of fine descriptions of great moments of acting, which will add distinction to his forthcoming volume of collected dramatic chronicles and reinforce his claim to be regarded as a latter-day Hazlitt: he is convinced that the dramatic critic is above all a camera-eye, a recorder, a witness to the living impact of acted drama, a reporter serving future generations who want to know what it felt like to have been present at this performance.

At the same time Mr C is keeping an eye open and an ear cocked to pick up some lapse on the part of actor or author which will enable him to display his well-known flair for brilliantly amusing mockery and invective: he regards himself as an entertainer, whose job it is to furnish the maximum of amusement to his readers who love to watch him spew his venom upon aging leading ladies or bumbling playwrights. He knows that in making fun of the failings of dolts and dodderers he panders to mankind's ever insistent urge to find reassurance and comfort in the misfortune of others.

Mr D on the other hand, is looking for grist to some ideological or political mill; totally uninterested in the skill of the performers or the elegance of the writing, he judges the performance entirely from the point of view of whether it helps or harms his own cause.

Mr E is also a doctrinaire, but his interest is aesthetic rather than ideological, he is for *one* style of acting or writing and therefore against all others; Mr F is completely unconcerned about ideological or aesthetic points of view, the eyes of history or the needs of the consumer: he is an impressionist who merely records what he feels about the performance, on the assumption that being an *homme moyen sensuel* such a feat of self-observation will tell his readers something about the play—and if he happens to be in love with one of the actresses or allergic to one of the actors he will faithfully set it all down without bothering—or even realizing the need —to declare his interest.

Mr G on the other hand uses the play merely to display his own wealth of information. The late James Agate belonged to this school; he was fond of opening his article with a reference to some performance by Garrick or Kean as recorded in some obscure source, thereby causing the mouths of his readers to gape over their Sunday breakfast about so much erudition. In fact, the illusion of such erudition is all too easily produced. All one needs is a good library of books about drama with usable indexes.

There is no need to go on, although the list of conflicting and differing objectives and motivations among critics in the daily and weekly press could be prolonged almost indefinitely.

But if the confusion of objectives is frightening, how much more frightening is the divergence of the premises, the basic assumptions, the basic training, the basic standards from which all these different reviewers start out: there is no common denominator of terminology or expertise which must be the foundation of any genuine debate, argument, comparison of varying views. The racing tipsters in the daily press all know something about horses and their performance. They may differ among themselves in the assessment of these horses' capabilities, but at least they start from shared—and verifiable—basic assumptions. Likewise the football correspondents all know the basic rules of soccer, the aeronautics correspondents have a shared assumption about what it is that makes aircraft fly. But the dramatic critics have no such common ground. Precious few of them have any technical knowledge of stagecraft, even fewer would agree on what constitutes a good play, good acting, good design, lighting, direction, let alone what theatre is about, what theatre is for —entertainment, enlightenment, uplift, purgation of emotions or what? And, indeed, what it is that *constitutes* entertainment, catharsis, enlightenment.

And yet the sum total of all these completely differently motivated verdicts, arrived at from totally divergent premises, eventually amounts to an apparent consensus, a collective opinion, which may make or break a new playwright; launch an actor into the big money or condemn him to a decade of starvation; or reverse a whole trend in the development of drama, change the cultural scene itself. It is, if one reflects upon it, too ludicrous to be funny.

The daily and weekly reviewers, the short-term critics, are of course severely handicapped by the unseemly haste with which they have to work in the English-speaking world. In many European countries the reviews may appear several days after the first night. The public there has learned to wait patiently till the critics have had time to digest what they have seen. Of course, in those countries the theatre is not predominantly commercial and frequently presents its plays as a genuine *repertoire*; hence after the first night days may elapse till there is a second performance; and in any case, the decision to go and see the play is not made on the spur of the moment—a large proportion of the audience has subscribed to its seats at the beginning of the season and will go to see the play regardless of what the critic had to say. Which has an important advantage for the art of criticism: a negative verdict in the press will have to be capable of standing up to the verdict of a large body of spectators, whereas in New York or London a negative verdict on the part of the critics kills the play and at the same time deprives the public of any chance to verify the critics' opinion. No wonder that such killer-critics tend to be more irresponsible: they are like judges who execute the accused *before* the jury has a chance to listen to the evidence. Indeed some of these critics—those whose papers go to press a little earlier than others—never even have a chance of properly meeting the accused. I know of at least one who has to sneak away before the end of any play that lasts a little longer than normal and who—being an honest fellow at heart—has developed a nice line in equivocations about the end he has not had a chance to see, such as 'such a hero surely must come to a bad end' or 'the programme announces that the fifth act takes place at dawn the next morning, that says it all ....' Those who are in the know are not deceived. But what of the mass of innocent readers? Yet one can only sympathize with the plight of these reviewers, who have to base their articles on a few hasty notes scribbled on the back of the programme, without time to reflect, look up the text, let the deeper message of the play work in their subconscious. I shall always remember and sympathize with the critic who phoned me the morning after a first night we had both attended and announced that he had been thinking all night about the play we had seen (and in defence of which I had argued with him during the intermission) and he had come to the conclusion that there lay a profound and important meaning behind the surface of eccentric goings-on, that the play was in fact a masterpiece. Alas, he regretted, he had arrived at these results thinking and worrying about the play throughout a sleepless night, *after* he had already delivered himself of a devastatingly negative notice which rejected the piece as pretentious non-sense. Indeed, I had just read that venomous and contempt-uous notice (which helped to bankrupt the backers of the play) over my breakfast. Ludicrous—but far from funny!

It would be wrong to blame the short-term, journalistic critics alone for this state of affairs. They are, among other things, the victims of an idiotic system. The commercial theatre *demands* such instant criticism, because the sale of tickets depends on the immediate availability of guidance to those members of the public who want to know whether it will be worth their while to buy tickets to a new show. A newspaper strike which keeps instant reviews from appearing immediately proves that tickets to new shows do not sell without such guidance. As long as the bulk of the theatre in the English-speaking world depends on the sale of tickets on impulse (rather than on intelligent long-term habits of theatre-going) the journalists will have to supply such instant notices.

The long-term critics, who are exempt from this tyranny of the deadline, may escape this particular handicap. Yet their work is by no means free from other, and perhaps even less excusable, defects. Is it permissible to lump these serious essayists, these specialists, experts, and academics together with the journalistic reviewers at all? Are they not a totally different species? I do not think so. It is very difficult to define the frontiers between journalistic reviewing and serious dramatic criticism. Some of the greatest serious critics were in fact journalistic reviewers—one has only to think of Lessing, Hazlitt, Otto Brahm, Archer and Shaw—while a fair proportion of at first glance serious work in book form turns out to have been just as ephemeral as journalism, but more lengthily and tediously written. Indeed, many of the long-term writers of criticism are afflicted by precisely the same confusion about the scope, aims and use of criticism as their hard-pressed journalistic colleagues. In addition they have a number of endemic shortcomings that are all their own: above all a much greater and more damaging remoteness from the living reality of dramatic performance on the stage, an even more flagrant ignorance of the practical and technical problems of production. How many academic writers on aesthetic theories of acting, for instance, treat the theoretical writings of Stanislavsky and Brecht like philosophical systems that exist in a vacuum rather than as prescriptions for practice which may or may not work on the stage—and which are constantly tested (and accordingly continue to develop by trial and error) by multitudes of directors and performers.

And indeed—long-term, academic critical writing on the theatre also merges gradually at the other end of the spectrum into purely literary criticism, theatre history, textual criticism. It is important to be conscious of the dividing line in this area as well. What then, in fact, is the proper definition of dramatic criticism itself? If I may venture a purely personal view on the matter, it is this: Dramatic criticism must essentially be related to drama in *performance*; the word performance being here used in the widest sense, which includes the performance of the playwright, as well as that of director, actor, designer, and also the work of theorists influencing performances of drama. True dramatic criticism helps the performers in assessing their own work, it helps their audiences to understand the work of the performers. The dramatic critic thus stands *between* the performers and the audience and functions as the vital feed-back mechanism that supplies a constant corrective to both sides. Without such a constant stream of expert and sensitive criticism, the performers, who need an authoritative summing up of audience reaction in order to develop artistically and to test their ideas in practice, no art, and certainly no performing art like drama (which cannot exist without a reacting audience) could continue to grow and keep in touch with the general move- ment of the culture of which it forms part. Likewise, without a constant stream of authoritative interpretation of the per- formers' ideas and intentions no audience could intelligently keep pace with, and react to, the new forms and experiments which a living art is bound to be constantly producing.

Thus to the performers the critic is the voice of the audi- ence, to the audience he is the informed spokesman of the performers. Good dramatic criticism will, in this light, be seen as the very hub and turntable of a healthy theatre. Defined thus, as 'descriptive, factual, and evaluative analysis of drama which will assist the creative process of the per- formers in the theatre and helps its audience to understand that creative process', dramatic criticism will be seen to cover both the writing of the daily critic who makes relevant con- structive suggestions and supplies information designed to show prospective theatregoers what they should look out for in a performance, as well as that of academic critics like Dover Wilson or Jan Kott who have actually shaped the work of directors and at the same time have helped to create an audience with an ability to follow what the directors con- cerned were trying to do; such a definition will also cover the efforts of theoreticians of the theatre like Brandes, Artaud, or Brecht, who have likewise shaped the practice of performers while simultaneously educating the tastes of audiences. Such a definition would however exclude purely historical or archaeological writing on the theatre, textual criticism of plays, the analysis of concepts such as romanticism, classi- cism etc., the tracing of literary sources, biographical mono- graphs on actors and playwrights. All these are of immense importance and can become raw material for dramatic criti- cism, without themselves falling into that category.

Let us, in the light of this definition, examine briefly how the various types of approach, motivation and attitude among contemporary reviewers and critics which we listed at the beginning of this article, fulfil a useful function:

The sales-tipster critic: insofar as a journalistic reviewer *merely* evaluates a performance from the point of view of its supposed entertainment value, or suitability for a certain type of audience, his activity may be of some social use (by, for instance, preventing parents from taking young children to a play they might not understand) but it certainly will not be criticism. On the other hand, of course, any true critic, in evaluating the performance and assessing its creative content or intention, in reflecting the reaction of an exceptionally well-informed and sensitive member of the audience, will incidentally perform that very service and furnish much more valuable consumer advice than the reviewer whose sole aim was the giving of no more than such consumer guidance. The sales-advice type of critic also exists in the longer term academic criticism—in the shape of those introductory essays on hitherto little known authors on which the adoption or rejection of a playwright or school of dramatists into the academic syllabus, and thereby ultimately into the conscious-ness of a civilization, depends. But here too this aspect of the critics' work must ultimately be the by-product of deeper analysis, never an end in itself.

The critic as recorder of performance, the taker of snap-shots for the future historian of the theatre. Insofar as the description of performances, scenes, even single gestures, serves to elucidate the value, technique, method or personal style of a performer, to help him to assess the effect of his work, and to open the audience's eyes to a new type of excel-lence in a performance, insofar this approach is of consider-able value and fully justified. But where, as is so often the case, it becomes an end in itself, a self-indulgence on the part of the critic concerned, an occasion for the display of his virtuosity (often ignoring the actual performance that is allegedly described), or for wallowing in sentimental adora-tion of a performer's personality rather than his work, such criticism, however brilliantly written and evocative, loses its usefulness and value as a historical record. Nothing smells quite as musty as those long-forgotten adolescent enthusiasms that one sometimes encounters embalmed in the pages of collected reviews.

Criticism as an occasion for the display of wit and invective. The practitioners of this form of journalism tend to be among the most famous and the most influential of journalistic reviewers. In those cases where their wit and gift for entertaining invective is not backed by any true knowledge of what they are writing about—and these cases are by no means infrequent—they are also the most pernicious and harmful of parasites. One of these gentlemen once explained to me that his editor had briefed him to be amusing at all costs, never mind the rightness or wrongness of the views expressed. I retorted that he reminded me of a judge who had condemned a man to death and was proud of the witty way in which he had summed up the case, although he knew the condemned man to be innocent.

The ideological, moralistic, or political critic. This approach is equally frequent, and not only among the purely journalistic critics. It is typified by that very well-known and brilliant left-wing critic who once admitted that he thought a play he had highly praised in his weekly article was bad, yet he had simply found it impossible to condemn a play with such a worthy tendency. It is easy to sympathize with such an attitude; yet it seems to me profoundly wrong. For in suppressing strictures, both the audience and the performers are set wrong standards; and ultimately this will result in a further lowering of quality. On the other hand, a writer's political attitude *has* an artistic relevance of its own. If he claims to discuss the real world (as a politically or ideologically committed writer invariably must) then the truth or falseness of his view of the real world becomes an artistic consideration. A copyist of reality must be judged by the quality of his likenesses. It is on the other hand totally wrong to reject a portrait which is a true likeness of the object portrayed on the grounds that such an object must not be portrayed under any circumstances (for example a play about homosexuality or drug-addiction on the grounds that such vices should not be dangled in front of an audience). The most glaring example of the consequences of ideological criticism of this type is furnished by the Soviet Union, where almost the totality of critical writing follows a strict ideological line and content is paramount over the form, quality and truth of the dramatic statement. The result is drama of appalling dullness, which has become ineffective even as political propaganda, simply because the audience knows the ideology already so well beforehand that there can be no surprise, and all drama becomes totally predictable. Indeed, one could argue that the ideological effectiveness of drama is in inverse proportion to its openly expressed ideological intent, and that ideologically actuated criticism of drama which ignores or underplays formal and artistic aspects tends to reinforce this tendency. In long-term academic critical writing a moralistic or ideologically oriented bias is equally reprehensible. On the other hand, in such longer term criticism it is not only legitimate, but highly desirable, that the ideological, political, sociological and moral *implications* (which are frequently at variance with the explicit intentions) of the works concerned should be brought out—as an aid to the understanding and evaluation of the play, not in a spirit of reprobation or approval.

The critic who pursues an aesthetic line. So long as this bias is openly expressed I see no harm in it. On the contrary, a standpoint of this kind, systematically and consistently developed and maintained, may produce a body of critical work that sets the seal on an epoch or movement. Lessing's pursuit of his standpoint in support of the English as against the French model for German drama in the eighteenth century, Shaw's advocacy of Ibsenite views in his theatrical criticism at the turn of our century, or Siegfried Jacobsohn's consistent support for the ideas of Reinhardt are cases in point. Here important critics developed a whole body of aesthetic doctrine by the day-by-day assessment of a wide variety of different plays and performances; and it is difficult to say to what extent it was the creative artists involved who inspired the critics, to what extent it was the critics who spurred on the creative artists and helped them to evolve their views and methods. We need more rather than fewer critics with a strongly held aesthetic doctrine, provided always that these doctrines are tenable, relevant and useful as constructive foundations for practical work. Of course, there are also those critics whose aesthetic doctrines are half-baked, out of date or reactionary. We know them only too well; but even they are of some use: so long as they make their standpoint clear they can be valuable as tests of the reactions of those quarters which they represent and helpful in crystallising issues in a debate. Jean-Jacques Gautier, the influential critic of the Paris *Figaro*, for example, admirably plays his pre-assigned part as the mouthpiece of traditional opinion in the French theatre.

The impressionist critic, who is concerned to record his own reaction untainted by aesthetic or political bias and who refuses to be an expert because he maintains that it is his job to represent the ordinary playgoer who is equally naïve in his approach. There is an element of truth in this attitude, but also numerous sources of error. Above all, no professional critic *can* be representative of the ordinary playgoer, because the ordinary playgoer does not go to all first nights, does not know all actors from having seen them dozens of times, etc. The pretence that a critic, however assiduously he may try to cultivate his naïvety and ignorance of the professional side of theatre, can retain this virgin approach, is therefore in itself a dangerous fallacy. The critic who succeeds in convincing himself that he possesses this innocent eye is deceiving *himself*, and consequently also his readers. And he will tend to grow incapable of discounting his own bias. Eager to record the nuances of his own feeling, he will become unaware of the subjective factors that enter into his reaction. It is fairly easy, for instance, to tell from the output of some of the practitioners of this school when they are going through a marital crisis: their reviews become increasingly more acid as their personal gloom deepens. Others are liable to react through the chance sequence of first nights: a competently performed light comedy of no value coming after three or four more difficult and demanding pieces with slight flaws, will suddenly take on the hues of a perfect work of art, simply because it represents a welcome change. At the extreme end of this spectrum, we would find the critic who would feel perfectly entitled to write: 'I could not sit through this play' at a time when he suffered from a bad attack of piles. Yet there is a core of an important truth in this attitude, insofar as all criticism will contain a very considerable element of personal bias and taste; insofar as every good critic must *start out* from an analysis of his own reaction. This remains the irreducible emotional factor in any critic's work and it must be faced with honesty and without illusions. The description of this personal reaction must be present— and present as an explicit element to enable the reader to discount it, if he so wishes—but it must be counterbalanced by rigorous self-critical analysis of all other knowable factors. The innocent eye *is* attainable, up to a point, not by passive surrender to, but by analysis of one's impressions. It demands an effort of the imagination, a conscious elimination of the fortuitous factors, the professional fatigue, the jaded palate. The ability to attain this state of self-induced naïvety is capable of being trained, but to some extent it is part of the critic's inborn equipment, his talent for his calling. (It is analogous to a director's need for the ability to see a play he knows by heart with the eyes of a spectator who is confronted with it for the first time. If a director lacks this ability he will never succeed in communicating his ideas to his audience.)

The critic who is concerned with displaying his own learning. This variety is more frequently encountered on the continent of Europe than in the English-speaking countries. In Germany or Switzerland one often finds reviews of performances which are straight out of a university lecture on the play and which almost totally disregard the performance.

Such essays have their usefulness and value (provided the learning they display is sound, which is by no means always the case) but they miss the point to a considerable extent.

A word must also be said about the critic who is actively engaged as a performer—in the widest sense—in the theatre. (I have to declare my own interests here, as I myself belong in this category, being responsible for a vast output of radio drama and occasionally directing myself.) Much of the best work that periodicals like *Encore* and TDR publish belongs into this category, either in the form of articles or in that of interviews with the personalities concerned. In itself active work on the creative side of drama does by no means preclude criticism of the highest order. Provided always that the built-in bias of involvement is made clear. Moreover descriptions by an individual of his own creative processes and methods are not in themselves criticism; they may be valuable autobiographical source material, they may be raw material *for* criticism; if they come disguised *as* criticism, and even more so disguised as aesthetic dogma, they are potentially dangerous. A good deal of the mists of confusion generated by Brecht's theoretical writings (and indeed those of Stanislavsky) can be traced to this. For creative men of genius of this stamp tend to be in need of rationalizations and generalizations to reach their own very concrete personal—and nevertheless instinctive—results. To elevate the reasonings behind a particular creative problem into a generally applicable dogma, however, is potentially dangerous and harmful.

This leads to one of the main types of academic critical writing: gropings towards generalized theories of aesthetics and poetics in the theatre. These are undoubtedly important and may be immensely useful. There is one note of caution however: as a practitioner I have noticed a tendency to overestimate the validity of any such theory and in particular of any categorization and classification, any working out of rules and aesthetic laws. Concepts developed in order to explain one or the other concrete phenomenon have a tendency to be taken so literally that they gradually assume a concrete existence of their own as though they were Platonic Ideas floating around in the heavens and jealously demanding that critics and performers observe their operational code. The pernicious influence of this type of attitude can be seen in the history of drama in the tyranny exercised by such concepts as the three unities or the supposed Aristotelian laws of tragedy. There are, that should by now be clear, no rigid rules in art. Criticism, tracing its line of descent, as it does, from schools of rhetoric, still seems to adhere, at least subconsciously, to the notion that its analysis of a given work of art will eventually lead to the establishment of the rules by which it functions, and thereby make it possible to produce others of a similar kind and standard of excellence. This may have been true of the stylistic tricks of ancient oratory (and even there it produced stilted and boring performances); it certainly can no longer be maintained of any artistic activity of our time. In dramatic criticism the old ghost still lives in concepts such as the 'well-made play', and a multitude of conventions and rules that are still adhered to, though by habit or subconscious assumption rather than by deliberate choice. And many academic critics still judge by such old—or even newly developed—rigid rules. It also often happens that, when they believe they have deduced such rules from an author's work, they apply them rigidly to his further output, censuring him for breaking his own stylistic code. (I once met Harold Pinter in a fury about such a critic who had demonstrated that his latest play had violated the code of Pinteresque style.)

So much for a rapid, and fairly random, enumeration of some of the prevailing archetypes of critical writing about drama. It must, of course, be stressed that this list is neither exhaustive, nor claims that any of the archetypes here described habitually exists in a pure state. All critical writing contains *elements* of one or several, perhaps even all of these archetypal underlying assumptions. One or the other of them may so predominate that it stamps the character of the entire work of the critic concerned; in that of others one may come to the fore at one time, another at other occasions. An honest critic sincerely striving towards a degree of objectivity should however be conscious of the admixture of different implicit assumptions, and—wherever possible—make them explicit. It is in this respect that critics are most frequently at fault.

To what extent is dramatic criticism at all capable of arriving at a degree of objective validity, of objective truth? Can one say of various reviews or critical essays about the same work that one of them embodies the truth about that work, while another is totally mistaken about it?

The assumption that there is such an objective standard of truth in critical activity about the drama (as in any other field) *does* in my opinion underly much of critical writing, journalistic as well as academic. And this, I feel, is the most dangerous fallacy of all, the source of much needless acrimony, anger, and meaningless debate. I am convinced that the degree of objective truth that is attainable by any kind of critical writing is very small (although not totally absent).

My own, long-held, views on this particular subject, were confirmed and reformulated for me, by a remarkable study by Professor Morris Weitz, *Hamlet and the Philosophy of Literary Criticism*.[1] A linguistic philosopher of the Wittgenstein school, Professor Weitz made the bold attempt to reach his own conclusion about the logical validity of critical pronouncements through an empirical analysis of the whole body of extant criticism concerning a single play; having read a vast amount of critical work stretching from the eighteenth century to our own day, he tabulated the kinds of questions that the critics had asked and grouped them into four main categories: (1) Questions demanding *descriptive* answers, such as 'Does Hamlet love Ophelia throughout the play?' (2) Questions demanding *explanative* answers such as 'Why does Hamlet delay?' (3) Questions demanding *evaluative* answers, such as 'Is *Hamlet* a great play?'; and (4) Questions demanding answers from the realms of aesthetic theory such as 'Is *Hamlet* a tragedy?' And after exhaustive, and highly

[1] Chicago University Press 1964, Faber & Faber, London, 1965.

convincing logical analysis, Professor Weitz comes to the conclusion that objectively true or false, i.e. verifiable, answers are possible only to the first category of questions, the category demanding *descriptive* criticism. Whether Hamlet loves Ophelia throughout the play can be demonstrated verifiably through a close study of the text. But as soon as we embark on explanatory criticism about the motives of characters etc; or evaluation, i.e. attempts to establish a hierarchy of excellence, standards of greatness etc; or into the realm of poetics and its shifting concepts, we are in a sphere that is not logically reducible or verifiable, simply because at the end of the line we always come to purely *subjective* opinions, primarily existential reactions of individuals which are, logically, of the irreducible nature of statements about whether a day is fine or not, whether a bowl of soup is hot or not, whether a woman is beautiful or not. Ultimately therefore all literary criticism of drama (and even more so all criticism of performance) comes down to being in the category of the critic who feels compelled to give the most honest possible description of his own personal and idiosyncratic reaction. Does this invalidate or devalue dramatic criticism? Not in the least. It merely enables us to adopt a more logical, a more detached and therefore a more controlled, a more scientific attitude towards it. Certainly Professor Weitz did not bring anything new to me, much as I admire the rigour of his approach, the elegance of his demonstration. The critic's activity is part of an artistic, not a logical or scientific process. A dramatic performance is not a mechanical, mathematically predictable process, but a living, organic event. Its elements are basically two: a work of art and an audience. A dramatic work is a dialectical unity, a dialectical tension between these two components. One cannot exist without the other. If the audience reacted with the uniformity and regularity of a physical process, its reaction would be totally predictable. (And this is the fallacy of the rules in art which underlay so many now exploded systems of aesthetics.) In fact each individual in the audience, each individual audience, the audience in each individual historical epoch, reacts totally differently to a work of art.

To take Professor Weitz's own example, *Hamlet*. The Elizabethan audience certainly reacted in a different way to different aspects in the play from those to which a contemporary audience reacts. And indeed an audience in Eastern Europe reacts differently today from an English or American, from an African audience. (I remember talking in Tanganyika to Africans who had recently seen a performance of *Hamlet* and who had found in it all the problems of their own tribal society.) Each audience consists of as many critics and critical responses as it has members. The professional critics are merely the elite among them, those who are most sensitive in expressing their reaction, best able to mould the reaction of their fellow-members of the audience, best qualified to inform the performers of the audience's reaction. It follows conclusively that there can be no absolute standard of criticism, but that each critical opinion is important insofar as it is an inalienable part of the work of art itself. Without its body of criticism, *Hamlet* would not be *Hamlet*. A work of art is an organic, living thing, which is, for its living existence, dependent on the total body of audience reaction it has evoked. Criticism is the sole record of this response and it is more than a mere record: it is a feedback, an influence which alters the work of art and conditions its organic growth as a continuing living entity. Just as a live performance of a play grows under the influence of each succeeding audience, so the literary existence of a dramatic work grows and expands in the light of the criticism it has evoked. Hence the quality of that criticism is of immense importance to the work itself and to the total climate of the culture in which the work exists.

Far from devaluing criticism this view emphasizes the importance of each individual critic's reaction. The absence of logical verifiability by no means makes it impossible to evaluate the *quality* of criticism itself. We know a good poem from a bad poem, even though such qualitative judgments are not logically arguable. In the same way we can judge the quality of criticism. Above all, the purely factual, descriptive elements *are* logically verifiable. The critic who thinks the heroine committed suicide (because he was asleep in the third act) while in fact she lived on happily ever after, can be condemned in the most scientific manner and so can the critic who is ignorant of the technical problems and factual background of a dramatic work. These criteria already eliminate a large body of critics whose factual information about the author, the play, its background etc. is habitually false, or non-existent. Beyond this, the quality of a critic's writing, the intelligence, clarity and perception of his style will allow us to judge his level of intellect and insight, the degree to which what he says deserves attention. There are also clear criteria which enable us to judge a critic's fairness and sincerity, notably the degree to which he plays with unmarked cards, the degree to which he declares his interest, seeks to overcome his bias etc. There remains the irreducible element of the individuality of a personal reaction. All good criticism presents a work of art seen through an individual sensibility. The more clearly important and worthwhile the individual concerned, the more valuable becomes his criticism, not because it brings it nearer to any objective standard of truth or taste, but because it makes it a more relevant portion of the total available body of critical reaction to that particular work of art.

The reader of criticism will never get an objective standard of evaluation. What he can derive from his reading is a rich human experience, the opportunity to match his reaction to a work of art against those of particularly sensitive and valuable individuals. By such a process of continuous challenge the reader of criticism will gradually be able to school and refine his sensibilities, regardless of whether he accepts any individual critic's view on any given work of art, or merely uses it as a view against which he himself reacts. This after all is also how all true education works, not by the handing down of unalterable valuations, but by providing the student with a standard against which he can whet his own reasoning power and perceptiveness. Dramatic criticism therefore (as any other criticism) is not a science producing results but an art embodying human experience in all its variety and individuality. The artist records his experience of nature, of the world, with varying degrees of technical skill. The critic records his experience of art with varying degrees of technical skill and verifiable expertise. And as art exists on a higher order of being than the amorphous and crude experience of life itself, the critic who describes his experience of this higher order of experience must himself be a human being of exceptional sensibility and creative power for the technically expert expression of such highly complex existential experiences. That is why there are so few truly great critics. That is also why the truly great critics deserve to be very highly valued.

Contemporary English Drama
and the Mass Media

We still tend to think of the electronic mass media as a very new development, too new in fact to deserve as yet to be looked at from a historian's point of view. Hence the contribution which the mass media have already made to English literature and cultural life as a whole has hitherto been relatively neglected in those circles whose business it is to chronicle and to evaluate these matters.

Yet this impression of the mass media as a very recent phenomenon is a false one. It probably arises from the fact that they *were* very new when the generation which is now middle-aged passed through its most impressionable period of development. After all, radio started more than forty-five years ago. The British Broadcasting Company was formed in 1922, and the BBC in its present form, as a public service corporation, started its operations on 1 January 1927, forty-two years ago. Even television has by now acquired a quite venerable tradition. The first television drama production—admittedly an experimental one—was broadcast from Baird's laboratory in Long Acre a full thirty-eight years ago—in July 1930: Lance Sieveking's production of Pirandello's *The Man with a Flower in his Mouth*. And the BBC's regular television service, the first in the world, began operations as far back as 1936, more than thirty-two years ago.

That the development of the electronic mass media has already produced a fundamental revolution in man's modes of perception, his sense of time and space, his manner of communication and perception of ideas, is, for me at least, beyond a doubt. And that such a change will, of necessity, have far-reaching consequences for literature and drama also as its ability to get inside a man's mind—the radio play, after all, comes to life not on a stage but in the listener's imagination, and is therefore ideal for dramatizing the inner life— in *The flowers are not for you to pick* (1930), which takes place inside the mind of a drowning man. Radio was also beginning to find its own poets: D. G. Bridson's *The March of the 45* (28 February 1936) was the first of a long line of fine poetical dramas on historical subjects. In the war, when, during the long nights of the blackout, radio drama reached enormous mass audiences, this trend became a veritable movement towards verse drama, which continued the efforts of Ashley Dukes, T. S. Eliot, Auden, and Isherwood, and produced a considerable number of noteworthy achievements. Louis MacNeice's *Christopher Columbus* (with music by William Walton—1942), Edward Sackville-West's *The Rescue* (with music by Benjamin Britten—1943) were followed, after the end of the fighting, in the equally bleak post-war period, by Laurie Lee's *The Voyage of Magellan* (1946) and MacNeice's *The Dark Tower* (with music by Benjamin Britten—1946), to name but the most outstanding examples. The Third Programme, which opened on 29 September 1946, became the vehicle for bold experimentation. Here Dylan Thomas's masterpiece *Under Milk Wood* had its first performance in 1954; here Giles Cooper (1918–66), one of the most original writers whose best work was for radio, developed his laconic, ironical style of black comedy with plays like *Mathry Beacon* (1956), *The Disagreeable Oyster* (1957), and *Unman Wittering* and *Zigo* (1958); here Samuel Beckett's plays, specially written for radio, spread the fame of their author: *All that Fall* (1957), *Embers* (1958), and *Words and Music* (1964).

It was radio drama which furnished Harold Pinter, after his first near-disastrous failure with *The Birthday Party* at the Lyric, Hammersmith in 1957, with further commissions for plays and helped him to continue as a dramatist: *A Slight Ache* (1959), *A Night Out* (1960) and *The Dwarfs* (1960) were the fruits of this policy. John Arden's first work as a dramatist *The Life of Man* (1956), was written for radio as an entry in a radio play competition organized by the BBC's North Region. Robert Bolt, whose greatest stage success *A Man for all Seasons* started life as a radio play in 1954; Alun Owen, Bill Naughton, Willis Hall, David Turner, James Forsyth, John Mortimer, Henry Livings, James Hanley and many other prominent playwrights made their impact on radio before they achieved recognition on the stage.

The development of drama on British television was somewhat slower. The fact that television drama did not suffer from the handicap of invisibility led at first to the mistaken idea that it could rely solely on performances of stage plays, which, in the first pre-war years of television, were regularly repeated a few days later and broadcast with an interval, after which a bell summoned the audience back to their seats from kitchens and bathrooms. Even after the television service was reopened—it had been suspended during the war years—on 7 June 1946, television drama continued to be mainly theatrical in origin. But gradually, as the medium conquered the masses—the breakthrough here came as late at 1953, the year of the Coronation of Queen Elizabeth II—the barriers of traditional form began to break and the realization spread that television was different in its basic aesthetics from both the cinema and the live theatre. What are these differences?

They spring, essentially, from the size of the television screen—at least at its present stage of technical development; the conditions under which television programmes are broadcast; and the conditions under which they reach the audience. The small size and low definition of television pictures reduce the impact of 'long-shots' (whole landscapes, rooms filled with many people, etc.) so that, effectively, the director is forced to rely mainly on 'medium shots' and 'close-ups'. It is difficult to get more than two characters into a 'medium shot'; hence television drama, on the whole, is most effective in dealing with conflicts between few people. The closeness of the audience to the performers, and of the performers to each other, in turn, favours muted dialogue: one cannot shout at a person only a foot away. Much of the best television drama, therefore, falls into the category which Strindberg termed 'chamber play'. Moreover, because television is a photographic medium, television drama, in the programme schedules, tends to be preceded and followed by a mass of documentary material. Hence the tendency among some television writers and producers to get television drama as close as possible to the documentary itself. Jeremy Sandford's *Cathy Come Home* is but one example among many for the effectiveness of this approach.

The playwrights of the generation which came to the fore after the breakthrough of John Osborne's *Look Back in Anger* at the Royal Court Theatre in May 1956 have, almost without exception, also written television drama: Osborne himself a historical documentary (*A Subject of Scandal and Concern*); John Arden (*Soldier, Soldier* and *Wet Fish*); Harold Pinter (*The Collection, The Lover, Night School, The Tea Party, The Basement*); John Mortimer (*Call me a Liar, The Headwaiter* and a number of other plays); Arnold Wesker (*Menace*); Alun Owen, Bernard Kops, Bill Naughton, Willis Hall, Charles Wood, Tom Stoppard have also contributed their share. A further group of dramatists of comparable stature must be considered primarily as television dramatists, although they, too, may have had plays produced on the stage. Among these are, above all, Clive Exton (*No Fixed Abode, The Silk Purse, Where I Live, The Big Eat, The Trial of Doctor Fancy*, etc.); David Mercer (*Where the Difference Begins, A Suitable Case for Treatment, In Two Minds, Let's Murder Vivaldi, On the Eve of Publication*, etc.) and John Hopkins, whose tetralogy *Talking to a Stranger* portrayed the same events through the eyes of different members of the same family; Leo Lehmann; Nigel Kneale (author of the famous *Quatermass* science fiction series); Colin Morris; Rhys Adrian; Dennis Potter; Troy Kennedy Martin, to name but a few in a long list.

The heyday of radio drama as a mass entertainment is over; the sound medium now retains its importance primarily as a field for experiment in new forms and as a training ground for young talent. But television drama is certain to continue to increase in importance and in its impact on the national culture and mode of life. Hence it may be of some value to examine some of the wider, more general aspects of the implications of the present situation—in which television reaches well nigh the whole of the population of Great Britain (well over 95 per cent of all households have a television set).

Above all, in the age of mass media, drama no longer is synonymous with live theatre. The theatre, which served as the sole outlet for dramatic writing from the ancient Greeks to the turn of this century, is now one among *four* dramatic media and reaches infinitely smaller numbers of people than the three others: the cinema, radio, and television. Moreover, perhaps for the first time since the days of the Greek city state, and perhaps the medieval mystery plays, which were seen by a majority of the population of the cities concerned, drama has become a genuine *mass medium* again. No more than about 5 per cent of the population ever go to the theatre, whereas a single performance of the most popular drama on television may be seen by up to twenty million people; on the average, drama audiences on television tend to lie around five to seven millions for a single performance. These are quantitative rather than qualitative considerations, but I don't think there should be any need to apologize for mentioning them. They must have far-reaching implications on the quality and nature of the material offered to such immense numbers of spectators. There is another very important quantitative aspect of the development of the mass media, above all television, which is of equal importance: it concerns the quantiy of material consumed by the mass media.

Forty years ago the total production of *new* plays in this country can hardly have been more than one hundred to two hundred per year; the capacity of the London and provincial theatres could not possibly have been higher. Today, if one counts the vast numbers of series and serial instalments (which also have to be written by professional dramatists) the television networks alone broadcast well over a thousand dramatic items, which have to be newly written every year; and radio broadcasts something in the order of another thousand. Thus the demand for dramatic material in Britain today—if one also counts films and the theatre—must be about *thirty times* what it was before the rise of the mass media. The economic incentives for writing drama have increased concurrently with this upsurge of demand. As a result more and more talented people are tempted to try their hand at writing dramatic dialogue; even those who start with hack-work acquire valuable practice and professional polish. Here, in my opinion, lies an important contributory factor to the present renaissance of dramatic writing in this country. (I have already mentioned another: the fact that young writers have been—and continue to be—exposed to vast quantities of drama from their earliest childhood. How much potential dramatic talent lay fallow in previous epochs merely because the people concerned could not get into contact with theatre in the most impressionable period of their lives?) No wonder that the social range of British playwriting has widened immensely in the post-war years. If drama, once upon a time, tended to be produced by gentlemen for middle-class audiences, today writers drawn from all classes and regional language areas are writing for the millions, the large majority of whom belong to the working class. Hence the vast success of serials like *Coronation Street*, of series like *Till Death do us Part*.

These are some of the effects of the upsurge of mass drama in the electronic media on the *creators* of drama. What about the effects of this state of affairs on its *consumers*, the vast— and relatively new—mass audience? The decisive, the really epoch-making, aspect of television and radio is not so much their ability to put news, music, or drama into everybody's drawing-room, as the truly unprecedented fact that, in the

Western world today, the entire population has a *continuous stream* of entertainment and information on tap, to be turned on and off at will, like the water or electricity supplies. Whereas in the pre-electronic age to see a play required an effort and was bound to produce a sense of occasion, now the knob is casually turned on, and, if the play proves not interesting enough, equally casually turned off. Dramatic conventions have become familiar to the masses: people who would have been hard put to work out the implications of the exposition of a play now tend to be as expert at this as they are in following the complex rules of football or cricket. This familiarity is bound to speed up their capacity to follow dialogue, to take in the salient points of a plot, and to foresee its possible solution.

What are the consequences of this state of affairs on the writers of television drama, and indeed of all drama? The absence of a sense of occasion and the audience's ability to abandon the play at any given moment, forces the writers to sharpen the *initial impact* of their plays; once a really strong and riveting situation has been created, the audience will be, as the professional jargon has it, 'hooked'. The increased familiarity of audiences with dramatic techniques and conventions, on the other hand, allows the writer to be more economical in his exposition, to save himself excessive 'pointing' and 'signposting'. It is noteworthy that in producing plays by writers even of the stature of Ibsen nowadays one tends to want to cut a good deal, simply because one has become aware of excessive repetition of important points; today's audience can see what the author is driving at far earlier than in previous epochs, and, indeed, they can also often see the joke coming too early in old plays. These are developments which, inevitably, spill over into the area of live theatre. The mass media *are* exercising a wide influence on writing for the stage. Even theatre audiences today are bound to have been conditioned by radio, the cinema and television.

To list just a few of the ways in which these influences operate outside the aspects already mentioned: television and radio present their audiences with an almost unending stream of spontaneous, unrehearsed speech: in interviews, parlour games, features. The fictional elements of the mass media—its dramatic output—are embedded in these vast tracts of unrehearsed talk. This inevitably forces the television and radio dramatist to try and make his dialogue as real as he can; otherwise the contrast, the unnaturalness, the theatricality of fiction as against the real world would become too obvious and totally inhibit the necessary suspension of disbelief. This seems to me to be one of the chief reasons for the upsurge of the vernacular, the 'tape-recorded' type of dialogue in modern drama, in the live theatre as well. Beyond this there is the influence of the techniques, which arise from the nature of the mass media, on the live theatre: in radio drama, for example, a *narrator*, a story-teller is essential in many cases. This familiarizes audiences and playwrights with the device. Occasionally successful radio plays are transferred on to the stage: Dylan Thomas's *Under Milk Wood* or Bolt's *A Man for all Seasons*, for example. The narrators are retained, and because the audiences are already familiar with the technique they are not found objectionable. As a result more and more drama, directly written for the stage, now also employs the narrator. In radio, moreover, its narrative, epic possibilities and its capacity to take the audience into the author's or the chief character's consciousness, have led to the development of techniques employing several levels of consciousness. In Bill Naughton's highly successful radio play *The Little Life of Alfie Elkins*, for example, the story is told by the chief character, Alfie, a working-class Don Juan, who is looking back into his own past. This leads to flashback scenes in which Alfie in turn is heard in past dialogue, but also in past interior monologue. That is, he tells the story of how he one day met a girl. We are then transported into that scene and hear him accosting the girl and talking to her. We also hear his thoughts, while he is making up his mind what to say to her. Thirty years ago it would have been axiomatic that it was impossible to use this technique in the live theatre. Yet, under the title *Alfie*, the play *was* transferred to the stage and the audience completely accepted the hero's passing from narrator to actor in dialogue and interior monologue. (The latter, incidentally, could then be seen as a reversion to the technique of the 'aside' proscribed by the rise of the naturalist school.)

Television plays tend to be more intimate and also shorter than full-length stage plays. The success and subsequent transfer to the stage of television drama has thus led to a revival of the one-act play (e.g. Pinter's *The Collection* and *The Lover*, which have become a popular double bill on the stage). The transfer of television plays, which can switch from one set to another instantaneously and therefore tend to be written in short, cross-cut scenes, has also contributed to the erosion of the well-made play. We are more and more, in the theatre, becoming familiar with sets embodying a multitude of locations with quick cross-cutting from one to the other through lighting changes. Here again Pinter's *The Collection* is a case in point. When it is done on the stage we see simultaneously the two flats involved with a section of the street in front of one of them—in fact, therefore, a reconstruction of the set used in the television studio.

These are just a few of the direct and positive influences of the electronic media on the live theatre. Even more important, however, are the *negative* influences, the things the theatre can, or should, no longer do because of the existence of television and radio, and the things it must do to survive their competition. For example: with so much drama constantly and freely on tap in the home, the theatre cannot offer fare which is already so widely and easily available. It is forced to explore those areas of its capacity where the mass media simply cannot follow: the rise of the spectacular musical can thus be seen—as was the rise of large-screen cinema—as an answer to the small television picture. The theatre's increasing preoccupation with subjects like sexual perversion, or explicit sexual situations in general, seems to me to be due to the fact that these are themes with which television—a mass family entertainment—cannot deal. The same is true of the increased emphasis on theatre as ritual (television has no sense of occasion—ritual is pure sense of occasion) and improvization, audience participation, happenings, which stress the *live* character of theatre and its ability to react instantly to the reactions of its audience.

These are some of the short-term effects of the rise of the mass media on the theatre. It, in turn, constantly influences the mass media: largely because the live theatre has, and will have, to remain the training ground for actors, directors, designers—and indeed to a large extent also playwrights, simply because the theatre, thanks to its being a *minority* medium, can experiment in front of small, sympathetic audiences. The long-term effects of the electronic revolution are, as yet, only dimly discernible in the future. There is, for instance, the long-term effect of television's continuous stream of programmes. Instead of the sense of occasion this produces the routine, the habit. Hence the immense popularity, in television and radio, of the regular recurring item. In terms of drama this leads to the prevalence of series (self-contained episodes using the same central character) and serials (continuing stories in instalments). This seems to be the form of the future, the form wholly in tune with the medium. Here there is no need to 'hook' the audience's attention. They are already hooked when the episode opens, because they have already become addicted to the story, the chief characters. Such serials cannot be the work of a single writer, they are produced by teams of writers. And once the characters are established, they develop a life of their own. With these series and serials we are, in fact, back in the world of myth: Barlow, Dr Cameron, Ena Sharples are the folk heroes of our time, as familiar to the people as the heroes and gods of Greek myth, as folk heroes of the stamp of Robin Hood or Baron Munchhausen. The writers may change, the heroes go on. Even the vast success of an adaptation of a work of literature of a past age, like *The Forsyte Saga*, depends, undoubtedly, on the habit-forming, myth-making nature of the long serial. These folk heroes, like those of former ages, embody the aspirations and dreams of the masses. Those of today, however, unlike those of the past, are, it might be objected, not the outcome of genuine creativeness, but the manufactured products of calculation by an entertainments industry. That is certainly true. Yet some of these products succeed, many others fail. Those which succeed must, therefore, correspond also to the hidden dreams and aspirations, the folk psyche, of the masses of our age. Compared to the folk heroes of the past, these new folk heroes—and the aspirations and fantasies they embody—may look paltry, trivial, unheroic, vulgar. And perhaps they are: but then, the myths and heroic sagas that have come down to us are, most probably, only the very best, the most beautifully shaped, that have survived the test of time. Thousands of others must have perished in oblivion.

The mass media which have turned the world into an electronic village, by the very fact that they have spread drama to the millions, have also vulgarized it, have turned into a branch of industrialized folklore rather than the high art created by the romantic ideal of the lonely artist. Yet out of folklore, out of folk art, have come some of the greatest examples of high art: the *Iliad*, Elizabethan drama; and in our own time the great works of popular entertainers like Charles Chaplin or Buster Keaton, which, I am convinced, are among the greatest artistic achievements of the century. There is no reason why, in the course of the decades, the centuries to come, the electronic folk art should *not* also generate works of high art.

There is no certainty in this hope. Much depends on factors outside the control of those directly concerned with creating the entertainment of the masses: the economic and political situation, changes in society, education, modes of life. Much will depend on chance: on the presence of the right men with the right talent in the right places at the right moments. But the possibility does exist that the new mechanized mass culture might generate a new high culture. I, for one, am at least not *wholly* pessimistic.

The Role of the Theatre

The anti-theatre has today become the mainstream of theatre. In what direction will this mainstream now move on? It is by thinking about the future that we may influence its development, and already its shape is discernible around us in the most significant new work. The question is to see what is significant in the work of the newest playwrights.

Undoubtedly, and not least through the revivifying impetus provided by the most exciting work of writers like Brecht, Beckett, Ionesco, Genet, Pinter, Albee, the live theatre has again become important, hotly debated, an issue of considerable social importance. In the English-speaking countries this phenomenon manifests itself in the upsurge of writing about the theatre (and the impressive sale of serious critical books about drama) and in the ever growing movement to provide live theatre as a social service, a social necessity as distinct from a luxury industry confined to metropolitan areas, in every civilized community. In Britain the creation of a National Theatre and a multitude of municipal and civic theatres and the revolutionary innovation of a minister responsible for the arts in Harold Wilson's government eloquently emphasize this trend. In the United States an analogous movement is taking place through different organizational channels but with very similar aims.

Why is it that the importance of live theatre—as against the mechanized mass media—should have become such an important issue at this very moment? It is, I believe, because of the nature of the social function of live drama in the future development of culture. Live drama contains elements that cannot be purveyed by mass media that may well be essential for the culture and psychological health of a nation.

What are these elements?

First of all, there is the element of direct communication, the contact between live performers and a live audience. The introduction of canned laughter into television shows is a grotesque tribute to the continued craving for the *collective* enjoyment of dramatic entertainment that is at the very root of the social function of drama throughout its long history. Clearly the theatre of the future must exploit its advantage vis-à-vis the mass media by making the fullest use of the presence of a live audience.

Secondly, in the mechanized mass media the screen not only presents the audience with a photographed picture of a scene, it also *selects* the aspect of the scene on which it wants to focus the attention of the spectator. Hence the mass media eliminate the element of choice in the spectator; they tell a story with a fixed pattern of stresses seen from a single vantage point. In the theatre the spectator must select his own close-ups and do his own editing. This not only offers the spectator much greater intellectual freedom, it also allows the director to present an action on multiple levels with multiple foci of emphasis. A play in the live theatre can therefore be not only far more complex, far richer in its potential of expressiveness, it can offer each individual spectator a slightly different spectacle in the creation of which he has actively cooperated by selecting his own points of emphasis, angles of vision, etc. The mechanically recorded dramatic performance is a *closed system*; the live one is *open* —and open also in the sense that the reaction of the spectators in turn influences the emotional response of the actors. And so in the live theatre not only has each spectator to cooperate in creating his own individual spectacle, each collectivity of spectators, each audience cooperates in eliciting a different kind of performance from the actors. An open form that produces a unique experience, spontaneously varied from spectator to spectator, from performance to performance:

that, in the age of mechanized mass media, is the decisive characteristic that distinguishes the live theatre from its competitors. The ever greater and continuing emphasis on the improvisational element in theatre (as indeed in other arts today) is another aspect of the craving for spontaneity and open form that is the healthy reaction of our time against closed, mechanical substitutes for art.

The open form may also be used as a call to action. Indeed, in the Communist countries of Eastern Europe we now find an increasing number of brilliant young dramatists who use the techniques of the Absurd to make social points and propagate social reform. In *Tango*, for example, the Polish playwright Mrozek attacks the older generation in his country in a style modelled on but in many ways surpassing that of Ionesco; but the subject he deals with is wholly social: he shows a world in which the old and the middle-aged are wild, beat revolutionaries while the young crave conformity and respectability. In Czechoslovakia, Havel's *The Garden Party* and *The Memorandum* also take their tone from Ionesco's fooling with language and logic (as in *The Lesson*) but argue, with devastating effect, political points.

Genet himself has been fusing the social epic and the absurd. In *The Screens* he deals with the problem of colonialism in Algeria, and undoubtedly at the time it was written the play was a call to action to help the Algerian rebels in their fight against the French. At the same time the play contains some of the most brilliant inventions in the field of an open-form theatre. One scene from it was to me one of the strongest experiences I have ever gone through in any theatre —the scene in which the insurgents set fire to the plantations of their oppressors. This was done in the production I saw according to Genet's instructions, by letting the actors *paint* the fire on the empty white paper screens that formed the setting for the play. As the rebels surged in with large brushes that had been dipped in red paint and violently daubed the screens with more and more flaming colours, the excitement became almost unbearable. We were witnessing a fusion of action painting with theatre! And miraculously the emotion generated by the situation in the play produced the most fabulously exciting action painting, so much so that after the performance some of the spectators hurried to secure fragments of the newly painted screens. Emotion had been aroused, we had seen it express itself on the screens, and the screens now held congealed white-hot emotion. The possibilities of development for the theatre in this direction seem to me literally limitless. It is a matter of developing ritual actions capable of expressing the deepest emotions about the most profound psychic contents and archetypes through which actors and audience can merge in a collective act of communication at the very deepest level. This is where the theatre originated. This is the direction in which it is tending.

In other words, in a world from which spontaneous human experience is more and more disappearing through the cancerous growth of overorganized, overmechanized, and ready-made patterns of work, behaviour, thought, and even emotion, the genuine need for theatre is growing apace—for a theatre in which human beings can regain their autonomy of feeling, in which the denizens of a thoroughly secularized, demythologized, emotionally dehydrated society can return to the roots of what need not be called religious experience, but which might be called a contact with the ultimate archetypes of the human condition, the awe and mystery, the grandeur of man's lonely confrontation with himself, the universe, and the great nothingness that surrounds it. The greater the automatism, physical and psychological, of our age, the greater becomes the danger that Aldous Huxley foresaw in his *Brave New World*, that men will be reduced to the status of permanently hypnotized zombies. The spontaneity of individual, artistic experience, and above all the collective artistic experience that only the live theatre can provide, are thus vitally important antidotes to a very dangerous development.

From this it follows that the live theatre (which is of immense importance also as the experimental laboratory and training ground of the dramatic mass media) must increasingly become a public concern. In continental Europe the commercial theatre is already very largely a thing of the past. Like public libraries, schools, museums, or hospitals, theatres are part of the essential social services of civilized communities. In countries like Sweden or Norway, moreover, state-supported touring companies bring live theatre to even the most remote communities.

How should the artistic policy of such a public service theatre be shaped? Is there not a danger that such a theatre will become a mere museum of established and therefore already fossilized masterpieces? Such a danger certainly exists, but the experience of a considerable number of outstanding theatres of this type amply proves that there is no inevitable need for such a development.

A repertory theatre of this kind has a twofold task: to re-interpret past masterpieces in the light of the present, and to present the new on the basis of the mature experience of the past. It is quite wrong to assume that the classical dramatic literature of any country or civilization is a fixed immutable quantity. Beckett has given us a new insight into Shakespeare; we must therefore renew our image of Shakespeare in the light of Beckett. Moreover a current development like the vogue of Brecht or of the Theatre of the Absurd gives new importance to long-forgotten dramatic styles of the past. In the light of Brecht's achievement the work of Büchner or Wedekind may become of fresh relevance and interest; in the light of Beckett or Ionesco certain Baroque dramatists suddenly emerge as forerunners of the present and as highly topical and relevant. It is thus in dealing with the past that a responsible theatre of this type can reflect and inspire the present. Similarly, in providing a platform for new writing and experimental work, a firmly established repertory theatre can draw on its familiarity with a variety of established styles to develop new ones. In England, Peter Hall's policy of using the company of the Stratford-on-Avon

Shakespeare Memorial Theatre in the most avant-garde plays at his second theatre in London has greatly benefited the acting of avant-garde plays as well as those of Shakespeare.

Thanks to the theatrical developments of recent years, the road that links the great dramatic rituals of Greek tragedy and Aristophanic comedy with the naïvely religious and at the same time riotously grotesque medieval mystery play, with the Elizabethans and the great Spanish classical theatre, with the theatre of Racine and Corneille which still awaits discovery in the English-speaking world, the great German eighteenth-and early nineteenth-century poetic drama, Restoration comedy, and the rich poetic theatre of today is now clear. The revolution of the past twenty years to which pioneers like Brecht, T. S. Eliot (*Murder in the Cathedral* will come into its own as an example of ritual drama), Thornton Wilder, Beckett, Genet, Ionesco, and a host of brilliant younger playwrights have contributed has given the dramatist of today the technical means and the vocabulary of stagecraft to develop a poetic theatre that is thoroughly up to date and yet able to give new insight into the age-old paradoxes of the human condition.

Acknowledgments
and Index

Acknowledgments

'New Form in the Theatre' first appeared in *The Nation* April 1961.

'Naturalism in Perspective' first appeared in *Drama Review* Winter 1968.

'Ibsen' is based on introductions to editions of *Hedda Gabler*, *The Master Builder* and *An Enemy of the People* published by Heinemann Education Books, 1965 and 1967.

'Pirandello' is an expanded version of an article in the *New York Times* 25 June 1967.

'Brecht in 1969' is based on an essay in *Drama Review* Autumn 1967, and an article published in *Encounter* August 1966.

'Brecht and the English Theatre' first appeared in *Tulane Drama Review* Winter 1966.

'The Neurosis of the Neutrals' is based on an essay on Frisch in *German Men of Letters*, Vol. III, published by Oswald Wolff, 1964, and on articles on Dürrenmatt which appeared in the *Guardian* February 1963, and in *Plays and Players* March 1963.

'Ionesco and the Creative Dilemma' first appeared in *Tulane Drama Review* Spring 1963.

'"Truth" and Documentation' first appeared in the *New York Times Magazine* 19 November 1967.

'Slawomir Mrozek' first appeared in *Drama at Calgary*.

'Vaclav Havel' was written as a programme note for a performance in Sweden.

'Günter Grass' is an enlarged version of the Introduction to *Four Plays* by Günter Grass, published by Secker & Warburg 1968.

'Edward Bond's Three Plays' is based on reviews in *Plays and Players*.

'Peter Weiss' contains passages from an article in *The Year in Sweden* Stockholm 1966, from correspondence in *Encounter* March 1966, and from 'The Meaning of Marat/Sade' by Martin Esslin which is taken from The Theatre Recording Society Production Folio for *The Persecution and Assassination of Marat as Performed by the Inmates of the Asylum of Charenton Under the Direction of the Marquis de Sade*, and is used by permission of Caedmon Records, Inc. Copyright © 1966 Caedmon Records, Inc.

'Pinter Translated' appeared in *Encounter* March 1968.

'Violence in Modern Drama' is the text of a lecture delivered at the Institute of Contemporary Arts, London, and published in *Encore* May/June 1964; it also contains passages from an article in 'The Theatre of Cruelty' which appeared in the *New York Times Magazine* 6 March 1966.

'Nudity: Barely the Beginning?' first appeared in the *New York Times* 15 December 1968.

'The Theatre of the Absurd Reconsidered' contains material from an article first published in *Playbill*.

'Epic Theatre, the Absurd, and the Future' first appeared in *Tulane Drama Review* Summer 1963.

'The Happening' first appeared in the *New York Times Magazine* 11 September 1966.

'Contemporary English Drama and the Mass Media' is based on the Arthur Skemp Memorial Lecture, Bristol University, 15 November 1968; it was published in *English* Spring 1969.

Index

WESTFIELD
UNIV.
LONDON
COLLEGE